LIBERATED CINEMA

LIBERATED CINEMA

The Yugoslav
Experience

Daniel J. Goulding

INDIANA UNIVERSITY PRESS • BLOOMINGTON

Manufactured in the United States of America

Library of Congress Cataloging in Publication Data

Goulding, Daniel J.
Liberated cinema.

Bibliography: p.
Includes index.
1. Moving picture industry—Yugoslavia.   I. Title.
PN1993.5.Y8G68   1985   384'.83'09497   84-42835
ISBN 0-253-14790-5

1 2 3 4 5   89 88 87 86 85

Contents

ILLUSTRATIONS

ACKNOWLEDGMENTS

The preparation of this book has spanned nearly a decade and involved me in a complex and stimulating journey through a diverse and dynamically changing film culture, whose outlines are often as subtle and elusive as the multinational character of the peoples it mirrors on the screen. During my several research visits to Yugoslavia I have been treated with unfailing courtesy, good humor, and friendship. While it would be impossible to name all of those who have served as generous and expert guides, I would be remiss not to mention certain key institutions and individuals without whom this study never would have been initiated or completed.

I owe an enormous debt to Filip Aćimović and Stevan Jovičić of Jugoslovenska kinoteka for arranging special screenings of films housed in the Belgrade film archives, and to Đorđe Babić and Milomir Marinović of Jugoslavija film for arranging screenings of a large number of more recent films. Momčilo Ilić, recently retired director of the Institut za film in Belgrade, was unstinting in his personal support and in making the research resources of the Institut fully available to me. Dejan Kosanović, professor of the Faculty of Dramatic Arts in Belgrade, was very generous in sharing his insights and capacious knowledge of the economics and organization of the Yugoslav film industry. Dušan Stojanović, professor of the Faculty of Dramatic Arts in Belgrade and one of Yugoslavia's leading film critics and theoreticians, provided me with constant friendship and intellectual sustenance during the entire period of my research and writing. Without his encouragement and support, I doubt that the book would have been completed. I am also grateful to a wide circle of film critics, artists, and directors of the film enterprises in Zagreb, Sarajevo, and Ljubljana for their lively discussions, hospitality, and generous support in providing interviews and arranging for screenings of important films. Since this book charts new territory, it is more than usually necessary to offer the customary disclaimer that any factual inaccuracies, faults in the general conceptual framework, or dubious interpretations are entirely my own.

Oberlin College has been very generous in awarding me research status to support a year's stay in Yugoslavia in 1979–1980 and in granting me research and travel funds for additional research visits in the summers of 1974, 1977, and

1981. I owe a special debt to Alexandra Podwalney for tutoring me in the intricacies of Serbo-Croatian and to the staff of the Institut za strane jezike (Institute for Foreign Languages) in Belgrade for providing me further language instruction. I am also grateful to Miodrag Čertić and Dr. Nina Drndarski for offering translation assistance during the early phases of my research.

Margaret S. Jennings, senior writer-editor for Aspen Systems Corporation in Washington, D.C., provided detailed and expert editorial assistance in the final stages of preparing the manuscript, and Priscilla Scott typed the entire manuscript and numerous revisions with unfailing efficiency and cheerfulness. Finally, I want to acknowledge the unswerving and loving support which I received from my wife, Elizabeth, and my two sons, Gregory and Michael. Elizabeth's strong encouragement and resolute faith sustained me during periods of doubt and waning enthusiasm. It is to her that I gratefully and affectionately dedicate this work.

INTRODUCTION

In the four decades of its development since the end of World War II, Yugoslavia has attracted and sustained a level of international attention disproportionate to its size and relative military and economic strength. In 1948, Yugoslavia was the first Communist state to assert its independence from the domination of the Soviet Union. In the ensuing years Yugoslavia demonstrated an imaginative capacity to chart its own "separate road to socialism," paved with innovative experiments in decentralization of party control, with socialist market mechanisms inserted into and replacing a command economy, and with the development of pluralistic self-management systems of decision making at the factory level, in local and republican government, and in cultural, health, and education areas. [1]

Yugoslavia's nonconformist ventures in the political, ideological, and economic spheres have been widely studied and analyzed by international scholars, while comparatively less attention has been paid to the equally significant and sometimes unique innovations which have occurred in the areas of press, radio, television, and film. Gertrude Joch Robinson's recent and extensive analysis of the organization, power relationships, and functioning of the press, radio, and television in Yugoslavia makes a major contribution in redressing this balance, but, as she herself acknowledges, her discussion of film is quite fragmentary and represents an area in need of systematic study. [2] The only attempt by outside scholars to describe and assess the evolution of Yugoslav film since the end of World War II was undertaken by Mira and Antonín J. Liehm. [3] The evaluation of Yugoslav film, however, is fitted into the much broader context of detailing the general development of film in the Soviet Union and in six other socialist countries: the German Democratic Republic, Czechoslovakia, Poland, Bulgaria, Rumania, and Hungary. While their book is a seminal and important work, its very breadth prevents a detailed discussion of the most important individual films and trends of Yugoslav cinema and permits only the broadest identification of relevant sociopolitical and economic influences.

Even within Yugoslavia there exists no systematic and critical study of Yugoslav film. The most impressive recent contribution toward filling this void is the book *Leksikon jugoslovenskog filma*, edited by Dejan Kosanović, which serves as a kind of prolegomenon and prod to further and more detailed historical analysis. [4]

Scope and Purpose

This study focuses upon a thematic and critical analysis of the most significant feature films produced in Yugoslavia from the end of the Second World War to the present, with primary emphasis given to the period from 1961 to 1972—a period widely regarded by Yugoslav and foreign critics as Yugoslavia's most innovative and fecund period of film development and achievement—and to the period from 1977 to the present, which some critics are now referring to as a *new Yugoslav cinema*, as a *second new wave*, or more simply as a period of "resurgence" or "rebirth" of a nationally and internationally significant Yugoslav cinema.[5] The critical and thematic discussion of individual films and film trends included in this study is developed in relation to 1) the analysis of historically evolving and changing patterns of funding, organization, and management of film production, distribution, exhibition, and trade, i.e., the export of domestic films and the import of foreign films; 2) the development of a Yugoslav film culture,[6] comprising professional film critics and theoreticians, film journals, festivals, prizes, professionally trained cadres of technicians and film artists, and the formation of artistic "collectives," "schools," or aesthetic movements and trends; and 3) changing patterns of political and ideological control.

As a schematic and initial orientation to the scope of this study, the evolution of Yugoslav film from the end of the Second World War to the present is conceptualized as falling into four broad periods of development.

Administrative Period—1945–1950

This period was dominated by the Soviet model of hierarchical and centralized organization under strict party control. Films were conceived of as serving heuristic and propagandistic purposes and reflected the aesthetic principles of *nationalist realism*—Yugoslavia's moderate variant of the Stalinist-Zhdanov narrowly conceived socialist realism dogma. Films made during this period were often technically crude and naively propagandistic. Thematically the films were most often devoted to: 1) the idealistic glorification and confirmation of the revolutionary past—the War of Liberation, its legitimizing symbols, and its heroes, including, of course, the further reification of its supreme leader and commander, Josip Broz Tito, and 2) the reinforcement of revolutionary élan and heroic struggle to construct a new socialist state built on the shattered ruins of war. Even in this period, however, there were some films which chafed against the boundaries of socialist realism and anticipated thematic perspectives, genres, and stylistic innovations which were further elaborated in the next period.

Decentralization and Breaking the Mold—1951–1960

This period was characterized by a general evolution toward the decentralization of the organization and control of the Yugoslav film industry, and by the introduction, quite slow in the beginning, of the principles and practices of workers' self-management into all phases of film production and film distribution. It was also characterized by considerable maturation in the infrastructure and material base for film production; the elaboration of more sophisticated networks for film distribution and exhibition; a steady rise in the professionalization of film technicians and artists; the development of a livelier, "freer," and more informed group of film critics, who were able to express their views in a proliferating number of serious film journals, newspapers, and weeklies; a progressive opening of Yugoslavia to cultural and artistic influences from the West; and a significant increase in the number, range, and genres of films produced.

The initial phase of this period was distinguished by polemic and ideological efforts to stretch or to break the narrow propagandistic mold of the first period and was followed by increasing experimentation with new styles of realism— most notably influenced by Italian neorealism and the British school of realism of the late 1940s and 1950s—and by greater thematic complexity, variety of genres, and emphasis upon character development and psychological individualization. It was during this period as well that Yugoslav film began to gain an increasing international audience and recognition, with recognition occurring primarily in the realm of short, documentary, and animated films and accruing secondarily, and to a lesser extent, to a relatively small number of "quality"-produced feature films.

Republican Ascendancy and New Film—1961–1972

This period witnessed the further decentralization of the Yugoslav film industry, accompanied by a significant rise during the latter half of the period of political and economic control vested in the six republics of Slovenia, Croatia, Serbia, Bosnia-Hercegovina, Montenegro, and Macedonia and later in the autonomous regions of Kosovo and Vojvodina. It was during this period that Yugoslavia achieved its highest levels of film production and film export, with most of this rise occurring in the area of feature films. It was also a period of intense creativity and experimentation, in which Yugoslavia's vanguard of film critics, theorists, and film artists rallied loosely and with varying degrees of commitment under the banner of *novi film*[7] (*new film*) or *open cinema*.[8] While lacking a specific program or coherent aesthetic perspective, the advocates of *new film* sought to increase the latitude for individual and collective freedom of artistic expression, to promote stylistic experimentation in film form and film language, and to involve film in the expression of *savremene teme* (contemporary themes), including the right to critique the darker, ironic, alienated, and gloomier side of human, societal, and political existence, all within the context and premises of a Marxist-Socialist state—at a time in Yugoslavia's evolution when these very premises were a focal point for heated philosophical and ideological debate. While films associated with these new tendencies provoked the most controversy within Yugoslavia and garnered the greatest attention internationally, they coexisted with a much larger number of films produced during the same period which affirmed more orthodox aesthetic values and thematic perspectives or represented the growing trend toward "commercialism"—the production of light-entertainment films designed to please the average (or below average) tastes of the domestic film audience.

The apogee of feature film production both in quantitative terms and in terms of the progressive liberalization of film content and expression was reached in the years 1967 and 1968. However, from about 1968 to 1972, the counteroffensive against *new film* tendencies intensified under the banner of *black film*, which attacked these films for their negative and pessimistic view of Yugoslav socialist development, for the expression of themes associated with Western-style liberalism and individualism, and for their anarcho-individualistic nonconformism. This campaign was stimulated, in part, by events occurring on the larger political stage: the 1968 student demonstration in Belgrade, the Warsaw Pact invasion of Czechoslovakia, and especially the Croatian nationalist-separatist crisis of 1971. These events ushered in a period of increasing ideological stringency aimed at nonestablishment Marxists, intellectuals, student leaders, and artists, which, in the area of film, led to banning some films and subjecting others to more subtle styles of bureaucratic intervention. This constricting ideological climate was also accompanied by a severe financial crisis in the Yugoslav film industry (in part characteristic of world cinema), which occurred at the end of the 1960s and continued into the early 1970s.

Accommodation and Resurgence—1973–1983

During this period the Yugoslav film industry adapted to the complex new forms of self-management mechanisms and accountability instituted after the 1974 Yugoslav Party Congress, and by the end of the seventies it had experienced a rise in feature film production which rivaled that of the earlier period. This renewed higher level of production opened the way for a new, young generation of filmmakers, who have spearheaded the resurgence of an artistically more interesting and diverse Yugoslav cinema, which once again is returning to a greater level of filmic experimentation and the exploration of contemporary social and political themes.

Limitations of the Study

While this study adopts a general chronological framework as the clearest mode for analysis and presentation, it does not purport to be a systematic historical study of the overall development of Yugoslav film from the end of the Second World War. First, the focus of critical attention is upon fiction feature films. This emphasis is not meant to minimize, especially in the Yugoslav context, the interest and value of animated film, news films, short and documentary film, and amateur film. Indeed, developments in these fields are often commented upon as they reflect or sometimes anticipate new directions and thematic perspectives found in feature film production. Second, the primary emphasis of this study is upon feature films which represent "liberated" or "liberating" tendencies in the evolution of film content and in varying modes of stylistic expression.

In the first two periods (1945–1950; 1951–1960), critical attention is focused on feature films directed by Radoš Novaković, Stole Janković, Živorad Mitrović, Veljko Bulajić, Branko Bauer, Fedor Hanžeković, France Štiglic, Vladimir Pogačić, and others. Among the most important of the more than twenty film directors receiving critical attention in the period of *novi film* (1961–1972) are Ante Babaja, Zvonimir Berković, Bata Čengić, Boro Drašković, Puriša Đorđević, Boštjan Hladnik, Matjaž Klopčič, Dušan Makavejev, Vatroslav Mimica, Krsto Papić, Živojin Pavlović, Aleksandar Petrović, Mića Popović, and Želimir Žilnik. The newest generation of filmmakers, whose work will be discussed in the final chapter, include Rajko Grlić, Goran Marković, Goran Paskaljević, Miloš Radivojević, Lordan Zafranović, Srđan Karanović, and Bogdan Žižić.

Finally, it should be noted that the analysis of the most recent developments in Yugoslav feature film production is necessarily more provisional than that of the earlier periods, because the contour and shape of its major tendencies have not yet clearly emerged.

SOCIALIST FEDERAL
REPUBLIC OF YUGOSLAVIA

---- Republic   ······ Autonomous
     boundary   region
 ⊛ Federal capital   ⊚ Republican capital

1

Establishment and Evolution of a National Cinema, 1945-1950

It is difficult to envision a more unpromising set of conditions for establishing a national film industry than those which existed in Yugoslavia immediately following the Second World War. Before the war the Yugoslav film industry had been practically nonexistent, and what did exist was concentrated in a few major urban centers, most notably in Belgrade, Zagreb, and Ljubljana. Unlike other small countries, Yugoslavia did not adopt legislative measures to protect an indigenous film industry—laws that would limit the import of foreign films and ensure the distribution and financing of domestically produced films. In an attempt to compete with foreign-produced films, the small and struggling Yugoslav community of film artists relied primarily upon imitation rather than innovation, and the films produced revealed little of the remarkable diversity and unique character of the nations and nationalities composing Yugoslavia. Mira and Antonín J. Liehm have stated that "all efforts at making motion pictures in Yugoslavia before World War Two were purely commercial and of no cultural interest, and were also outside the framework of national traditions."[1]

At the same time, foreign firms, most notably American, exploited the film distribution market in Yugoslavia and lobbied heavily against any efforts to foster an authentic national cinema.[2] In the production of films, Yugoslavia was chiefly exploited by foreign studios for the attractiveness of its geographical locations and the cheapness of its manpower, so that even the films coproduced by foreign and Yugoslav film companies in the thirties could be called Yugoslav "only in their geographic location or in the presence of Yugoslav actors."[3]

Shorn of a sophisticated film history and film tradition such as that of the other newly formed socialist governments in Hungary, Poland, and Czechoslovakia, Yugoslavia found itself after the Second World War with an almost complete lack of trained film professionals, with film equipment which was scarce and antiquated, and with practically nonexistent systems of film production and distribution. There were fewer than five hundred cinema houses in all of Yugoslavia, many of which were damaged by the war and ill-equipped.[4] What did exist, however, was strong support from the state and a determined will to succeed. Immediately after the liberation of Belgrade in 1944, a film section was

1

established in the department of propaganda of the high command of the liberation forces; it later formed the basis for the organization of Yugoslav film.

Not only were the conditions and resources for the development of film in Yugoslavia scarce or nonexistent, they were also framed by a country savaged by a war of resistance against the occupying forces and a civil war waged among Partisans, Chetniks, and Ustashis. With the exception of Poland, no country had experienced such wide loss of life and destruction of its basic economic infrastructure. In the double holocaust of civil war and the resistance, the loss of life in Yugoslavia was staggering. Out of a population of 16 million, the Yugoslavs lost 1.9 million, of which 1.1 million deaths were directly attributed to the war and to massacres.[5] Especially devastating was the loss of lives in the age groups just entering their productive years and among those with skills and education. The average age of the fallen was estimated at twenty-two years; they included approximately 90,000 skilled workers and 40,000 "intellectuals." In addition:

> Some 822,000 buildings had been destroyed, 3.5 million were homeless, and an estimated 35 per cent of prewar industry, 289,000 peasant homesteads, between 50 and 70 per cent of various categories of livestock and 80 per cent of ploughs and harvesting equipment had been lost or put out of operation. Over 50 per cent of railway trackage, 77 per cent of locomotives and 84 per cent of goods wagons had been destroyed.[6]

In the first year after the war, mass starvation was avoided only by the intervention of aid from the UN Relief and Rehabilitation Administration, and the first factories, railways, roads, bridges, and buildings were put back into operation by a massive Yugoslav government-directed program of volunteer and forced work brigades.[7]

Faced with such a massive and complex set of priorities for rebuilding a war-torn country, it is a significant testimonial to the high importance which the new socialist regime placed upon film that the first concerted efforts to establish and build a new national cinema occurred in these early years of struggle against severe odds and deprivations.

The first period of establishing a national cinema in Yugoslavia was dominated by the Soviet model of hierarchical and centralized organization under strict party control. Films were conceived of as a powerful mass medium for serving heuristic and propagandistic purposes, as well as for reflecting the development of a distinctive socialist art based upon the principles of *nationalist realism*—Yugoslavia's variant of the Stalinist-Zhdanov narrowly conceived socialist realism dogma. In the initial five-year period following the Second World War, Yugoslavia produced only thirteen feature films—nearly all of which dealt with patriotic Partisan war themes or socialist reconstruction. The first feature film, *Slavica*, directed by Vjekoslav Afrić, was not completed until 1947; it centered upon Partisan guerrilla actions against the Italians along the Dalmatian coast of the Adriatic. During this same period, however, there were over five hundred documentary and short films made, along with a large number of newsreel segments,[8] which frequently provided a searing, firsthand account of war-torn villages, cities, and countryside of Yugoslavia and documented the early efforts to rebuild the shattered country. This period also witnessed the establishment of a basic infrastructure in the areas of film trade, film production, and film distribution upon which an independent national cinema could be built.

Early Stirrings

In the last days of October 1944, soon after the liberation of Belgrade, a film section was established in the department of propaganda of the high command of the liberation forces. The film section was provided with the task of organizing film activities in the liberated parts of the country. It undertook the distribution of films received from the Allies, approved film showings, established the price of admission tickets, supervised the production of news films, and operated the then relatively small number of nationalized film theaters.[9]

These temporary wartime arrangements for the organization of film activities in Yugoslavia were supplanted on 3 July 1945 with the formation of the Film Enterprise of the People's Republic of Yugoslavia (FPNRJ). After the first elections of the new Tito-led socialist government, at the end of 1945, its name was changed to the Film Enterprise of the Federation of People's Republics of Yugoslavia (FPFNRJ). It represented the first centralized effort to organize cinematography in the new state. Placed under the ministry of education, with centralized funding and control, the state film enterprise was given the tasks of:

1. Administering all production of film documentaries, news films, and cultural-educational films.
2. Maintaining exclusive control over the licensing and regulation of the import and export of films.
3. Organizing and distributing of films throughout the country.
4. Organizing and administering the nationalized film theaters and the private owners of permanent and movable projection facilities.[10]

In less than a year, the inadequacy of this form of organization to meet the diverse needs and ambitions of a young film industry was recognized. In June 1946, a much wider and deeper commitment to film was made by the central government when it formed a separate committee for cinematography as the highest state organ for the development of film, and placed at its head the well-known Yugoslav writer Aleksandar Vučo, who was appointed by Tito himself.

When the old organization was disbanded, on 30 July 1946, it could claim that, despite working against considerable odds, it had produced sixty numbers of film journals—eleven from Croatia, six from Slovenia, and the remainder from Serbia—and twenty-seven different short and educational films, with fifteen of these produced in Serbia, seven in Croatia, and five in Slovenia.[11]

Committee for Cinematography

The new federal committee for cinematography quickly established separate regional committees for cinematography in each of the six republics, except Montenegro, where a special commission was formed. On the federal level, two film production houses were formed, Zvezda film in Belgrade, which specialized in film journals, and Zora film in Zagreb, which specialized in cultural-educational films. The committee also set up a separate enterprise (which evolved into Jugoslavija film) to regulate the import and export of films, and rapidly established separate production centers in each of the republics. The largest film studio, Avala film, in Belgrade, where the first feature film, *Slavica*, was produced, was founded on 15 July 1946. One day later, Jadran film was established in Zagreb, the capital city of Croatia: it produced its first feature film, *This People Must Live* (*Živjeće ovaj narod*), in 1947. On the same day, 16 July, Triglav film in Ljubljana, Slovenia was established, and nearly a year later, on 1 July 1947, Bosna film in Sarajevo, Bosnia-Hercegovina and Vardar film in Skopje, Macedonia were formed. The last of the six Yugoslav republics to found a studio was Montenegro, where Lovćen film was established in Budva on 3 July 1948.[12]

The Committee for Cinematography also elaborated a five-year plan for the development of all areas of film activities, which established as its main tasks: 1) to develop a network of film theaters and film projection halls which would provide an average of one film-showing facility for every ten thousand inhabitants, 2) to build and organize film production and technical facilities capable of producing annually no fewer than 40 short and feature-length fictional or "art" films, 100 documentary and educational films, and 124 weekly and monthly news journals, and 3) to create a production base for the domestic manufacture of needed technical supplies and film materials.[13]

In addition, the committee began the ambitious task of planning, building, and equipping a new Film City (Filmski grad) at Košutnjak, on the wooded outskirts of Belgrade; established the first film school in Belgrade and two technical schools in Belgrade and Zagreb for the training of film technicians; and founded a serious monthly journal, *Film*, as an outlet for film discussion, criticism, and polemics.

The goal of this first five-year plan was no less than to establish a national film structure which would permit Yugoslavia to stand on its own feet and to free itself, in a relatively brief time, from the necessity of depending on foreign assistance and support.[14]

In assessing the results of the first year and a half of this plan, one of the important figures in the early development of Yugoslavia's young film industry, Jakša Petrić, outlined both the initial results and the numerous problems and impediments which stood in the way of moving toward a more sophisticated and mature film industry. In summarizing the accomplishments of this initial period, Petrić could point to a significant increase in film production, including the completion of the first two feature films, *Slavica* and *This People Must Live*, thirty-one documentary films, forty-six weekly news films, twenty-eight monthly news journals, and four educational films. As opposed to the first year after the war, this period also witnessed the first film productions from the less-well-developed republics of Bosnia-Hercegovina and Macedonia, with Montenegro the only remaining republic not yet prepared to enter into active film production. This period also revealed a notable increase in the number of film theaters—from 576 in 1946 to 635 in 1947—along with a dramatic growth in film viewers—from 25,988,127 admissions in 1946 to 40,613,419 admissions in 1947. This growth was especially strong in the poorer republics of Bosnia-Hercegovina, Macedonia, and Montenegro. In Bosnia-Hercegovina admissions grew from 2,716,000 in 1946 to 3,373,436 in 1947; in Macedonia from 1,827,880 to 2,843,291; and in Montenegro from 371,090 to 706,684. Through the operation of approximately thirty movable projection facilities, many villagers in the poorer sections of Yugoslavia had the opportunity to view films for the first time.[15]

These accomplishments were made possible in part by the move from a totally centralized form of organization at the federal level to a pyramidal structure which allowed for more initiative and planning on the republican level, and in part by the more than tenfold increase in state funding[16] which became possible after the worst damages of the war had been repaired.[17]

Along with the accomplishments, however, were a number of weaknesses and unresolved problems. According to Petrić, film distribution and film showings were not coordinated between the central distribution firm, Jugoslavija film, and republican agencies. This situation often led to delays of as much as a month or more in scheduling and rotating films; a lack of planning and publicity at the local level for film showing; low initiative in making films available to more-remote villages; a shortage of trained projectionists, resulting in frequent breakdowns and damage to film prints; poor packing, inspection, and mailing of prints, which greatly reduced their usable life; and local administrations which were top-heavy with office workers and lacking in skilled operators.[18]

In the area of film production, Petrić acknowledged that the material and technical base for film, though improved, was still inadequate for the ambitious demands made upon it. He nevertheless argued that its effective utilization was severely undermined by poorly organized shooting schedules of inexperienced directors, poor lab and studio utilization, the lack of trained personnel in all artistic and technical areas, and even a lack of trained mechanics to maintain cars and other means of transport adequately for location shooting.[19] In the area of general organization of the film industry, Petrić was one of the first to see the need for greater development of local and republican organizations and the necessity of separating and distinguishing the administrative tasks of the three major areas of film activity—film trade, i.e., import and export of films; film production; and film distribution and theatrical showings.[20]

Underlying all of these problems, however, and the most important and difficult issue to address, was the need to build cadres of skilled film artists, technicians, and administrators capable of leading the young Yugoslav film industry to a higher plane of technical and artistic achievement and toward a more rational utilization of scarce resources for the production, distribution, and showing of films. While for the first time in its history, at the end of 1946, Yugoslavia had established a state film school for film acting and film direction (in Belgrade) and two middle-level technical schools (in Belgrade and Zagreb) for the training of film technicians, these centers of education and training lacked the facilities, courses, and personnel to meet the needs of a rapidly expanding industry and to free Yugoslavia completely from dependence on the advice and support of foreign experts and film artists—most notably during this period, Russian and Czechoslovakian.[21]

Although the multiple problems facing the Yugoslav film industry during this formative period were by no means completely resolved when the Committee for Cinematography was disbanded in April 1951 in favor of a more decentralized film structure, the committee could lay claim to several impressive achievements—achievements all the more impressive when seen in the context of the shattered condition of the country immediately following the war and of the severe economic and political crisis which occurred following Yugoslavia's break with the Soviet Union in 1948. During the nearly five-year period in which film activities were centered in the hands of the federal committee for cinematography and its surrogate republican organizations, a sufficiently modern organization and material and technical base had been established to support the annual and continuous production of domestic films. A slow but steady improvement in the growth of trained and experienced cadres of film artists and technicians had been achieved. Film production had risen to levels which exceeded by several times the annual production of prewar Yugoslavia and included the production of 13 feature films, 270 documentary and short films, and more than 300 numbers of film news and journals. Moreover, production had expanded during this period to include all of Yugoslavia's six republics, including a modest output by the smallest of its republics, Montenegro.[22] The network of film theaters had increased substantially, from 576 in 1946 to more than 920 by April 1951, and viewers had increased from 31,520,000 in 1946 to more than double that number by the end of 1950, 67,926,000. During the same period, state investments in the development of all areas of film activity had grown by more than ten times.[23]

Ideological and Aesthetic Perspectives

As important to the early Yugoslav leaders in film as the task of building a new film industry was the development of a set of ideological and aesthetic principles which would guide and mold the content and direction of Yugoslavia's young Marxist-socialist cinema. From its inception, the newly founded national cinema was guided by party-line orthodoxy, which conceived of film as the most important mass medium for reaching all levels of society and possessed as its greatest goals: 1) the idealistic confirmation and reification of the revolutionary past, i.e., the National War of Liberation and its heroes, and 2) the confirmation and reinforcement of revolutionary élan required to construct a new Marxist-socialist state.

On the aesthetic level, the films of this period, for the most part, adhered to the principles of socialist realism inspired by the Soviet Union, with deviations from these principles found primarily on the level of nationalistic thematic perspectives. At its most rigid, the doctrine of *socialist realism* emphasizes the strict delineation of good and evil, approved genres, and set character types. This combination of socialist orthodoxy with classical patterns of film narrative—based on directed logical coherence, rationally presented character motivation, in which characters represent their value systems explicitly, and a predictable "clockwork" functioning of intentions, causes, and effects—made the serious contradictions and paradoxes inherent in the human and sociopolitical condition nearly impossible to explore or to reveal. The rigid application of socialist realist norms in the area of film creation, as Herbert Eagle has pointed out, leads to films that "serve the explicit, immediate needs of socialist construction by fostering appropriate attitudes" of depicting reality "not *as such* but in terms of its 'revolutionary development'—that is, that contemporary social reality is presented not *as it is*, but with a substantial (though inaccurate) admixture of *what is supposed to be* according to ideological positions," that the films be "didactic and clear-cut," and finally that the film's assessment of a situation, past or present, "be ultimately optimistic."[24] In their most sterile realization, such films are replete with coarse propagandizing, ideological posturing, and sloganeering set in the context of socially important but banal content; involve a mechanical analysis of reality through sharply defined antinomies such as reactionary-revolutionary, individual-social, subjective-collective; and deny any connection with worldwide artistic traditions.

While it is sometimes asserted that Yugoslavia escaped the worst consequences of Zhdanovism[25] through the development of its own more moderate variant of socialist realism, there is little to distinguish the two variants in the area of film expression except, as previously mentioned, in the area of nationalist-inspired thematic orientation. In the lead article of the first issue of the monthly journal *Film*, the director of the federal committee for cinematography, Aleksandar Vučo, outlined the orthodox strictures which should guide the early development of Yugoslav film production. Vučo asserted that the dominant traits of the new cinema should be:

> . . . high principles and feelings of responsibility by our film workers toward their film viewers, toward their nation, and toward their country. Our film art cannot and must not allow itself to have any other interests than the interests of our national authority, no other tasks than the task of educating the wide mass of viewers in the spirit of our national and cultural revolution. In her first stages . . . our film production, so much of which is still undeveloped and unskilled, nevertheless has proved that it is inextricably linked with the life of our country and that all her efforts are informed in a direction that shows the nations composing our country involved in an unparalleled aspiration to change all of the old relations and ideas and in an unparalleled struggle to achieve a richer and better future for man.[26]

Conceiving of film as the richest resource among all the artistic media for reaching and informing all levels of society, and for "uniting truth with artistic strength," Vučo argued that "our nations have the right to demand of film artists that they know well the social and political nature of our state and the internal nature of its historical process" and that each viewer "can see and has the right to see on the film screen all the stages of our heroic and cultural past, all the stages of our national war of liberation throughout the entire country, involving all her nations, in the struggle to create new material, cultural, and human values."[27]

According to Vučo, it is at the level of film "truth" and not at the level of technical prowess (as desirable as it is to achieve higher standards of technical excellence) that the young Yugoslav film industry should be measured and where its deepest value to the nations of Yugoslavia can be found. It is a mistake for the young film industry of Yugoslavia to measure its accomplishments or to be guided in its future development by invidious comparisons with the highly developed film industries of America and the countries of Western Europe. The rich material and technological base for film production which these countries possess is often employed for light and "vulgar entertainment" or for purveying values and ideological perspectives alien to a society built upon socialist principles, and consequently it poses a danger to viewers who may be seductively led by these films into the artificial spheres of "mysticism, stereotypes, melodrama, and lies" and away from the sphere which embraces the "problems and demands of a socialist worker's state." As for the more "serious" film experimentation in the West, Vučo warns against the dangers of formalism, into which film can so easily fall, leading to the creation of films devoid of meaningful social content and characterized only by "abstraction and pure exterior technical beauty." Against all such tendencies and influences, Vučo urges unremitting battle. [28]

Vučo also compares the young Yugoslav film production with the Soviet Union's "peerless work in cinema," and suggests that at the level of social and political truth, i.e., "truth in words and images," the Yugoslavs' early film efforts need not take a second place to the Soviets' and need not be a cause for shame. He insists that the most valid comparison of the early news journals and documentary work of the Yugoslavs could most accurately be compared to the Kino series and Agitprop films of the Soviet Union made during and immediately following the First World War, when their film industry was in a similarly developing state. At the same time, Vučo, in a manner typical of this period, acknowledges that, while the sources and stages of development of Yugoslav and Soviet cinema were certainly different, there was, nonetheless, reason to suspect that Yugoslav film would turn to "those clear and well-lit paths which the Soviets are following, orienting itself to the millions of working people actively sharing with them and strengthening them in the knowledge of our national consciousness, and of its power and its great tasks." [29]

In describing the proper approach to the creation of film works, Vučo also warns against the creation of a "star" system and the elevation of leading personalities, and emphasizes instead the necessity for collective work and cooperative efforts among film artists (directors, scenarists, cinematographers, actors, and editors) and workers in all the technical areas. He ends with the exhortation that the collective efforts of film workers in concert with the wide national masses should struggle for "a new life and a new culture, instructing the nations in the spirit of new human relations and in a spirit of love toward homeland and toward freedom." [30]

The themes which Vučo enunciated in this early manifesto were often repeated and elaborated upon by other film artists and critics throughout most of this initial five-year period: 1) Films should be based on principles of socialist realism, avoiding abstract experimentation, and instead should be oriented toward clear and effective communication with the masses of viewers; 2) they should serve heuristic and propagandistic purposes aimed at inspiring viewers with a deeper understanding of the revolutionary struggle which the country as a whole, as well as its various nations and nationalities, had just passed through, and they should forge a deep collective bond in meeting the challenges of creating a new socialist state; 3) the cinema of the Soviet Union offered the best prospect for illuminating the path which Yugoslav cinema should follow; and 4) film work itself should be fashioned on collectivist rather than individualistic principles.

One of the more interesting transformations of these basic themes, of course, was the reversal in polemics regarding the Soviets' role in the initial growth of a new Yugoslav cinema which occurred after Tito's dramatic break with Stalin and the expulsion of Yugoslavia from the Cominform on 28 June 1948. While the initial reaction of the top members of the government and Communist party of Yugoslavia following this expulsion was guardedly mild and conciliatory, by the end of 1949 and the beginning of 1950, a tough counteroffensive was beginning to take shape, which led to resolutions of support for the Tito-led government from all sectors of the society and sharp attacks on the Soviet Union and the Cominform.[31] Vučo, again, was among those in the forefront of the Yugoslav film community, attacking what he characterized as the Soviets' arrogant assumption that they possessed absolute superiority and dominance in all spheres of politics, knowledge, and culture, and of their habit of "falsifying history whenever it touched on the role of other socialist states."[32] Vučo then analyzed a number of Russian films produced after the Second World War, which he asserted reveal a progressive degeneration of the Soviet Union's great socialist experiments in film of the 1920s and 1930s toward portrayals on the screen of "great Russian hegemonic and nationalistic chauvinism."[33]

A similarly sharp and more detailed attack on Soviet "revisionist" tendencies in film culture was made by another early leader of the Yugoslav film community, Vicko Raspor. He asserted that a long time before the resolutions of the Cominform in 1948, it was clear that the Soviet film advisors who had been sent to Yugoslavia after the war were working along the lines of the "general revisionist understanding of the Central Committee of the Soviet Communist Party" and that their objective was to subvert rather than to promote the development of an authentic people's socialist film art and industry in Yugoslavia. In short, said Raspor, "it was necessary, from their point of view, that we stay clear of 'bad business,' and that, in our film development, we build a culture which was socialist in form, and nationalistic (that is, hegemonic and great-Russian) in content."[34] Because of the resolution of the Cominform, it had become much clearer, asserted Raspor, "that harmful influences on our film can originate not only from the West but also from the East."[35]

Raspor argued that it had always been clear that it was necessary to protect "our national artists and the reflection of reality in our artistic works from the influence of bourgeois films which preach the most heterogeneous kinds of 'philosophy,' 'science,' and 'aesthetics.'" Among these Raspor listed "mysticism, antihumanism, individualism, nationalism, pessimism, surrealism, and existentialism."[36]

Now it was clear, stated Raspor, that "we must also protect ourselves from the aesthetic dogmatism of the Central Committee of the Soviet Communist Party and the revisions of Marxist-Leninist thought and decadence in the field of culture to which it has led." [37]

It is evident that these polemic declarations of independence and reassessments of Soviet leadership and influence in the development of Yugoslavia's film art did not immediately signal an opening toward Western culture and art. Indeed, the deformation of socialist ideals which was now being attributed to Soviet film art following the Second World War was seen, at this period of time, as intensifying the need for Yugoslav film artists to assume the mantle of protectors of true socialist realism or *nationalist realism* dogma. [38]

Thematic Perspectives

Of the thirteen feature films produced in Yugoslavia by the end of 1950, all but one dealt either with the National War of Liberation or with socialist reconstruction following the war. The one exception was the film *Sofka*, directed by Radoš Novaković, which was a filmic adaptation of a classic novel of the turn of the century, *Impure Blood* (*Nečista krv*) by Bora Stanković (a film which is discussed in greater detail later).

The War of Liberation

The National War of Liberation waged by the Communist-commanded Partisans in Yugoslavia was the central founding myth upon which the new Tito-led postwar government was built. In order to understand the filmic transformations of its primary legitimizing symbols and motifs, it is necessary first to trace out the broad historical schematics of this dramatic and complex event. [39]

The invasion of Yugoslavia by the Axis forces began on 6 April 1941 with a savage bombing attack on Belgrade under the code name "Operation Punishment" and ended only eleven days later, on 17 April, with total capitulation. King Peter II and his government, which had been newly installed less than a month before (27 March) by a military coup d'etat and widespread anti-Axis demonstrations in Belgrade and elsewhere, had already fled the country and subsequently formed a government in exile in London.

Following their swift military victory, the Axis occupiers proceeded to dismember and obliterate the political structure and boundaries of Yugoslavia, the "land of the South Slavs," which had been newly created at the end of the First World War. Defeat was total, and Yugoslavia ceased to exist. The largest defeated territory of Yugoslavia was formed into the "independent" State of Croatia and placed in the hands of the Fascist and terrorist leader Ante Pavelić and his Praetorian Guard, the Ustashis, operating under Italian and German suzerainty. The new state included Bosnia and Hercegovina, a long-time dream of Greater

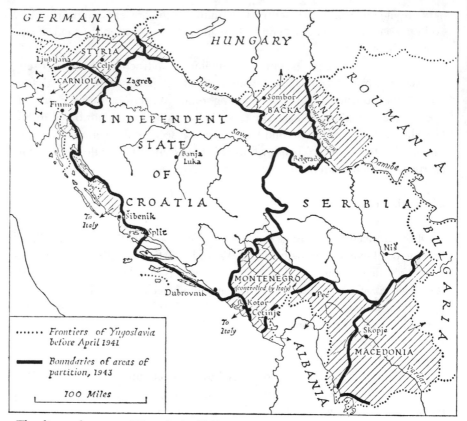

The dismemberment of Yugoslavia, 1941.

Croatian nationalists, but was deprived of a large part of the Dalmatian coastal region and the Adriatic islands, which were annexed by Italy. Pavelić quickly established a brutal dictatorship, which assumed as its first task the racial and religious purification of the region, which meant the forced conversion or extermination of the Serbs—nearly fifteen percent of Croatia proper and over a third of the population of Bosnia and Hercegovina—as well as the persecution of Jews and other non-Croatian minorities. This program was carried out with primitive ferocity, and included desecration of churches, rape, drownings, pillage, and well-documented cases of atrocities involving driving stakes through living skulls, mutilation, and Ustashi executioners who carried, as trophies, sackfuls of human eyes.

Slovenia disappeared from the map, with the more highly developed region of the north annexed by the German Reich and the lower half by the Italians. Montenegro was again declared a kingdom, and its crown was united with that of the Italian occupiers. The Kosovo region, with its majority population of Albanians, became a part of Albania, already under direct Italian rule. Bulgaria claimed a large section of Macedonia, formerly a part of Yugoslavia, and proceeded to institute a harsh program of Bulgarization. In similar fashion, Hungary annexed and initiated a program of Magyarization in the former Yugoslav region of Bačka, lying south of Hungary's border. The Germans administered the Banat, lying along Rumania's border, and recruited their administrators from the large population of immigrant Germans which lived in that area. Serbia itself, which had been the heart of patriotic and pro-Allied demonstrations against pacts of friendship and cooperation with the Axis powers, and had led the coup d'état which had installed the short-lived regime of King Peter II, was reduced to a rump state under the military occupation of the Germans. Although hard pressed to find reliable collaborators from the ranks of the rebellious Serbs, the Germans had succeeded by August 1941 in establishing a puppet regime under General Milan Nedić, a former minister of war and commander of the southern group of Yugoslav armies. He was given carefully circumscribed limits of authority to form a government of "national salvation" and raise a small military force called the Serbian State Guard.

The rapidity and deadly completeness of this catastrophe initially left the Yugoslav peoples prostrate and demoralized. Before the summer was over, however, based in part on the inspiration and new hope engendered by the German invasion of Russia on 22 June 1941, the series of small skirmishes and acts of resistance against the occupying forces which had taken place up to that time developed into full-scale rebellions in Serbia and Montenegro. These initial and remarkably successful uprisings were led by a small but well-organized Yugoslav Communist party under the leadership of Josip Broz Tito, along with his talented and tightly organized inner circle of seasoned conspirators and leaders, and by the Chetniks under the leadership of Draža Mihajlović, a colonel on the general staff of the prewar royal army, who refused to recognize the surrender of the old Yugoslav army and had established his headquarters on the wooded slope of the Ravna Gora in Western Serbia. The uprising in Serbia succeeded in routing the Germans from most of the countryside and from the towns and villages throughout central and western Serbia. Liberated areas were partly under Chetnik control and partly under Partisan control. It was in these circumstances that Tito and Mihajlović met in mid-September in the village of Struganik at the foot of Ravna Gora and worked out tentative and limited agreements of cooperation. Despite occasional clashes, the uneasy alliance between Partisans and Chetniks held together, and on 26 October another meeting was held between Tito and Mihajlović in the village of Brajići—which, however, resulted in no firm or workable agreements for further cooperative efforts in prosecuting the resistance against the Germans. Following this meeting, clashes between partisans and

Chetniks became more serious, and on 1 November a major engagement was fought, in which the Partisans captured the town of Požega from the Chetniks. In the meantime, the Germans had prepared a massive counteroffensive and, aided by the growing internecine rivalry between Chetnik and Partisan forces, were able to drive the Partisans out of the town of Užice, where Tito had set up his main headquarters, and across the border of Serbia into the mountain fastness of Bosnia, while the Chetniks retired to their retreat around the area of Ravna Gora.

In Montenegro, where a history of resistance to foreign invaders was a proud national tradition, a rising had occurred which was even swifter and more spectacular than that which had occurred in Serbia but which ended with no-less-tragic results. Following the proclamation of a puppet regime on 13 July, a spontaneous national uprising occurred, which again was spearheaded principally by Partisan and Chetnik forces. Fighting in common cause, the combined nationalist forces of Montenegro succeeded in driving the Italian occupiers nearly to the sea. Under the influence of Milovan Djilas and the Marxist intellectual Moša Pijade, however, the Partisan forces in Montenegro followed an extremist political line, in direct variance with Tito's own policy, in attempting to impose Communist orthodoxy in the liberated territory. This policy, which led to many excesses in liquidating opponents, played into the hands of the Italians, who were able to win over the "nationalist" Chetniks—loosely aligned to Mihajlović's forces in Serbia—and to join with them in direct collaboration to drive the Partisans out of Montenegro.

From that point on, the war that was waged in Yugoslavia was forged on the anvil of both civil war and resistance against the multiple occupying forces which had dismembered and obliterated the old Yugoslavia. In that struggle the Partisans steadily gained in strength and prominence, while their arch rivals, the Chetniks, faded and became irretrievably compromised by "agreements," "understandings," and, finally, direct collaborative military efforts with the enemy occupiers. This already complicated picture, of course, was further compounded by the war that was waged against the Ustashi forces of the "independent" State of Croatia, which from the outset were wed to the military and political fortunes of the Fascist occupiers.

The growth, bravery, and military successes of the Partisans are legendary. The Partisans had grown from a general staff without an army in July 1941, to a force of about 80,000 at the end of that year, to some 230,000 organized in "divisions" and "corps" (therefore not including scattered, smaller guerrilla units) by the autumn of 1943, to a full-scale and well-equipped army of more than 350,000 by the end of the war.[40]

The Partisans had been equally successful in winning the political battle to determine the shape of a postwar Yugoslav socialist state. The boldest of these moves was taken on 29 November 1943, when representatives from all regions of

talent for bold initiative a
, enjoyed three advantages
"a better and more discipline
with flexibility and generous r
d advantage was "consistent imple
onstantly and everywhere . . . disrega
on and defining the enemy as the forc
o fought with them." And, finally, and p
lution to the national question, blazoned
ty' and in the promise of a federal state an
mposition of their leadership." [43]

m such a brief sketch, the epic proportions which
n had assumed in Yugoslavia and the rich resource
resentation and for propagandizing and legitimizing
socialist government. However, all of these early film
exception of France Štiglic's first film, *On Their Own*
bed by the prevailing strictures of *nationalist realist*
aive and inept scenarios, exaggerated pathos, simplistic
imitations, and theatrical histrionics. They were films
ce, neither known nor remarked outside of Yugoslavia.
zations, however, should not obscure the enthusiasm with
de and the sometimes enthusiastic, or, at least, tolerant,
y were received by Yugoslav viewing publics. Viewers for the
to see indigenously produced films which reflected, however
stically, their own cultures and past experiences. At the same
mics, discussions, criticism, and self-doubts were expressed by
critics and film artists impatient to see Yugoslav-produced films
r plane of technical and artistic expression.
ture film in postwar Yugoslavia was *Slavica*, produced by Avala
de in 1947 and directed by Vjekoslav Afrić. Afrić had picked up
film direction he could as an assistant director to the well-known
or Abram Room, in shooting the film *In the Mountains of Yugoslavia
ma Jugoslavije*) in 1946. His primary training, however, was in the-
eceived his diploma in acting from the School of Dramatic Art in
the 1920s and subsequently pursued a successful career in the prin-
aters in Split, Sarajevo, Belgrade, and Zagreb. During the war he served
e Partisans and helped to establish and to direct the Theater of National
tion. After the war he combined his film work with a continuing career
ater and was appointed as the first rector of the School of Film Art in

In Partisa...

the Partisa...
domestic oppo...
zation, combining...
autonomous local initiati...
tion of the decision to fight the...
reprisals against the civilian popula...
all occupiers and of all Yugoslavs w...
haps most important, "was their s...
the slogan 'Brotherhood and Un...
manifested in the all-Yugoslav c...

Early Partisan Films

It is easy to discern, even fr...
the National War of Liberati...
that it provided for filmic re...
the newly founded people's...
efforts, with the interesting...
Ground, were circumscr...
dogma and plagued by...
stereotyping, technical...
frozen in time and pl...
Such broad character...
which they were ma...
spirit with which the...
first time were able...
crudely and simpl...
time, serious pol...
more discerning...
move to a high...
The first fea...
film of Belgr...
what skills i...
Soviet direc...
(U planina...
ater: he...
Zagreb i...
cipal th...
with th...
Libera...
in t...

tio...

P...
exile...
ments a...
whether th...
Finally, the...
in the Istrian...
given over to Ita...
course, was to co...
formed Yugoslavia a...

The sessions at Jajc...
war of resistance and in...
forces greatly outnumbere...
towns and the most importa...
to face major confrontations a...
fore the basic outlines of a newly...
ized in actuality.[41]

Dennison Rusinow has claimed th...

> . . . were on the one hand the strateg...
> brilliance of Tito and his Party comrades,
> on the other the continuous blunders of the.
> disparate and contradictory motives and goals
> than a fraction of the populace.[42]

Belgrade. Afrić sketched out the initial scenario for the film *Slavica* while work-ing on the Room film and chose as his setting the Adriatic coast, the region where he had served as a Partisan and one which he knew intimately, having been born in 1906 on one of the major southern islands of the Adriatic, Hvar, not far from the major coastal port city of Split.

The story takes place in Afrić's home town and covers the whole span of the war, from the time that the Italians occupied the Dalmation coast to their capitu-lation to the Allies in 1943; it shows the consequent German presence and cul-minates in the liberation of Split by the victorious Partisan forces. The principal protagonist of the film, the fisherman Marin, and his brave comrades conceal a fishing boat from the Italians in order to outfit it as a gunboat. Their efforts are thwarted by stereotypically presented local informers and sneaky, buffoonlike col-laborators, and they are captured and put in prison. Their subsequent rescue is effected by a local Partisan guerrilla unit under the command of an ever-smiling, bold, compassionate leader, who is as adept in leading his men in full-throated renditions of patriotic Partisan songs as he is in leading them into strenuous com-bat. Using the rocky retreats of the coastal island for protection, the brave fisher-folk use their makeshift gunboat for missions to nearby islands. Slavica is a courageous young maiden in love with Marin but too constrained by the rigors of battle to express more than an occasional comradely embrace. The summary battle occurs on the sea, where the Partisans, making toward Split with Marin at the helm, manage, miraculously, to sink a formidably armed German gunboat, and to board and subdue another at the moment that their own badly damaged boat is listing precariously. The brave Slavica loses her life to German bullets while she is in the hold of the ship trying to caulk the holes made by German shells. Her dead body is discovered floating in the water of the listing ship after the smoke of battle has cleared. The ship is named *Slavica* in her honor and is celebrated as one of the first of a crude Partisan navy. The last scene of the film takes place in liberated Split, with celebration, marching, and flags. Marin finds the parents of the slain Slavica, and he and the grief-torn parents join the march-ing throngs, flags unfurling in the wind behind them, framed by a tight three-shot from below—heroically transforming grief into exalted revolutionary vic-tory—facing resolutely forward, against time and grief, to form a new nation of brotherhood and unity of all the nations and nationalities of Yugoslavia.

The film abounds in such simplistic melodramatic sequences, acted out with theatrical flourish and excess and accompanied by very simple stereotyping of collaborators and satraps; of evil, indolent, pleasure-loving Italian occupiers; of harsh, unfeeling Germans; of exceptionally brave, fair, enthusiastic, ever-victorious Partisans, joining hands and hearts in song and heroic deeds; and of simple, strong fisherfolk, learning for the first time the magic legendary name of "Tito" and discovering the real meaning of the National War of Liberation, in

On location. *Slavica*.

Marin and Slavica. *Slavica*.

Marin and his brave comrades. *Slavica.*

which their own destinies are merged with a new Yugoslavia reborn from the ashes of the old and characterized by brotherhood, unity, and victory for all the peoples of the country.

Despite its naiveté and crude propagandizing, the film, nonetheless, does capture well the Dalmatian coastal setting and the dialects and authentic culture of that region in a way that is almost entirely lacking in the professionally better-made Soviet film *In the Mountains of Yugoslavia.* The film is also imbued with an intense nationalism and pride, which, despite all simplifications, is a more accurate rendering of the indigenous all-Yugoslav character of the War of Liberation than that given in the Soviet film, which portrayed the Yugoslav Partisan movement as deriving its force and direction from overarching Soviet leadership and from the might of the Red Army, where the true source of Partisan successes are to be discovered. There is even a sequence in the film in which two extraordinarily brave and resourceful soldiers of the Red Army fight off vastly superior enemy forces to "rescue" an entire unit of Partisans.

Finally, the film *Slavica* is built on a structural model which was to be emulated by most of the other early Partisan films of this period. It is a pattern which begins by affirming Partisan-led local initiatives in specific locales, involving the distinctive nationalities of the region, and builds organically to an affirmation of the epic all-Yugoslav character of its leadership and heroes—with Tito presented as the preeminent heroic unifying symbol—and of the all-Yugoslav character of the Partisan fighting forces, which becomes the essential guarantor of ultimate victory in war, as well as the basis upon which to build a completely new Yugoslavia.

Perhaps for these reasons, and perhaps because *Slavica* was simply the first Yugoslav feature film after the war, its reception by audiences throughout the country, at least as measured by numbers of viewers and comments from contemporaries, was strong and enthusiastic. During the forty-three days it was shown in Belgrade, it attracted 173,000 viewers; in Zagreb over a twenty-one-day engagement, it attracted 68,000; in Skopje, 40,000 in seven days; in Ljubljana, 20,000 in eleven days; and after its first year, *Slavica* had attracted nearly 2,000,000 viewers throughout all regions of Yugoslavia.[44] This strong showing was not matched by other early Partisan war films made in the same naive, epic mold. These were nonetheless widely viewed, with the second feature film, *This People Must Live* (*Živjeće ovaj narod*), by the Croatian director Nikola Popović, attracting in its first year over 1,200,000 viewers, and *Immortal Youth* (*Besmrtna mladost*), directed by Vojislav Nanović and produced by Avala film in 1948, attracting nearly 750,000 viewers in less than six months.[45]

At the same time, the more discerning critics and members of the Yugoslav film community expressed increasing impatience with the level of technical and artistic achievement revealed in these early efforts. The literary and film critic Eli Finci, writing in *Borba*, the official Communist daily newspaper, praised the authentic nationalist character and overall theme of the film but was nonetheless unsparing in pointing out its obvious weaknesses in scenario, naive portrayals etched only in simple extremes of black and white, and lack of both internal cohesion and clarity of overall purpose, and he questioned whether such was the path that future Yugoslav feature films should follow.[46] This critique became the subject of a "round-table discussion"—a form of polemic confrontation and sometimes lively exchange of views which is popular in the Yugoslav film community to the present time—held in the editorial club of *Borba*. Present at the meeting were the critic Eli Finci, the director of the film, Vjekoslav Afrić, and seven other Yugoslav critics and film artists: Jovan Popović, Milan Bogdanović, Velibor Gligorić, Hugo Klajn, O. Bihalji-Merin, N. Hercigonja, and Marijan Stilinović. The majority of those present agreed with Finci's assessment of the weaknesses of the film, to which they added their own elaborations, but they were highly critical of the failure of the critic to properly understand the process of film creation and the limiting technical and artistic milieu in which the film was made and, more importantly, to properly assess its positive and inspiring influence on the masses of viewers.[47]

Teodor Balk addressed the same problems as they were revealed in the early short films and documentaries of the period in an article in the second number of *Film*. He asserted that cliché-ridden film texts, character presentation, dialogue, and thematic oversimplification might be the death of film in Yugoslavia—not only of "artistic values but also the death of their social utility and effectiveness."[48] Writing toward the end of the period, Jovan Popović asserted that the complex and rich materials suggested by Yugoslavia's immediate revolutionary past and socialist reconstruction had too often received only surface film treatment abounding in repetitive stereotypes and formulaic rigidity. He also called for the elaboration of new thematic perspectives and genres, including historical dramas and filmic adaptations of the traditional literatures of the nations of Yugoslavia—the rich possibilities of which had already been suggested by Novaković's film *Sofka*—as well as films dealing with contemporary life, films of social satire, and the development of animated films.[49]

Liberalizing Tendencies

Of the small number of feature films produced in Yugoslavia during the initial five-year period following the Second World war, three stand out as suggesting deeper and more mature possibilities for future filmic development: France Štiglic's *On Their Own Ground*, dealing with Partisan war themes; Vladimir Pogačić's *Story of a Factory*, centered on postwar socialist reconstruction; and Radoš Novaković's *Sofka*, the only film produced during the period which effectively suggests the possibility of filmically portraying prewar historical subjects and adapting traditional Yugoslav literary sources to the screen.

On Their Own Ground

France Štiglic, in his first feature film, *On Their Own Ground* (*Na svojoj zemlji*), produced by Triglav film of Ljubljana in 1948, early established himself as one of Yugoslavia's most gifted film directors and helped to stimulate a tradition in Slovenia of producing numerically few but stylistically distinctive and professionally well-crafted feature films, a tradition which has persisted to the present time. Štiglic was born in 1919 in Kranj and studied law and drama in Ljubljana. During the war he served as a Partisan and journalist, and immediately following the war he was an actor in avant-garde theater, a film scenario writer, and a director of documentary films. His documentary film *Youth Builds* (*Mladina gradi*) was the first Yugoslav film to receive an international prize, the "Bronze Lion of San Marco," and his first feature film was quickly recognized by Yugoslav critics as revealing a richer use of film language and greater verisimilitude of settings and psychological milieu than was present in the other war films of the period.[50]

On Their Own Ground opens with a still shot of rocky mountain landscape

On Their Own Ground (Na svojoj zemlji).

with the titles superimposed. Early morning is suggested by shots of mist rising in the forest, revealing a small file of Partisans making their way to the crest of a hill that overlooks a small Slovenian village nestled picturesquely in the alpine mountains, whence members of the small guerrilla band have been recruited. The film initially portrays the intertwining destinies of Partisans, Italian occupiers, and members of the village. It tells of local skirmishes; of one family in the village which has given seven sons to the cause and tries in vain to prevent the youngest from finding his way into revolutionary battle; of a young villager, Drejc, who attempts to stay aloof from the struggle but is finally goaded by internal pressures and obscenities perpetrated by the occupiers to gun down some Italian soldiers in the village, and then makes his way to the mountains, only to lose his life in a guerrilla action; and of older villagers who are executed by the occupiers in retribution for guerrilla actions. The hard march to Trieste follows; there the small guerrilla units are merged with the swelling numbers of Partisans making their way to claim the surrounding territory for the new state of Yugoslavia against the Italian claims of the 1920 and 1924 treaties.

Throughout the film there is a strong visual sense of time and place and a realistic, and sometimes chilling, portrayal of retribution, and of the long march of single files of Partisans threading wearily over rugged terrain, carrying their wounded with them, fighting as much for simple survival as for a noble cause.

One of the most skillfully presented sequences, done without melodramatic insistence, is the simple act of the villagers being led to execution who first remove their shoes so that they can touch their feet to native soil and prepare themselves to stand and die on their own ground. This central metaphor achieves larger meaning when the combined forces of Partisans fighting against superior forces reach the area of Trieste to stand upon and claim "their own ground" in the name of the new state of Yugoslavia. Along with these strengths, the film does not escape the sometimes arbitrary verbalizing and "set" speeches about fighting for an independent Slovenia in concert with the liberation of all the peoples of Yugoslavia, reverent tributes to Tito, and allusions to the perfidy and lack of reliability of the Western Allies when contrasted to the constancy and common cause forged with the great socialist homeland of the Soviet Union.

On Their Own Ground shares with the more naive Yugoslav war epics of the time an intense nationalism and patriotism. The unique circumstances in which the Communist party of Yugoslavia came to power as the leader of a combined war of socialist revolution and resistance can scarcely be overemphasized. Yugoslavia was the only European Communist government established after the war whose legitimacy was founded primarily on its own efforts and not on the sponsorship and the political and military domination of the Soviet Union.[51] The filmic transformation, reinforcement, and reification of this distinctive national experience and its national heroes and leaders clearly distinguish the Yugoslav films of this period from the Soviet-dominated thematic perspectives found in the films of newly formed postwar Eastern European Communist states.[52] As an increasingly important and popular mass medium of the time, it also appears likely that these films contributed in some measure to the reinforcement of public support for the Tito-led government during the dramatic break with the Soviet Union and the harsh aftermath of Cominform-imposed economic sanctions against Yugoslavia.

Story of a Factory

Although most of the documentary and short films of this period dealt with the theme of socialist reconstruction after the war, there were only three feature films which fell clearly into this category.[53] In these films the revolutionary élan developed during the war was transferred to the heroic task of rebuilding a war-ravaged country, restoring agricultural production, and establishing the infrastructure for the industrialization and urbanization of Yugoslavia. These films celebrated the achievements of "shock" workers, who compensated for antiquated machinery and lack of technology and technical expertise with human will, exertion, and muscle; of volunteer workers and youth brigades, who, against forbidding natural barriers—and often, in the films, against the work of reactionaries and saboteurs—rebuilt and extended railways, roads, factories, mines, and bridges; and of agricultural workers, who combined new technologies with old to solve the great problem of providing enough food to feed a reviving nation and to provide a valuable export to other countries. The fighters and earnest political commissars who had gained some experience during the war in the administration of liberated areas and regions of Yugoslavia were favorably depicted as the vanguard and cadre leaders of this new revolutionary struggle in nation building. The films are permeated by symbols of the new state: large banners and slogans—including the central slogan of the War of Liberation, *Bratstvo i jedinstvo* ("Brotherhood and Unity")—which had now become the symbolic informing principle for building up all the regions of Yugoslavia, from the poorest to the richest; outsized likenesses of Lenin, Stalin, and Tito—with Tito often placed between and not below the other two great leaders of Communist revolution; Communist party songs, workers' songs, and Partisan songs, which saturated the sound tracks; and brigades of youth, upon whom so many propaganda efforts were expended, who carried in their hearts and emblazoned on their banners the central unifying slogan, *Mi smo Titovi, Tito je nas* ("We are Tito's, Tito is ours").

And it was Tito who sounded the note for continued heroic exertion after the war in a speech delivered from the balcony of the National Theater in Belgrade on 27 March 1945, seven days following the city's dramatic and emotional liberation:

> The day when all the regions of our country will be free is not far away. Victory is very near. But let us not be too carried away by our successes in the battlefield, but rather think of how we are going to build our towns, our railways, our roads, our villages and fields, so that the coming generations will be able to say that their fathers did everything they could to leave them a better inheritance. . . .[54]

Pogačić's *Story of a Factory* (*Priča o fabrici*) shares the idealism and patriotism which characterized these early films of socialist reconstruction and reveals some of the same simple stereotyping of heroic workers and irredeemable reactionary types. At another level, however, the film also provided a more interesting and complex sense of time and setting, a more believable and natural style of film acting, and more sophistication in character development—especially in the portrayal of the film's principal protagonist. He is an engineer and member of the prewar bourgeois intelligentsia, who is first accused of collaboration in sabotage operations against the factory, is then cleared of the charges, and comes to a personal decision to join his efforts more fully with the vanguard of the new state, personified in the film by the local Communist party cadre leader and organizer of the factory.

The film *Story of a Factory* begins with a scene of a hearing attended by factory workers, with the chief engineer of the small textile factory answering charges of collaboration in sabotage operations involving an explosion which had damaged some of the machines and nearly caused the death of a heroic young female worker, who was at the moment of the explosion demonstrating new worker techniques for operating several machines simultaneously to increase production. Through testimony and flashbacks, the story is told of reactionary elements— including the former owner of the factory, a priest, petit bourgeois underlings, and the wife of the accused chief engineer—trying through desperate contrivance to thwart the development of the new order and to hold onto and restore old privileges. On the other side are the workers acquiring new political consciousness and solidarity through the patient efforts of the party cadre leader and new organizer of the factory—who backs words with deeds by rolling up his shirt sleeves and joining his hands with those of the workers when the occasion demands. Not only are the workers engaged in increasing production by superhuman toil in the antiquated factory, they are also simultaneously building a new and better one to replace it. The film includes obligatory sequences of bannerbedecked workers' meetings, in which shy but inspired workers vie with each other in expressing their resolve to meet and exceed production goals and to pledge additional volunteer hours of labor. The only note of protest to this growing sense of solidarity is sounded by the husband of the film's principal worker heroine, who sees little to recommend such extra exertions in the face of low pay, minimal living conditions, and shortages of the basic necessities of life. By the end of the film, however, the husband is brought firmly into the circle of worker solidarity as much by the exemplary deeds of his wife and her escape from death as by her serene vision of a better future built on the sacrifices of the present. In the end, as well, the villains are apprehended, the new factory is built, the chief engineer and the Communist organizer of the factory are cooperatively bound by a handshake, and the last words of the film are spoken by the Communist leader, who says that "this was not so much a story about a factory, but a story about people."

Despite the predictable conformity of the film's overall plot and structure, as previously indicated, the film does contain moments of real conflict and believable characterizations and a strong visual sense of the rude and simple conditions in which the workers lived and toiled. There is also an interesting dramatization, in the character of the chief engineer, of the process of accommodation with the new order made by many members of the prewar bourgeois intelligentsia, whose knowledge and skills were sorely needed at the time.

Sofka

One of the most interesting and skillfully produced films of this period, and the only feature film which departed from themes of war and reconstruction, was *Sofka*, directed by Radoš Novaković. Born in 1915 at Prokuplje, Novaković was one of the most experienced, widely educated, and gifted of the early Yugoslav

The Communist leader of the factory. *Story of a Factory (Priča o fabrici)*.

The worker-heroine. *Story of a Factory* (*Priča o fabrici*).

The engineer's indolent "luxury-seeking" wife. *Story of a Factory* (*Priča o fabrici*).

film artists. He had first studied law at the University of Belgrade and then graduated from the Belgrade Academy of Dramatic Art as a dramatic producer. In the prewar period he was active in the cultural life of Belgrade and, while still a student, had become well known for his reviews and essays in such literary periodicals as *Mlada kultura* (*New Culture*), *Nova stvarnost* (*New Reality*), *Izraz* (*Expression*), and others. A Partisan fighter during the war, Novaković was withdrawn from the front in 1944 to work in the newly created film section in the high command of the liberation army; after the demobilization in 1945, he was appointed production director of the State Film Company. Having served as one of the founders of the new Yugoslav film industry, Novaković relinquished his responsibilities as production director to devote full energies to the direction of a number of short films before undertaking the more complex task of realizing his first feature film, *Sofka*, produced by Avala film in 1948.

Set in the latter part of the nineteenth century in the village of Vranja in old Serbia, the film is adapted from the classic Serbian novel *Impure Blood* (*Nečista krv*) by Bora Stanković. This popular tale relates the story of a beautiful young girl from the home of a prominent member of the old aristocracy with roots in

Sofka as mature heroine. *Sofka*.

Rural exile. *Sofka*.

the era of Turkish domination, whose family is falling into material decay and want. As a means of maintaining the facade if not the substance of his former position, the father sells his daughter in marriage to a young son of a rough, untutored, "new rich" farmer-merchant, against the strong protestations of Sofka's mother. Sofka leaves the genteel surroundings of her home, where she has been shielded from the knowledge of her family's failing fortunes and the dissolution of the old order, and goes to the rude, primitive, sprawling farm house to live with the family of her not-yet-of-age husband. She accepts her new position with grace and fortitude. The father dies, and the son grows of age and falls in love with Sofka, only to become proudly and passionately alienated from the arrangement when he discovers the true nature of the business transaction that has brought them together. Despite this cruel and unhealable breach between them, life goes on, and children are born—with Sofka deepening into a mature and beautiful tragic heroine. The last shot of her is in the crude surroundings of her home, surrounded by her children—a figure displaced in time and from her "natural" milieu, a victim who makes the best of her fate, sealed with the exchange of riches, which served only to perpetuate for a time the position of her father and family, which, in the context of the times, no longer had any meaning.

While the film lacks the complexity of the novel, with its subtle intertwining of the fate of this one girl and the era in which she lives, it does skillfully evoke the customs of the time, the sensuality of the settings, and the evocative beauty of Sofka in her transition from young girl to womanhood, and it contains a long and skillfully executed sequence of the marriage ceremony. It also suggests the distant sound of drums and cannon when, in 1876, Serbia joined cause with the Bosnian insurrection against Turkish rule, the success of which was ensured by the military intervention of Russia and resulted in the treaty of San Stefano in 1878.

Summary

It is not surprising that, in the initial five-year period of the establishment and evolution of a national cinema in Yugoslavia, the predominant energies of its leadership were directed toward creating the necessary organizational, material, and technical means for continuous independent film production. While the films produced were virtually ignored by the international film community, they nonetheless revealed a vibrant nationalism and a striving to express, to reinforce, and to legitimize a unique and complex national experience which had been forged on the anvil of a brutal war and the hardships of nationalist reconstruction. In the process a small but growing vanguard of skilled film artists had gained their experience, and the rudiments of a distinctive film culture had begun to take shape. There were already signs of increasing impatience to break the confining mold of socialist realist dogma, to expand, diversify, and deepen the possibilities for filmic expression, and to move toward greater flexibility and decentralization of film organization and production.

2

Decentralization and Breaking the Mold, 1951-1960

The second period of Yugoslavia's evolution of a national cinema is infinitely more complex and richly textured than the first struggling period after the war. It was a period characterized by a general evolution toward decentralizing the organization and control of the Yugoslav film industry through the introduction, quite slow in the beginning, of the principles and practices of workers' self-management into all phases of film production and film distribution. Partly as a consequence of these changes and partly as a consequence of the generally improved economic conditions and economic growth which occurred in Yugoslavia at the end of the decade, this period witnessed a considerable maturation in the infrastructure and material base for film production; the elaboration of more sophisticated networks for film distribution and exhibition; a steady rise in the professionalization of film technicians and artists; the development of a livelier, "freer," and more informed group of film critics, who were able to express their views in a proliferating number of serious film journals, newspapers, and weeklies; a progressive opening of Yugoslavia to cultural and artistic influences from the West; and a significant increase in the number, range, and genres of films produced. The initial phase of this period was characterized by polemic and ideological efforts to stretch or to break the narrow propagandistic mold of the first period and was followed by increasing experimentation with new styles of realism and by greater thematic complexity, variety of genres, and emphasis upon character development and psychological individualization. It was during this period as well that Yugoslav film began to gain an increasing international audience and recognition, with recognition primarily occurring in the realm of short, documentary, and animated films and secondarily, and to a lesser extent, accruing to a relatively small number of "quality"-produced feature films.

Decentralization

Perhaps the most famous and dramatic legislative act of postwar Yugoslavia was passed on 27 June 1950 by the National Assembly under the cumbersome title "Basic Law on the Management of State Economic Enterprises and Higher

32

Economic Associations by the Work Collectives," which came to be more generally known as the law on worker's self-management. Encapsulated in this law were the principles, continuously evolving to the present time, of Yugoslavia's unique system of self-management socialism, which now extends to all levels of social, economic, political, educational, and cultural institutions and constitutes the second founding myth (along with the National War of Liberation) of the postwar Yugoslav state.

The law on workers' self-management attempted to codify the ideological reinterpretation of Marxist-Leninist thought which had evolved in Tito's innermost circle of leaders after the break with the Cominform in 1948.[1] Tito presented the new law personally and underscored the major questions which it addressed. First, the law was necessary to initiate the process of the "withering away of the state," which Stalinism had prevented by strengthening hierarchical, central techno-bureaucratic control in the transitional phase of the "dictatorship of the proletariat," effectively postponing the millennium of the "withering" process to the distant and unforeseen future. From this perspective it was Stalinism and Cominform ideology which represented revisionism and deformation of Marxist-Leninist thought, and not the Yugoslav-initiated system of decentralized self-management socialism. Second, the new concept of self-management was necessary to protect the integrity of the Yugoslav Communist party as the progressive vanguard and force for a constantly evolving socialist system from the tendency to become a totalitarian elite, in which the party was merged with the central state apparatus and the entire economic system in a monolithic command structure which dictated from the top downward to all levels of economic, cultural, educational, and political activity. Finally, it was argued that true Marxist-Leninist thought held that nationalization and state ownership of the means of production represented only "the first and lowest form of socialism," while the new law marked the beginning of a transition to a debureaucratized, decentralized, and self-managed "higher form of socialism" which was true to Leninism and oriented away from Stalinist deviation. In this new arrangement, Tito remarked, "lies our road to socialism."[2] Yugoslavia's independent path to socialism, as yet uncharted in this initial legislation, became widely known as "Titoism" and was accompanied by increasingly sharp attacks on Stalinism and the Soviet Union. By 1950 the Yugoslavs were heaping scorn upon the dictatorial nature of the Soviet regime, its imperialism, and its tyranny over and exploitation of the Soviet and East European peoples, and all of these were seen

> . . . as consequences of the Russian Revolution's fatal incompleteness, which had left all political and economic power concentrated in the hands of a highly centralized Party-State apparatus—a "State Capitalism" worse than the private kind—responsible to neither the people nor the Party itself and inevitably bureaucratized, corrupted and brutalized. The revolution, the Yugoslavs concluded, could be

saved from such an otherwise inevitable degeneration only by immediate steps to fulfill the rest of the Marxian socialist program: the State must begin to "wither away" as soon as its "last independent act," the nationalization of the means of production, had been completed, and it must be replaced—gradually but quickly—by "direct social self-management" by a "free association of producers" in all public and common affairs.[3]

The new law on self-management also introduced the concept of a socialist market economy, in which ownership is neither private (except in the case of small service establishments) nor solely in the hands of a centralized state. Under such a system, workers in each enterprise were theoretically to become trustees of that portion of socially owned property committed to their hands in the form of buildings, resources, and the means of production, and this trusteeship was to be exercised through

> elective organs, *workers' councils*, consisting of between 15 and 120 members (or of all the workers in small enterprises with less than 30 employees), and management boards of less than two dozen members, selected by the workers' councils and including the director of the enterprise as an *ex officio*, non-voting member.[4]

While the state continued to promulgate general plans of economic development, these were to be "indicative" rather than mandated and were to provide a general orientation for future development. As self-management socialism slowly evolved in Yugoslavia, it penetrated to all levels of economic, social, and political organization, including workers' councils or self-management in industry proper; self-managing bodies in social and cultural institutions such as schools, cultural enterprises, and health and other quasi-governmental bodies; and self-management at the commune (county) level. In 1956 the Communist party itself began to move toward a greater decentralization, as signaled by its change of name to the League of Communists of Yugoslavia (LCY) and the redefinition of the role of the party as a "social animator" functioning through persuasion rather than autocratic power.[5]

Despite these sweeping changes in form, there was no immediate transfer of real power to self-managing mechanisms. In the early 1950s a centralized, administrative system of planning remained in effect, and the Communist party retained its monolithic hierarchical structure:

> The State continued, as long as a Soviet-type command economy remained in effect, to control the quantity and assortment of inputs and outputs, income distribution and investment. Workers' councils were duly elected and consulted but played no real management role: they had no money to dispose of on their own initiative. Management boards had somewhat wider effective powers, but were too small, too indirectly elected and usually too dominated by the director to be truly representative or autonomous.[6]

As Bogdan Denitch has observed, it was not until the introduction of a market economy that the councils "began to assert at least minimal *enterprise autonomy*," and it was not until the councils began to have some authority in disposing of the major part of their income that "real economic power began to shift."[7]

The tensions and contradictions created in Yugoslavia by a self-managing, participatory, polycentric form of decision making which stresses consultation and consensus, on the one hand, and a one-party hierarchically organized state apparatus which stresses decision making flowing from the top down, on the other, have never been satisfactorily resolved to the present time.[8]

While it clearly falls outside the scope of the present study to present a detailed analysis of the theory and practice of socialist self-management in Yugoslavia, the above sketch of its major features provides a framework for understanding the process of reorganizing the Yugoslav film industry during this period and tracing out the main stages of its evolution.

Reorganization of the Yugoslav Film Industry

Following the passage of the law on self-management in June 1950, the Yugoslav film industry began to undergo deep and fundamental changes. In the new scheme, the three main areas of film activity—film production, film trade, and film distribution and theatrical showing—were decentralized, with film production falling under the category of economic activity with "special cultural significance"; film trade under the category of domestic and international commerce; and networks of film distribution and theatrical showing under the category of "service activities of a communal character."[9]

The most profound internal changes in organization occurred in the area of film production. They were introduced at the end of 1950 and in early 1951 and set the basic direction, with many emendations, of the development of Yugoslav domestic film production to the present time. These changes introduced a complex tripartite division to govern the relationships and economic activities associated with the process of film production—from initial script conceptualization to finished print. The first division included all the enterprises and workers involved in managing the technical bases of film. These enterprises were granted exclusive right to or trustee "ownership" of the instruments and technology of production, including cameras, sound equipment, and other technical means for film shooting, i.e., sound studios, sound-mixing facilities, and film-processing laboratories, which were leased or rented to film studios. The second division embraced the film production enterprises (film studios), which managed "social economic resources" for the actual production of films, including contracting with film artists and workers and renting resources, personnel, and services from the technical base, and which became the sole owners of the finished film. In December

1950, film production studios were organized into the Economic Association of Film Enterprises of Yugoslavia (with parallel organizations established in each of the six republics), which later ripened into the Society of Film Producers of Yugoslavia, again with similar societies formed in all of the republics.

The third division of film production fell into the category of free associations of film workers, which were formed in each of the six republics and together composed the Union of Film Workers of Yugoslavia (Savez filmskih radnika Jugoslavije), founded at the end of 1950. The Union of Film Workers included the artistic creators of film: film scenarists, film directors, directors of photography, sound composers, and their artistic assistants; assistant directors, cameramen, assistant scene designers, sound technicians, costumers, film editors, and production assistants. The *artistic* workers in film were the only category of film workers to be freed from direct employment in technical and production enterprises and were granted the right to negotiate contractual arrangements with film studios for the realization of scenarios and film projects.

In the film and technical enterprises themselves, the mechanisms of self-management workers' councils and self-management boards were established but, as in other areas of the economy, did not immediately assume any significant decision-making role. In the early 1950s, film production was still dependent on centrally administered film subsidies from the State Film Fund. Film producers were tightly restricted in their economic development by the newly established state and republican economic chambers, under whose authority and direction they were subsumed, and were guided ideologically by Communist party-dominated cultural commissions in each of the six republics.

With the establishment of this new decentralized organizational scheme, the Committee for Cinematography, which had been the centralized guiding force in the early development of film, was formally disbanded. The purpose of the newly reformed Yugoslav film industry was to free itself from excessive bureaucratic baggage and to introduce new incentives for the more rational management and economic utilization of the technical and artistic resources of film. It was envisioned that the new arrangements would forge a common interest in producing films in the quickest and most efficient ways possible and in foreshortening the time between creating a scenario and the completion of the film. Studios which owned the finished film would profit from more efficient completion of films through an earlier realization of domestic and, increasingly during the latter fifties, foreign distribution returns. Free associations of artistic film workers would be able to enter into new contracts, with their attendant additional fees, royalties, and salaries, and the enterprises and workers engaged in the technological dimensions of film work would realize increasingly effective utilization of technical resources, along with the leasing and rental fees which such utilization generated.

The theoretical promise of this new system, however, did not ripen more fully until the passage of the Basic Law of Film in 1956, which was designed to codify more fully the changes which had been introduced since 1950 and to set forth the regulations governing relations in the areas of production, trade, and film showing. The most substantial change ushered in by the film law of 1956 was the abolition of the system of state subsidies to film in favor of a system of taxes (seventeen to twenty percent) on film admission tickets, which became effective early in 1957.

The largest portion of this admission tax was used for the direct support of domestic film production, with a smaller amount set aside for the continued improvement of film distribution. This system of self-finance (*samofinansiranja*) also provided small allocations for the awarding of prizes to quality films and much larger allocations as bonuses for films which increased domestic film traffic, i.e., were "box office" successes.

In part as a result of these added incentives and in part as a result of the strong economic growth which Yugoslavia experienced at the end of the 1950s, the annual production of domestically produced feature films more than doubled in the latter half of the decade—from an annual rate of six films through 1954 to an average of fourteen films in the years from 1957 through 1960. 1954 marked the first year that Yugoslavia entered into coequal financial and artistic feature film production with foreign studios, and by the end of the decade, nineteen coproductions had been completed—many of them with Western countries. Among the most significant Western film directors involved in these coproductions were the Norwegian Kaare Bergström, who codirected with Radoš Novaković the film *Bloody Road* (*Krvavi put*, 1955), which dealt with the dramatic fight for survival of a group of escaped Yugoslav prisoners of war, set against the backdrop of Norway's snow-covered mountains; the French director Claude Autant-Lara, who made a film about conscientious objectors, *Thou Shalt Not Kill* (*Tu ne tueras point*, 1961); the West German director Helmut Kautner, who directed an antifascist film, *The Last Bridge* (*Die Letzte Brücke*, 1954); and the Italian directors Giuseppe De Santis and Gillo Pontecorvo, who each made a film in the Italian neorealist manner.[10]

During the same decade, admissions for domestically produced films more than tripled—from 5,656,000 in 1951 to 17,133,000 in 1960. Admissions to imported foreign films also experienced a strong surge, from 57,875,000 in 1951 to 112,991,000 in 1960.[11] This rise in domestic viewing of foreign films was tied to the dramatic opening and growth of film imports from the United States and Western Europe. In the years immediately following the war, the USSR clearly dominated the market, with only a small trickle of films from the United States, Great Britain, and Italy and a somewhat larger share from France. Beginning in 1950, however, this picture was reversed, with the United States emerging as the dominant exporter of films to Yugoslavia, followed by France and Italy.[12]

Despite the growth of a rapidly expanding domestic film market, the cost of film production from 1957 to 1960 often outstripped the available funds from admission taxes and sometimes led to large deficits. These were made up, in part, by special allocations from republican sources, bank loans, and profits from coproduction with foreign studios, and by shifting funds from the less-developed republics to the major producing centers in Serbia, Croatia, and Slovenia. This latter imbalance was partially corrected in 1962 by tying allocations for film production to admission taxes collected within the boundaries of each of the six republics on a proportional basis.

Social market incentives also led to the steady growth of the "commercialization" of the Yugoslav film industry, which reached its apogee in the late 1960s. According to many Yugoslav critics, the quest for box office success and the competitive struggle for more viewers sometimes led to a devaluation of the "social functions and artistic value of films."[13]

In assessing the positive achievements of the period of decentralization and reorganization of the Yugoslav film industry, Dejan Kosanović suggests that many meaningful successes were realized:

> . . . the physical resources of film production were expanded, new thematic breakthroughs occurred in feature films, domestic animated film was born, and documentary and short films ripened. With regard to professional and technical standards, Yugoslav production approximated world norms, domestic films found an export market and received their first prizes at international film festivals, and Yugoslav cinematography was affirmed as a solid partner in coproductions with foreign film producers.[14]

Breaking the Mold

At the same time that Yugoslavia was experimenting with new forms of decentralization and the insertion of socialist market mechanisms into a command economy, an intense struggle was taking place to free cultural and artistic expression from the sterile confines of socialist realist dogma. The primary locus of this struggle occurred in the established traditions of literature and the fine arts and only later in the decade found significant voice in the newly evolving community of film artists, critics, and theorists.

As early as 1946, the influential and distinguished Croatian writer Miroslav Krleža had eloquently warned against the sterilizing effects of reducing literature and art to dogmatic propagandistic formulas; he stressed the need for socialist literature to express a critical approach to existing conditions in the contemporary world.[15] This line of thought was submerged, however, by a rising tide of proletarian and revolutionary poetry and prose and a comparative literary silence from Yugoslavia's most gifted writers. From 1947 to 1950, the literary scene was dominated by the poet, critic, and politician Radovan Zogović, who later earned the unenviable sobriquet of "Yugoslavia's Zdhanov" and was characterized as a party hack and literary informbureauist. Until approximately 1950 there was strong party pressure to unify writers and painters along narrow ideological-aesthetic lines. Although socialist realism did not take over completely, it clearly dominated the literary-cultural scene.

After 1950 there was a strong rallying of writers against cultural Stalinism and against domestic dogmatism in the arts. It was all part of the larger struggle to forge an independent path for Yugoslav socialism and consequently received some partial and often ambivalent encouragement from top party ideologues. The most important turning point toward the liberation of Yugoslav culture from the dead hand of socialist realism came at the Third Congress of the Union of Writers of Yugoslavia, held in Ljubljana in 1952. The major speech was delivered by Krleža, who laid to rest once and for all the waning specter of socialist realism—and with it his old enemy Zogović. The congress called for a new dialogue and struggle of opinions and for the exploration of new modes of self-expression. Diversity and open discussion were to replace ideological conformity, and that was seen as the surest guarantee of the development of a strong and dynamic socialist culture in Yugoslavia.[16]

Following the Third Congress of the Union of Writers of Yugoslavia, several progressive journals were established to advance the polemics against conformism and for greater freedom of expression. In Belgrade this development was heralded by the brief appearance of the journals *Mladost* and *Svedočanstva* and similar liberal literary periodicals in Croatia (*Krugovi*) and Slovenia (*Beseda*). Paradoxically, these publications were first approved and funded by the party's ideological commissions and were later banned by them. Sveta Lukić explains this paradox by arguing that

> both the politicians and the ideologues at the time needed proof of freedom of ideas in literature and culture in order to undermine Soviet dogmatism. However, too much independence of mind in domestic literature went beyond official plans and desires. The League of Communists of Yugoslavia was more interested in scoring a foreign policy goal against the Soviet Union than in securing genuine internal freedom for Yugoslav culture.[17]

One immediate cause for a wavering cultural line appears to have been the conservative party reaction which had already set in and was further exacerbated by the dramatic fall from power of Milovan Djilas, who generally supported a liberalization of Yugoslav cultural life. Another was the ambivalent policy which developed toward the Soviet Union after the death of Stalin in 1953—which included both continued assertions of ideological independence and polemic attack, while at the same time cautiously searching for modes of rapprochement and normalization of relations.

Cultural polemics were overshadowed and colored in late 1953 and early 1954 by the dramatic "Djilas affair," which culminated in the expulsion of this prominent party ideologist and member of Tito's inner circle from the central committee for his public essays which advocated the radical democratization of the party and scathingly criticized the new privileges, powers, and decadent morality of the ruling cliques. At first, Djilas published his essays in *Kommunist* and the official daily newspaper, *Borba*, with at least tacit approval from some of his powerful peers in the central committee. As Djilas became increasingly aware of the uneasiness which his articles were creating in the highest reaches of the Communist party, he founded in late 1953 the short-lived journal *Novao misao* (*New Thought*) to serve as an outlet for the growing wave of criticism of political and cultural spheres of Yugoslav life. In the next-to-last issue of this journal, Djilas wrote his famous "Anatomy of a Moral," which directly precipitated the special plenum session of the central committee, assembled at Brioni on 17 January 1954, at which he was denounced by his powerful colleagues and deprived of all his party positions.[18]

Even without the Djilas affair, the laying to rest of socialist realist dogma did not immediately lead to a renaissance of literature and art in Yugoslavia. In the early 1950s there was a tendency to respond to the possibilities of new freedom and new thought by a retreat into what Lukić has described as "socialist aestheticism," or art for art's sake. In response to the absence of crude political pressure, "the humanist intelligentsia's ideal of social activity now turned inward, from a 'bad reality' to a pure, good, impenetrable, and hence unchallengeable, inner subjective reality."[19] Combined with this strategy was the retreat to safe historical subjects in which literary experimentation could take place without rubbing against sensitive areas of contemporary life and dealing critically with *savremene teme* (contemporary themes).

It was not until the late 1950s that confused and sometimes obscurantist polemics began to orient themselves around the polarities of modernists versus traditionalists and literary and artistic life became distinctly more lively. The infusion of these new possibilities was first realized in film in the witty and creative work of the Zagreb school of film animation and in short and documentary film. Feature films were also propelled into new genres and modes of expression but did not realize their richest potential until the next decade.

Preparing the way for the ripening of Yugoslav cinema was an increasingly sophisticated, well-informed, and lively group of film critics and theoreticians, who were able to find expression for their views in a proliferating number of serious journals, newspapers, and weeklies. In the early 1950s the journal *Film*, an organ of the Union of Film Workers of Yugoslavia, was the most important platform for film criticism, cultural polemics, historical and theoretical discussions, and reviews of both domestic and international festivals and film activity. In

1952, the editorship of the journal passed into the capable and vigorous hands of Vicko Raspor, who transformed it from an official intermediary between party ideology and film activity into a lively medium which ranged across a wide spectrum of artistic and cultural questions. Increasing critical attention was paid to important developments in world cinema, with films and film directors from the West given more detailed and expert analyses that were increasingly freed from stereotypical ideological reflexes—i.e., derision for decadent tendencies, inculcation of alien cultural philosophies, and commercially oriented deformations. Serious and often lively discussions centered on the works and distinctive cinematic styles of such American and British directors as Reed, Lean, Lubitsch, Wyler, and others. Important film movements such as post-Second World War Italian neorealism were treated in depth, and articles were written encouraging greater experimentation and broadening of thematic perspectives in Yugoslav films. Criticism of domestic films became less impressionistic and more demanding of higher artistic and social values and greater latitude for individual creative expression. Attracted to the pages of *Film* were some of the more gifted film essayists, film artists, and critics of the time, including, among others, Gustav Gavrin, Vladimir Petrić, Radoš Novaković, Branko Belan, Živorad Mitrović, Slobodan Glumac, and Aleksandar Petrović.

Other serious journals of the time which struggled to break the narrow bounds of film criticism and film expression that had characterized the first five years of Yugoslav film development were the bimonthly Zagreb periodical *Filmske revije* and the Slovenian monthly journal *Film*, published in Ljubljana. In the ripening years of the late 1950s, an even broader and more progressive platform for film discussion, criticism, and exploration of aesthetic questions was provided by the journal *Filmska kultura*, published in Zagreb, which has remained one of Yugoslavia's most important film journals to the present time, and by the short-lived but highly influential periodical *Film danas*, published in Belgrade under the sponsorship of Jugoslovenska kinoteka.

Filmska kultura was founded and published by the Association of Cinematography of the Socialist Republic of Croatia in Zagreb in 1957 under the experienced editorship of Stevo Ostojić and Fedor Hanžeković and was issued in five or six numbers annually. While regional in origin, the journal was from the outset all-Yugoslav in character, attracting to its pages the most prolific and talented film essayists, artists, and critics from throughout the country. The periodical dealt more fully than previous serious film journals with a broad range of questions dealing with film theory, history, and aesthetics, economic and artistic movements in international cinema, lengthy polemics, and discussions and criticism of Yugoslav films, and included critical texts and commentaries from foreign journals. While it would not be possible to mention all of those who contributed substantially to the development of this journal, among the most important were Milan Ranković, Vicko Raspor, Ante Peterlić, Milutin Čolić, Rudolf Sremec, Nedeljko Dragić, Dušan Stojanović, Branko Belan, Petar Krelja, Ranko Munitić, Fadil Hadžić, Dragoslav Adamović, Igor Pretnar, Mira Boglić, Slobodan Novaković, Vatroslav Mimica, Dušan Vukotić, Stevo Ostojić, and Fedor Hanžeković. Several of these were to assume a leading role in opening Yugoslav cinema to world trends in cinematic theory and practice, and in stimulating *new film* tendencies in the 1960s.

Perhaps the liveliest and most influential periodical of this period was *Film danas*, which described itself as a periodical for the "popularization of film art" and published thirteen numbers between 15 April 1958 and the end of 1959. Under the editorship of the distinguished film director and director of Jugoslovenska kinoteka, Vladimir Pogačić, and a gifted editorial board consisting of Dušan Stojanović, Žika Bogdanović, and Slobodan Glumac, *Film danas* involved itself in an eclectic, progressive, and free examination of new film trends in international cinema, a lively discussion of film aesthetics and theory, and stimulating critiques and reviews of domestically produced films. The editorial board encouraged complete freedom of expression by its contributors and made the unprecedented policy announcement in each issue that the opinions and stances expressed by individual authors were not "obliged to conform to the views of the editorial board." More imaginative in design, graphics, and layout than other film journals and periodicals of the time, *Film danas* associated itself with progressive and modernist tendencies in Yugoslav cultural life and attracted to its pages cultural writers in Belgrade who not only were widely conversant with film art but also were active and knowledgeable about related modernist trends in literature, drama, and the fine arts. Nor did the writers adopt an elitist view of film art; they often brought fresh perspectives and an open spirit of inquiry into the examination of popular films and film genres, including westerns, action-adventure films, criminal films, science fiction, and social comedies. They also examined popular film myths and sex symbols, including a treatise on film vamps and a two-part series on *Merilin Monro* (Marilyn Monroe)—generously and fulsomely illustrated.

Many of the most creative leaders and film artists of the *novi film* (*new film*) movement of the 1960s were able to express and to test their views and aesthetic perspectives within the lively format of *Film danas*, and to anticipate trends that would later be worked out in artistic practice. Among these were Dušan Makavejev, Branko Vučićević, Žika Pavlović, and others. The prolific film essayist and critic Ranko Munitić, who was not personally associated with the work of *Film danas*, stated that it was the most dynamic film periodical of the time and, in terms of the quality of its writing, layout, and design, "perhaps the best film periodical in Yugoslavia to the present." [20]

Alongside specialized serious film periodicals and journals, there was a rapid growth during this period of popular film magazines and reviews, some of them short-lived, and expanding opportunities for film reviews and criticism in major daily newspapers and weeklies. The vanguard of Yugoslavia's film theorists, critics, and essayists during this period more often led than followed trends in domestic film production and increasingly associated themselves with modernist and progressive tendencies in cultural life and expression, which at that time were found more abundantly in Yugoslav literature, drama, and the fine arts than in film. With perhaps a touch of professional hubris, Munitić declared that, with the exception of the Zagreb "masters of animation," there were in Yugoslavia of the late 1950s "many more good film critics than good film directors."[21]

Despite the gap that often existed between theoretical and critical expectations and actual artistic practice, Yugoslav feature films steadily progressed during the 1950s in terms of technical quality, expansion of thematic subject matter, and experimentation with new styles of realism. In the latter part of the decade, modernist tendencies in the feature films of the 1960s were anticipated in the internationally recognized creative work of the Zagreb animators, in short and documentary films, and in the growing strength of the amateur film movement.

Expanding Genres

The most immediate change from the heuristic and propagandistic filmic confirmations of the War of Liberation and socialist reconstruction was the expansion of the range of subject matter and genres. The 1950s ushered in films of light comedy and satire, children's films, action-adventure films, and historical-literary films, as well as transformed in various ways the subject matter and filmic approach to the Partisan war experience.

Film Comedies and Satire

The first successful film comedy made during this period, *Vesna* (1953), was directed by František Čap, an experienced Czech director who had emigrated to Yugoslavia after Yugoslavia's break with the Cominform in 1948. This film won first prize at the first annual festival of Yugoslav feature films held at Pula in 1954; it was a light comedy with a naive story about a girl named Vesna and a group of fellow students. Vesna falls in love with another student, only to learn that he has wooed her for the purpose of lifting the final exam from her professor father. This film was well received by the viewing public, and Čap followed it by a series of officially acceptable entertainment films.

One of the most popular of these light film comedies was directed by Yugoslavia's only woman feature film director, Soja Jovanović. Her first film, *Father Ćira and Father Spira* (*Pop Ćira i pop Spira*, 1957), was based on the classical light comedy of Stevan Sremac and satirized village life. The two fathers are members of the village elite, and their families live in peaceful and close under-standing and friendship. Consanguinity is disrupted and comedic contretemps ensue when a young male teacher, who is eligible to marry only one of the lovely daughters in the two families, arrives in the village. *Father Ćira and Father Spira* was the first feature film shot in color, received the first prize at the 1957 Pula festival, and was one of the largest box office attractions of its time.[22]

Brief mention should also be made of the two film satires on village life di-rected by Velimir Stojanović and produced by the small Montenegrin studio Lovćen film: *Cursed Money* (*Zle pare,* 1956) and *Four Kilometers per Hour* (*Četiri kilometra na sat,* 1958). Stojanović's promising career, however, was cut short by a premature death in 1959.

Literary-Historical Films

Another offically sanctioned haven for new themes and experimentation in film stylistics was the literary-historical film. The two most important of these were directed by Fedor Hanžeković, born in Bijeljina in 1913. Before the war Hanžeković had studied classical languages in Zagreb and in England and was active as a translator, critic, and essayist. After the war he worked as director of news films (*Filmske novosti*) and as chief of the screenplay department of Jadran film in Zagreb and served as a director and scriptwriter for numerous docu-mentaries. His first feature film, *Monk Brne's Pupil* (*Bakonja Fra Brne,* 1951), successfully transforms the 1892 story written by the Croatian Simo Matavulj into an effectively realized film drama. The film captures the atmosphere and life of Renaissance times and relates the story of Ivo, a desperately poor and wretched peasant, who is driven by material want into a monastery. A cunning and clever student, Ivo becomes a monk who learns how to combine spiritual progress with a discerning and lusty appreciation for worldly pleasures.

Hanžeković's best filmic contribution of the period was his adaptation of Slavko Kolar's play *Master of One's Own Body* (*Svoga tela gospodar,* 1956). This poignant satirical comedy takes place in a small rural village north of Zagreb (circa 1928). It concerns a peasant family threatened with hard times because of the sudden loss of their prize cow. The father, Jakob, decides to redeem the fam-ily's fortune by arranging for a marriage between his handsome young son, Ivo, and the lame and outwardly unattractive daughter of Jura, a nearby prosperous farmer. The arrangement is finalized against the bitter objections of the son, and the family receives a rich dowry. Ivo, who is at the full stretch of his young man-hood, resolves to be the master of his own body and never to consummate his marriage with his lame wife, Rosa. Rosa proves to be an industrious and caring wife, with inner beauty and grace and a not-unlovely face. Ivo, unknown to Rosa, shores up his vows of marital chastity with nocturnal visits to a local widow whose sensual charms he had enjoyed before his marriage. Rosa shyly attempts

Jakob (left) and his friends. *Master of One's Own Body* (*Svoga tela gospodar*).

to make herself more attractive to Ivo, whose resentment at the forced marriage she both understands and finds deeply humiliating.

The culminating scene of the film is a long and complex filmic sequence of the wedding party for Rosa's beautiful sister—who Ivo had originally thought would be selected for him and to whom he is still attracted. Once again—as at her own wedding—Rosa is an isolated figure, but this time she has determined to win her own long-delayed marriage rights by lacing Ivo's wine with an aphrodisiac prepared by a local sorceress. Ivo immediately detects the strange taste, forces Rosa to confess the contents of the wine, and upon learning of her design begins to slap her vigorously. With tear-stained face and resolute will, Rosa asserts that she is Ivo's wife, that she loves him, that she wants him, and that he has no right to deny her what is hers. Ivo is softened by the passion, strength, and vulnerable beauty of Rosa at this moment and seems, once again, at the point of yielding to the affectionate and tender feelings which have been growing within him. Instead, he turns away from her, but with less resolve, and begins to walk briskly away from the wedding party and its temptations, up the gently rolling hill. Rosa follows, limping. The film ends unsentimentally, leaving unresolved whether Ivo and Rosa will at last consummate their marriage in the physical sense, as well as grow closer together in affection and understanding.

This film was well crafted in writing, acting, and visual stylistics and won the acclaim of critics and audience alike. It satirizes the provincialism, hyprocrisy, and narrowness of rural life and half-castigates and half-condones the patriarchal and chauvinistic social structure which has placed Ivo and Rosa in such an absurd relationship. This ambiguity toward village life and the rural heritage of Yugoslavia is more sharply brought into focus in several of the most important films of the 1960s and will be discussed in greater detail later.

Action-Adventure Films

The most prolific and successful director of action-adventure films during this period was the Serbian Živorad (Žika) Mitrović. Born in Belgrade in 1921, Mitrović began his career in Yugoslav cinematography during its rebirth in 1944. He wrote screenplays and directed documentary films, was given a medal for the improvement of films in Serbia in 1948, and won a state prize in 1949 for his documentary film *First Lights* (*Prve svetlosti*, 1948). In the 1950s Mitrović turned to the direction of feature films and was influential in transforming the Partisan war film from heuristic national epics to well-crafted, tightly drawn stories of action, suspense, and bravado—which were enormously popular with the domestic audience. Two of his most successful films dealt with the struggle of Partisan forces against the *balisti*—a fascist organization of Albanian Shiptars— in the historic Yugoslav region of Kosovo-Metohija, bordering on Albania. His film *Echelon of Dr. M* (*Ešalon Doktora M*, 1955) details the heroic exploits of Dr. M, who leads an echelon of war-weary young and wounded Partisans across dangerous terrain to a nearby liberated town. Harassed and attacked by balisti bands, the Partisans are helped to victory by the defection and support of Ramadan, who is the son of the leader of the balisti forces. *Captain Leši* (*Kapetan Leši*, 1960) portrays the successful exploits of Captain Ramiz Leši in driving the balisti forces out of Kosmet—and in the process weaning his brave brother from the balisti to the Partisan cause. Also popular with the domestic audience was Mitrović's film *Signals above the Town* (*Signali nad gradom*, 1960), which depicts a band of Partisans who attack a German occupied town, escape from an ambush, and free their comrades from imprisonment.

Perhaps his most interesting film of the period, *Miss Stone* (*Mis Ston*, 1958), departed from Partisan themes to depict the adventures of an American missionary, Miss Stone, who is caught up in the maelstrom of Macedonian resistance to Turkish domination in the nineteenth century. Macedonian revolutionaries capture Miss Stone for ransom from the Turkish government. After an unsuccessful attempt to rescue her by force, the Turkish government agrees to the ranson, and Miss Stone, who has been won over to the rebel cause during her captivity, leaves them as a friend and convert.

A specialized variant of action-adventure films which emerged during this period was those made specifically for children. The first of these, *Kekec* (1951), directed by the Slovenian Jože Gale, won first prize in the category of children's films at the 1952 Venice Film Festival. It portrays the brave exploits of the child, Kekec, who overcomes the evil woodsman Bedanc and frees his youthful captives.

The most popular of the children's films made during this period were directed by the versatile and talented Croatian Branko Bauer. Bauer was born in 1921 in Dubrovnik and began his career in film in 1949 as a director of documentary, news, and short fiction films. His first feature film, *Grey Seagull* (*Sinji galeb*, 1953), was made for children and depicted the adventures of the child Ivo and his comrades, who are captured by smugglers, outwit them, and bring back a treasure to pay a debt owed by Ivo to his father. It was followed by his most successful and cinematically mature film in this genre, *Millions on an Island* (*Milijuni na otoku*, 1955), which relates the tale of a group of island children who discover a treasure and fantasize about travel and adventure on the high seas. Pursued by petty criminals, the children are rescued by the island militia, but, alas, a sharp wind blowing along the shore lifts and scatters the money, along with their dreams, far out to sea.

New Styles of Realism

Accompanying the growth and widening of popular themes and genres of film expression which occurred during this period was a searching reexamination of the war experience and its aftermath, as well as the first tentative steps toward dealing with contemporary themes and problematics. The revolutionary past began to take on an increasingly tragic and human dimension in the films of such directors as France Štiglic, Branko Bauer, Stole Janković, Vladimir Pogačić, Radoš Novaković, and Veljko Bulajić. The abstract and idealized epics of the first period were replaced by intimate psychological portraiture and realistic, sometimes brutally naturalistic, depictions of the war and its aftermath. Interesting problems of human survival and the cruel moral dilemmas of war are posed in concrete and eventful stories in which filmic narrative is advanced by freely linked visual sequences and is shorn of postured set speeches and abstract heroics.

One of the first of this type of film was directed by Radoš Novaković, who had already established his credentials as one of Yugoslavia's leading directors with his first film, *Sofka*. His film *The Sun Is Far Away* (*Daleko je sunce*, 1953) is based on Dobrica Ćosić's influential postwar novel of the same name. The film effectively captures the harsh winter landscape of the forbidding mountains where a unit of Partisans is being held down by a superior force of Germans. A brave peasant fighter from the region, Gvozden, leads an attack not sanctioned by the staff of the Partisan unit. In the interest of discipline, he is judged and executed by his own comrades, who are emotionally torn between the necessity imposed by iron discipline and the bitter act of killing one of their own who had served their cause devotedly and bravely. Lukić describes Ćosić as one of the most important of the postwar Yugoslav writers and one of the first to penetrate the official idealization and purity of the War of Liberation—to expose its sometimes disillusioning, cruel, and bitter side. [23]

Vladimir Pogačić also contributed significantly to more realistic screen portrayals of Partisan war themes in his films *Big and Small* (*Veliki i mali*, 1956) and *Alone* (*Sam*, 1959). The film *Big and Small* is an intimate psychological drama of an underground resistance fighter in occupied Belgrade, who is provided shelter and assistance by a ten-year-old boy and his friends. The boy's father, an old friend of the resistance fighter, had previously refused help and shelter, fearing reprisals for his family. In the context of the film, it is the "small" who rises to largeness of spirit and action, while the "large" (in the person of the father) chooses the safer path of compromise and survival. A more complex portrait of the Partisan experience is drawn in Pogačić's film *Alone*, which tells the story of a Partisan unit surrounded by the Germans in a ring, which is closing. The Partisans fight a desperate and bloody fight, which they win—but they then must break out of the ring at night across a narrow river gorge. Only a few survive the cruel enemy crossfire, including a baby recently born to a female member of the unit. The story derives its interest from the believable characterizations and adept visual imagery. The central character is a young Partisan, who is brash, resourceful, and insubordinate and openly questions the leadership of the unit for maneuvering them into such an impossible situation. He fights bravely in the initial victorious skirmish but then concludes that the situation is hopeless and deserts to the enemy. He is questioned at length by the Germans and commanded, as a certification of his sincerity as a deserter, to execute one of the wounded and tortured Partisans, his squad leader, who is tied by chains to a tree and is near death. German photographers are there to record the event, along with members of the German command. The Partisan lifts his rifle but cannot shoot his comrade. He tries again—and then in a final act of redemption quickly turns the rifle around and shoots the German commanding officer. He is immediately surrounded by German soldiers, who club him to death with their rifle butts. While the film contains some fairly improbable scenes of bravado and hand-to-hand combat, in which outnumbered Partisans toss German soldiers about like so much confetti, there is a hard grain of reality in the depiction of suffering, of tensions and dissent among the Partisans, and of the cruelty of the circumstances in which they are trapped.

The film begins with the evocation of German strength and military might as depicted in a Nazi propaganda film, replete with rolling tanks and goose-stepping Germans, which ends with a large "V for victory" sign. This scene is followed by shots of rugged mountain landscape—with titles superimposed—as the camera pans rocks and mountain gorges, with one carefully composed shot of a lone tree growing stark against a cloudy sky.

In the last scene of the film there are only five surviving Partisans and the new-born child carried in one of their back sacks; they are followed by the camera as they make their weary way, single file, up the rocky mountain pass—to fight again. The baby and the small band of survivors are framed like the lone tree in the beginning of the film—symbolizing the strength of the life force even in such a bleak and hellish landscape.

During this period, Slovenia's leading director, France Štiglic, realized his most effective film about the war experience in *The Ninth Circle* (*Deveti krug*, 1960). The film is a variation on the Anne Frank theme and provides a chilling portrayal of the persecution of Jews by the Ustashi regime in Zagreb. A Catholic family saves a lovely Jewish girl, Ruth, from being arrested with her family and sent to a concentration camp. They marry her, in name only, to their nineteen-year-old son, Ivo, and sequester her in their home. Ruth's family and Ivo's family were members of the professional middle class and had long been close friends. At first, Ivo rebels at the restrictions which this mock marriage has on his own life and student activities. However, as the dark seriousness of the situation becomes clearer to Ivo, he comes closer to Ruth, and a tender love develops between them. Ruth is sensitive and full of life and loves to watch the children playing under her window. She especially likes the nearby park and fountain where she cannot now go, and her days are increasingly marked by anxiety over the fate of her family.

One sunny day when there is an air raid warning, Ruth is drawn by the sunlight and empty streets to her beloved park to enjoy a furtive time of freedom. She sees a poster which announces the deaths of Jews and finds the names of her family among them. She breaks down and is observed by a young Ustashi, who is a school chum of Ivo. She is arrested and taken to a nearby concentration camp. Ivo, against the tearful protests of his mother, goes out to find her and bring her back. There are misty, dark scenes of the camp, with its forlorn watch towers, long barracks, and barbed-wire fence. Ivo's school acquaintance is there as a guard and gives him a nightmare tour of the facilities. Ruth is in a barracks where drunken Ustashis are dancing with the pretty girls, trampling their bare feet with muddy boots. Nothing can be done for Ruth. She is trapped in the ninth circle— which in the argot of the concentration camp means that she is scheduled for certain elimination. At the exit gate, alone with his former classmate, Ivo overpowers and kills him. He manages to free Ruth from the barracks, and they hide

Ruth and Ivo—no escape. *The Ninth Circle (Deveti krug)*.

in an abandoned watchtower, where they await their opportunity to avoid the sweeping searchlight and climb over the barbed-wire fence. They make love in consummation of their marriage. At the right moment they attempt escape. Ivo makes it over the fence, and freedom seems in view. Ruth, however, cannot negotiate the barbed wire in her bare feet. She tells Ivo to leave her, but instead he climbs back up to try to help her across the top. At the moment that their hands clasp and he vows not to leave her, the searchlight pinions them on the fence, the stark light fills the screen, and all hope of escape is banished.

The Ninth Circle is a visually arresting film, in which the play of sunlight and darkness achieves metaphorical significance; in which life is caught unaware, lived out in its dailiness against a backdrop of gathering tension and depredation of the human spirit. The realism of the concentration camp scenes, done without melodramatic insistence, serves only to underscore its dark luridness. The final scene of the film also affirms unsentimentally the possibility of human tenderness and love in the midst of an occupied city and even in the midst of the grotesqueries of a concentration camp.

Another film which captures realistically the atmosphere of occupied Zagreb is *Don't Turn Round, My Son (Ne okreći se, sine,* 1956), a film directed by the

Croatian Branko Bauer, who had already established his reputation as one of Yugoslavia's leading directors of the time with his two action-adventure children's films previously discussed. Bauer in this film relates the story of a man who escapes from a prison train on the way to a concentration camp and finds his way to his apartment in Zagreb, only to discover that his wife is being kept by a German officer and his son is enrolled in a special Ustashi school to learn Fascism and military skills. Helped by a painter friend and a network of Partisan sympathizers, he manages to spirit his son from the school and to establish contact with a nearby unit of Partisans. On the edge of the woods where the Partisans are secreted, the man and his son are pursued by a squad of Germans. The father turns to face their pursuers and tells his son to run straight for the woods and not to turn around. The Germans riddle the father with bullets, and a German on a motorcycle is about to overtake the running boy, when shots ring out from the

Near capture in a Zagreb apartment. *Don't Turn Round, My Son* (*Ne okreći se, sine*).

woods and the German is shot from his mount. The motorcycle careens riderless back to the dead body of the father and comes to rest at his side. An overhead shot captures this melancholy and forlorn tribute to the dead resistance fighter while his son melts into the woods and an uncertain destiny.

While this film captures well the betrayals, compromises, and furtiveness of characters playing out desperate roles in the twilight streets and apartments of Zagreb, the heart of the film, and that which gives it meaning, is the intimate psychological portrait of a son and a father who rediscover each other. In the process, the boy is freed by tenderness, understanding, and love from an alien and deforming ideology.

One of the most realistic and affecting Partisan films of this period was *Partisan Stories* (*Partizanske priče*, 1960), based on the literary work of Antonije Isaković and directed by the Serbian Stole Janković. Janković understood intimately the tragic dimensions of the War of Liberation; he joined the Partisans as a teenager in 1941 and served and fought in the war to its successful conclusion. After a distinguished career in film, Janković turned his attention solely to politics and rose to the influential position of member of the Central Committee of the Communist party in Serbia. While his credentials as a Partisan fighter and a loyal party member were never in question, he deplored films which idealized the war experience and obscured its human costs with shallow heroics. The film *Partisan Stories* consists of two separate narratives. The first story, *Return* (*Povratak*), relates the episode of a girl whose father is the rail station master in a small, German-occupied town by the Neretva River. A youthful fighter in a nearby Partisan unit is engaged in a sabotage operation against the railroad and is injured as he throws a hand grenade to take out an enemy machine gun bunker. He is carried to the house of the young girl. The parents are afraid of the danger which the wounded Partisan represents to them, but the daughter risks securing medicine for him at the town's pharmacy and gently nurses him back to health. When he is well enough, she helps him escape at night in a small rowboat secreted at the edge of the river. A German patrol finds her near the river with her dog and suspects her of complicity with Partisans. She is brought into town for questioning. The German officer in charge of the interrogation is deepened in his suspicion of the girl because he had earlier seen her in the pharmacy getting the medicine. The girl will not talk. In retribution for the Partisan attack, the town is bombed, and, in the morning, the girl is led out to be shot. She walks past the place where she is ordered to stand and begins to cross a swinging bridge arched gracefully over the river. Ordered to halt, she continues to walk. The last image is a closeup of the beautiful girl's face, her eyes closing in death, as she is shot in the back. This image is held in freeze frame while gradually a wintry blizzard is superimposed and the film makes its transition to the more powerful of the two stories, *The Red Shawl* (*Crveni šal*).

A guerrilla action. First episode of *Partisan Stories* (*Partizanske priče*).

The Red Shawl begins with a long line of Partisans carrying their wounded in a bleak mountain winterscape; the snow and ice cling to their coats and hair. The wind whistles, and its coldness penetrates to the bone. The climb is steep—the march is a forced one against fatigue, hunger, and numbing cold. A young teenage fighter reminisces about his family and his life before the war. The Partisans arrive at a small farm settlement nestled in the mountains and take rest and food. The peasants are suspicious and unfriendly, having been warned by Chetniks that the Partisans bring in their wake only deprivation, reprisal, and death. A peasant woman engages the commander of the unit in conversation and expresses skepticism concerning the value of the paper scrip, redeemable after the war, which was given by Partisans to peasants for food and shelter. She is openly scornful of the Partisans and their worthless pieces of paper given in return for scant supplies needed for the peasants' own survival. The Partisan leader wearily and solemnly avows that the Partisans, in the end, will triumph. Somewhat rested, the Partisans line up the next morning and prepare to resume their long march. The peasant woman rushes from the farm house and excitedly announces that her beautiful, large red shawl has been stolen. A small group of skeptical peasants has assembled to watch the departure of the Partisans. The leader begins to search for the red shawl, but the young boy immediately volunteers that he has taken it to ward off the cold. He removes it from under his coat and lets it drop to the ground. The woman is surprised and grateful that her shawl has been retrieved. But the Partisan leader must make a hard decision in enforcing the strict discipline of the Partisan code, which forbids theft from peasants on penalty of death. The Partisans were themselves composed chiefly of peasants and moreover owed their thin lifeline to the cooperation and sustenance of rural peasants and villagers. The peasant population was the branch on which Partisans stood and were upheld. The boy understands the penalty that must now be exacted. He is led off by his comrades. When the peasant woman understands what is happening, she pleads for leniency and mercy. A single shot rings out offscreen, announcing the boy's death. With a pained and drawn expression, the leader marches his unit, single file, into the gathering whiteness as the villagers watch in shocked and subdued silence.

Pogačić was the first to break through the chronic aversion to contemporary themes and problems, with his film *On Saturday Evening* (*Subotom uveče*, 1957). The film consists of three stories of ordinary people, with careful attention to small details of everyday life and a skillful rendering of milieu. The first story concerns a young couple, Mirko and Nada, who have married without the knowledge of their parents. The young man expects to secure an apartment through his job, but for the time being they must see each other on the sly. The film opens with a scene at a train station on a Saturday evening, where the young couple is discovered in tender embrace. The other passengers waiting on the platform become priggishly annoyed at this open expression of affection—although the couple is standing off from the crowd in an alcove. A policeman is asked to intervene and does so in a way that causes embarrassment, accompanied by remarks and joking from the people on the platform. Mirko assures the policeman that they are married, but his identity card contains no proof of his assertion, and Mirko is ushered off to the police station. Nada hurries home to her family's small apartment to retrieve the marriage certificate. Her younger sister is awakened, however, and witnesses Nada taking the certificate from a locked cabinet. In her rush to leave the room, Nada noisily awakens her parents. She runs out of the apartment, catches a bus, and goes to the police station. In the meantime, the police officers have begun to believe the young man's story and to sympathize with his problem in securing an apartment. Nada arrives, and the marriage certificate confirms everything. Nada's father has followed in a taxi and arrives at the police station in a state of disarray and anxiety. He is not pleased at the revelation of his daughter's secret wedding and takes Nada and Mirko off in a huff. At home the father has a family consultation while the young couple is in the next room. They kiss gingerly and are found in embrace when the father comes in to scold them for their premature and foolish decision to marry. Seeing the love that is between them, the mother softens, and the father finally relents and with gruff resignation invites the young man to live with them until the apartment is secured.

The second story is a well-drawn portrait of a gentle little man, "Doc," who haunts the sports stadium where boxing matches are held each Saturday evening. He proudly carries an old photograph of himself as a lightweight amateur boxer. He is rudely kidded by the regular patrons, but there are also signs of rough affection toward Doc's harmless fantasies and gentle good nature. Not having the price of admission, Doc sneaks into the stadium with the surging crowd to cheer on his favorite boxer, Edi. The fight sequence and noisy patrons are well presented in the film, as is the smoke-filled ambience of ringside. Doc is discovered by the stadium guard and roughly ushered out the gate, to the jeers of some of

Doc's isolation. Second episode of *On Saturday Evening* (*Subotom uveče*).

the regular patrons. Undaunted, however, Doc sneaks through the gates again when they are opened to let in a late arrival. This time the crowd prevents the guard from throwing him out, and Doc pushes up to ringside to offer his unsolicited advice to Edi's handlers. After taking a strong beating, Edi rallies and wins the match. Doc follows the crowd of well-wishers to Edi's dressing room but is shunted aside. He waits outside the stadium gate while the crowd melts away. He lights up with eager expectation when Edi appears with his entourage of handlers and prepares to drive off in a black car. Doc approaches to congratulate Edi, who immediately recognizes him and invites him into the car. The manager, however, impatiently and gruffly orders the car forward. The last scene poignantly frames the figure of Doc, standing alone, dwarfed by the large stadium gate. The camera slowly moves upward and above to accentuate Doc's smallness and isolation—a figure alienated and barred from the realization of his small and harmless fantasies.

The third story also deals with an ordinary and common Saturday evening pastime of the period—the open-air dance. In what is cinematically the most complex of the three stories, Pogačić captures the ambience of young people discovering each other on a Saturday evening. There are the would-be make-out artists, the bully boys and sharp dancers who menacingly threaten all those who would dare cock an eye at "their girls," and an appealing young man and woman who find each other and enjoy a moment of genuine tenderness. The young man and young woman are immediately attracted to each other but find it difficult to overcome a natural reticence and diffidence. They are further embarrassed by simple and inappropriate dress. The girl had soiled her one good dress before the dance by whirling around her apartment in eager anticipation of the evening's entertainment and knocking over a bottle, whose contents made a large stain. She had to wear an ordinary cotton dress instead. The young man had failed to borrow his roommate's one good suit and is likewise ill fitted out. As they are drawn to each other, the young man fantasizes a sequence in which he is dressed to the hilt and puts the bullies in their place. The young woman fantasizes that she is dressed in a new gown; she romantically meets the young man, and they walk together through a willowy path. The actual meeting is awkward and shy, but awkwardness soon gives way to simple affection and tenderness. It begins to rain, but the couple dances on in the rain—a slow dance—while others with bravado dance under umbrellas as the band plays on under the bandstand. The young man's friend has caught the fancy of the friend of the young woman, and they leave the dance terrace. But the young couple continues to dance in their magic circle of young love—alone now under the shimmer of light and softly falling rain.

Pogačić was alone among his contemporaries in filmically depicting a society returning to normalcy and everyday preoccupations. The terrible exactions of

Saturday evening dance. Third episode of *On Saturday Evening* (*Subotom uveče*).

the war and its aftermath, followed by the severe economic dislocations caused
by the Cominform blockade, were being replaced by an assertive and growing
economy. Pogačić gently satirizes petty bureaucratic interventions and continued
material and housing shortages and, in the episode "Doc," was the first to enun-
ciate the theme of the alienated outsider, framed apart from the rushing and indifferent crowd.[24]

Another director who contributed significantly to expanding the possibilities of
film realism was the Croatian Veljko Bulajić. Bulajić had received his training
at the Centro Sperimentale in Rome under the tutelage of Cesare Zavattini,
and the precepts of neorealism which he absorbed were imaginatively translated
to the Yugoslav screen several years after their force had been spent or transformed in Italy. After several years as a successful documentary film director,
Bulajić realized, in 1958, his first feature film, *Train without a Time Schedule*
(*Vlak bez voznog reda*, 1959), in which he depicted the immediate postwar
government-sponsored migration of farmers from the exhausted, rocky, and in-
fertile area of the Velebit region in Dalmatia to the rich farmland of Vojvodina
around Novi Sad. In neorealist fashion, the film provides a rich and detailed

Anticipating a better future. *Train Without a Time Schedule* (*Vlak bez voznog reda*).

portrait of the slow progress of the antiquated train and the conflicts, uncertainties, and cutural clash experienced among the travelers as they attempt to emerge from the bitter, shattering days of the war to anticipate the new possibilities which await them at the end of the journey. The film is characterized by a rough and convincing realism, which depicts a journey not only to a new land but away from old customs and values.

Bulajić's second important neorealist-inspired film from the period was *City in Ferment* (*Uzavreli grad*, 1961), which dealt with the struggles and conflicts surrounding the building of a foundry in Zenica in the post-World War period of reconstruction.[25] While not entirely avoiding idealization and simplification of the problems of postwar Yugoslav industrialization, the film treated the period with greater verisimilitude and searching realism and far less socialist bathos than was present in the earlier film on the same subject, *Zenica* (1957), directed by Jovan Živanović and Miloš Stefanović.

Having propelled himself to the forefront of directors seeking to expand the boundaries of realist film expression in the late 1950s, Bulajić later resolutely turned his back on the *new film* tendencies of the 1960s in favor of directing expensively produced, well-crafted, and enormously popular film epics of the War of Liberation.[26]

Anticipation of *New Film* Tendencies

The most significant modernist filmic experimentation in Yugoslavia in the late 1950s and early 1960s occurred not in the realm of feature film production but in the areas of film animation and documentary and short films and in the growing sophistication of the amateur film movement.

During the late 1950s, animated film production in Yugoslavia was concentrated in the specialized studio of Zagreb film, founded in 1953 as a successor to Duga film, which had pioneered postwar Yugoslav experimentation in animation under the inspiration of the multitalented Croatian Fadil Hadžić. Reaching its most fecund and imaginative period in the late 1950s and early 1960s, Zagreb animated films transcended national boundaries and achieved wide international recognition and renown. Less of a "school" than a loose collective or "family" of imaginative artists, Zagreb film animators produced a remarkable series of witty, abstract, ingeniously designed meditations on the tragi-comic paradoxes and ironies of the modern life; satires of popular art forms; and poignant evocations of contemporary humanity's frustrations, helplessness, and limitations. The most visible of the early leaders of Zagreb film were the Montenegrin Dušan Vukotić and the Croatian writer-director Vatroslav Mimica. Vukotić's films have now entered the classical repertoire of animated films, and his work was recognized by numerous international prizes, including the first Academy Award for animation granted outside the United States, for his film *Ersatz* (*Surogat*, 1961). Mimica likewise directed a series of highly recognized animated films, including *Alone* (*Samac*, 1958), which won the studio's first international prize at the Venice Film Festival, *At the Photographer's* (*Kod fotografa*, 1958), *The Egg* (*Jaje*, 1960), and *A Little Story* (*Mala kronika*, 1962).[27] Mimica alone among the Zagreb film animators successfully experimented with both animated film and feature films and became a leading figure in the *new film* tendencies which characterized Yugoslav feature film production in the 1960s.

Another source of experimentation and the development of original new talent in the late fifties and early sixties was found in the realm of documentary and short film production. As Liehm and Liehm have pointed out, documentary film in Eastern Europe lagged behind even fiction film, "because it had to surrender, a priori, one of its basic esthetic prerequisites; a direct, ideologically unwarped view of reality. Any exceptions, like Poland's 'black series,' were soon suppressed." On the other hand, Yugoslavia's "looser guidelines and its less stringent censorship of 'reality' facilitated the origin of an interesting documentary school there in the fifties."[28] The most important "schools" or centers of documentary film production during this period were the Belgrade school associated with Dunav film, the Sarajevo group associated with Bosna studio, and the Zagreb documentarists, associated mainly with Jadran film and later with the influential FAS—Film Authors' Studio—which was disbanded in 1973 for financial reasons. Garnering a number of international prizes and recognition, several of the prominent Yugoslav documentary and short film directors later emerged in the vanguard of feature film directors of the sixties, including, among others, Matjaž Klopčič, Puriša Đorđević, Ante Babaja, Aleksandar Petrović, Bata Čengić, and Krsto Papić.

Another source of stylistic filmic experimentation and the development of film artists was the Yugoslav amateur film movement, which began quite modestly in the late forties and early fifties but by the end of the fifties had attracted to its activities some of those who would become the most prominent feature film directors (as well as film writers, directors of photography, and film editors) associated with *new film* tendencies of the sixties, including, among others, Dušan Makavejev, Živojin Pavlović, Kokan Rakonjac, Boštjan Hladnik, and Želimir Žilnik. The most influential of the amateur film clubs was the kino klub group Beograd in Belgrade. Not only did this kino klub become a lively center of film experimentation—carried forward with quite modest technical and material means—it was also a center for lectures and discussions of classic films supplied by the Belgrade film archives, and for the development of a sophisticated understanding of film aesthetics and criticism, organized under the leadership of one of its earliest members and one of Yugoslavia's leading film theorists and critics, Dušan Stojanović. While amateur film clubs operated under looser ideological guidelines than professional cinema, several of the early experiments by the Belgrade group aroused the concern of more conservative official ideologues, still wed at the time to socialist realism, and led to the banning (even for showing in amateur film festivals) of some of the kino klub's more irreverent offerings. Among these was the fourth amateur film directed by Dušan Makavejev, *Don't Believe in Monuments* (*Spomenicima ne treba verovati*, 1958), which ironically and elliptically portrays the vain attempts of a young girl to make love to a nude reclining male statue, and *Rain and Love* (*Kiša i ljubav*), directed by Kokan Rakonjac, which was ostensibly banned because it depicted a militia man who behaved clumsily and was inappropriately dressed! More disturbing to ideological purists, however, was the resolutely morbid and abnormal ambience of Rakonjac's films, with their queer, pathological heroes, ill-fated desperadoes, lunatic ex-convicts, and others among society's castaways. Živojin Pavlović also aroused official concern, with his two films *Labyrinth* (*Lavirant*) and *Triptych on Matter and Death* (*Tripih o materiji i smrti*), which early established his preoccupation with depicting the dark underside of socialist life, with its portrayal of decaying living spaces, muddy courtyards, decrepit slums, and alienated heroes.

Eclectic in approach, the major participants in Belgrade's kino klub eschewed aesthetic conformity and experimented with a wide variety of themes and styles, including the poetic, symbolic films of Marko Babac—*The Cage (Kavez)*, *The Girl and the Wind (Devojka i vetar)*, and *The Little Wooden Horse (Drveni konjić)*, some of them inspired by the work of Maja Deren; experiments in surrealism by Rakonjac—*The Wall (Zid)*, and Babac—*Libera*; political satires by Makavejev—*The Stamp (Pečat)* and *Anthony's Broken Mirror (Antonijevo razbijeno ogledalo)*; and love stories with social overtones by Dragoljub Ivkov—*The White Handkerchief (Bela maramica)* and *Love Each Other, Men (Volite se, ljudi)*. Nonetheless, the more talented among the Belgrade group, although highly individualistic and sometimes bitingly acerbic among themselves, were united in their criticism of conformist, establishment films and increasingly impatient to move from the wings of amateur film to the center stage of Yugoslav film production.[29]

They did not have long to wait. With all of its polemic ups and downs, the decade of the fifties had witnessed a quickening and ripening of the Yugoslav cultural scene, which, in the realm of film, had led to imaginative breakthroughs in animated film, and in documentary, short, and experimental films. Feature films had likewise steadily expanded their repertoire of themes and genres, as well as broadened the "acceptable" boundaries of film expression. Moreover, the economic and material conditions for an accelerated rate of film production and film organization had been achieved, and by the end of the fifties, Yugoslav film was poised and ready to enter upon its most fecund and creative period—a period described, with justification, as its Golden Age.[30]

3

New Film and Republican Ascendancy, 1961-1972

The richest and most complex period of Yugoslavia's development of a domestic film industry was ushered in at the beginning of the 1960s. It began with high ambition and enthusiasm, evolved over a turbulent decade full of contradictions and struggles, and reached its lowest ebb in the beginning of the seventies—with its vanguard creators silenced or dispersed and the industry itself dispirited and beset with severe economic difficulties and challenges. This chapter attempts to trace out the complex ideological, organizational, and economic dynamics which framed the development of *new film* tendencies, while the next two chapters describe and analyze in more detail the thematic perspectives and stylistic innovations of the most significant feature films produced during the period.

The sixties witnessed a further decentralization and democratization of Yugoslav self-management film enterprises and a shift toward greater republican autonomy in the organization and dispersal of financial resources for film production, distribution, and exhibition. The Basic Law on Film was revised in 1962 to reflect this changed emphasis and ushered in a period of considerable reorganization of film activity throughout Yugoslavia's six republics, leading to a more richly textured filmic representation of the diverse cultures and languages of its nations and nationalities.

By the end of the decade, separate centers for film production were also established in the two autonomous regions of Vojvodina and Kosovo, with Neoplanta film founded in 1966 in Novi Sad, the capital of the autonomous region of Vojvodina, and Kosova film established in 1970 in Priština, the capital of the autonomous region of Kosovo. The decentralization of Yugoslavia's film industry into six republican and two autonomous regional centers is one of its unique and enduring features, and also has created complex problems of coordination and cooperation across republican and regional lines in building up Yugoslav cinema as a whole.[1] The tendencies toward republican and regional rivalries reached their peak in the late sixties and early seventies and led to some further readjustments after 1971 to achieve greater balance between federal and republican interests.

Toward the end of the sixties there was even a heated and inconclusive polemic exhange among leading film critics as to whether aesthetic and cultural criteria existed to distinguish separate and distinctive national schools of cinema in Serbia, Croatia, and Slovenia and perhaps later (with more mature development) in Bosnia-Hercegovina, Montenegro, and Macedonia. Slobodan Novaković was the principal proponent of the view that such clear aesthetic distinctions were already present and continuously evolving in the film work produced in separate national centers. Ranko Munitić, Rudolf Sremec, and others argued that such separate national characteristics of film (to the extent that they existed) were clearly secondary to the primary shaping influences on Yugoslav cinema of worldwide cultural trends and of the binding socialist premises and collective cultural and sociopolitical experiences through which Yugoslavia as a whole had passed since the Second World War.[2]

After reviewing the arguments and analyses presented on both sides, Bogdan Tirnanić asserted that the only conclusion that these recondite and sometimes hair-splitting discussions revealed was that there had evolved in Yugoslavia "*neither* a Yugoslav cinema, in the sense of possessing a unified aesthetic and a single federal view on matters, *nor* a collection of national cinemas which reflected *primarily* their own separate and distinctive national sensibilities and sociocultural experiences."[3] National rivalries and competition were sometimes expressed at a less exalted level among jury members charged with selecting Yugoslav films to be represented at international film festivals and within the juries which awarded top prizes to Yugoslav feature films at the annual Yugoslav feature film festivals held at Pula.

Such rivalries were even more manifest in the traditional and longer-established realms of literature and the fine arts. In 1967, for example, a "Declaration on the Name and Existence of a Croatian Literary Language" was promulgated from Zagreb. Although this declaration was officially condemned by politicians, according to Lukić, it acquired increasing momentum in the late sixties and early seventies. It was countered by a group of Belgrade writers with a "Proposal for Reconsideration," which stressed Yugoslav linguistic and literary unity but was attacked as a thinly veiled attempt to reassert greater Serbian nationalism of the type that had prevailed in prewar Yugoslavia. This attack was accompanied by further demands that the "various national literatures be clearly delineated," a task which Lukić described as "almost impossible in a country where each republic contains amalgams of traditions."[4]

Despite the difficulties encountered in reconciling and coordinating the enrichment and development of republican and regional centers of film production with the overall development of Yugoslav cinema, this period witnessed a substantial increase in levels of production, which was especially manifest in the area of feature films. In 1961, feature film production leaped to more than twice the annual level it had achieved in the previous decade, with thirty-two domes-

tically produced feature films and one coproduction. This high level of film production, however, proved to be overly ambitious (in terms of socially owned and
self-managed resources for film and in terms of the domestic and foreign market
for Yugoslav films) and was not achieved again until the peak years of 1967,
1968, and 1969. Both in quantity and in the progressive liberalization of film
content and expression, the apogee of Yugoslav feature film production was
reached during those years and has not been matched to the present time. In
1967, thirty-one domestic feature films and four coproductions with foreign
firms were completed; in 1968, thirty-two domestic films and seven coproductions; and in 1969, twenty-nine domestic films and ten coproductions. These
peak years, however, fell between years in which annual production was significantly less although still maintained at a level above the annual production of
the previous decade.[5] The lowest production year was 1963, in which sixteen
domestically produced feature films were completed, along with two coproductions; there were several other years in which domestic feature film production
did not rise above twenty.[6]

Such dynamic and variable levels of film production were in marked contrast
to the relatively more stable curve of ascending annual production averages previously experienced, and reflected not only the periodic ups and downs of the
Yugoslav economy as a whole but also the increasingly ad hoc system of annual
production planning and the ever-changing fortunes of Yugoslavia's several centers of film production which characterized this period.[7] Film production enterprises often overextended their credit and the availability of "self-managed social
resources," and several newly established film enterprises folded for financial
reasons.

An even more troublesome trend during this period was the steady decline in
the number of film viewers, which reached its strongest level of deceleration in
the late sixties and early seventies. The highest point of total film viewing occurred in 1960, with 130,124,000 admissions, but by 1971 this number had
fallen thirty-eight percent to 80,874,000. Toward the end of the sixties there was
also a deterioration in the ratio of admissions to domestic films to admissions to
imported foreign films. From 1961, the peak year for admissions to domestic
films (21,075,000), the numbers fell by 1971 to only 6,100,000, a drop of
seventy-one percent.[8] These trends reached crisis proportions in the early seventies and were further exacerbated by a drop in foreign earnings on the export of
Yugoslav films, which had experienced a significant growth throughout most
of the sixties.[9]

The most evident reason for the overall drop in film attendance which marked
this period was the spectacular growth and impact of television, reflected in the
rapidly increasing numbers of set owners, network expansion, and the increase in

program time and diversification of program offerings. In 1960 there was only one set for every 618 inhabitants, but by 1972 this number had grown to one set for every 10.

Along with this rapid diffusion of television sets came the expansion and organization of ever more sophisticated republican centers for television production. The original television centers (Ljubljana, Zagreb, and Belgrade), located in the more developed and populous republics of Slovenia, Croatia, and Serbia, were joined during this period by centers in the less-developed republics of Macedonia, Bosnia-Hercegovina, and Montenegro.

There was also a dramatic increase in program time and diversification of program offerings. Beginning the decade of the sixties with a schedule of four hours of evening programming, Yugoslav television ripened to the point that by the early seventies it was offering approximately twenty hours of programming daily, with about sixty percent of this programming domestically produced. Television had grown from "an experimental luxury providing four hours of programming for privileged set owners to a mass medium watched by over 90 percent of the total population."[10]

Television had usurped film's dominant role as Yugoslavia's most important popular medium of information, entertainment, and artistic expression and was met with increasing hostility and resentment from film workers and artists. It was not until the later seventies and early eighties that the Yugoslav film industry discovered how to "live with television" and find ways of entering into mutually advantageous creative and financial collaboration.

One of the consequences of the steady decline in the number of film viewers, and the loss of revenue on admission taxes which it entailed, was the expansion of other sources of republican and enterprise revenue to prop up the expanded level of domestic film production—especially in the most expensive area of feature film production. In the late sixties, a portion of income taxes used to subsidize cultural activities was siphoned off to support domestic film production, and a variety of republican and enterprise sources were tapped to finance promotional films, tourist films, filmed television commercials, and educational films. Despite all of these efforts, Kosanović estimates that by the end of the sixties only about one-fourth of the revenues to support domestic film production were derived from domestic film viewing and earnings on film exports, while the remaining three-fourths were derived from supplemental support from republican and enterprise sources.[11]

These generally negative trends led to a reduction in overall feature film production in the early seventies and created a significant crisis in the areas of film distribution and film exhibition as well. The dynamic implications of these adverse economic trends were combined with a tightening ideological climate which occurred in Yugoslavia in the late sixties and early seventies, and together they formed the twin millstones upon which *new film* tendencies were ground to a halt.

New Film and Ideology

In the sixties, Yugoslavia entered its most creative and innovative period of experimenting with new forms of self-management socialism and fostering an atmosphere of wide-open debate and discussion in social, economic, and cultural spheres of development. It was a period in which film advanced to the forefront of artistic experimentation and was often a lightning rod which attracted heated polemic exchanges on the "proper" role of artistic expression in a socialist state and on how far the boundaries of "free" expression and stylistic experimentation should be extended. Yugoslavia's vanguard of film critics, theorists, and film artists rallied loosely and with varying degrees of commitment under the banner of *novi film* (*new film*) or *open cinema*. While lacking a specific program or coherent aesthetic perspective, the advocates of *new film* sought: 1) to increase the latitude for individual and collective artistic expression and to free film from dogmatism and bureaucratic control; 2) to promote stylistic experimentation in film form and film language—influenced initially by early 1960s films associated with French *nouvelle vague* and vanguard Italian cinema, and later in the sixties by *new wave* tendencies in Eastern European countries, most notably Czechoslovakia and Poland; 3) to involve film in the expression of *savremene teme* (contemporary themes), including the right to critique the darker, ironic, alienated, and gloomier side of human, societal, and political existence; and 4) to do all of these things within the context and premises of a Marxist-socialist state—at a time in Yugoslavia's evolution when these very premises were a focal point for heated philosophical and ideological debate. One of Yugoslavia's leading film theoreticians and critics, Dušan Stojanović, perhaps best expressed the "spirit" and thrust of the *new film* movement when he stated that "the most valued distinction of the new Yugoslav film is that on the philosophical, ideological, and stylistic plane it extends the possibility—and that possibility is daily realized in practice—of transforming a single collective mythology into a multitude of private mythologies." [12]

New film was associated with the larger trends of the period toward greater decentralization and democratization of Yugoslav society, sometimes referred to as Yugoslavia's "second revolution," and claimed for itself the right to serve as a critic of all existing conditions and the freedom "to be a conscience—often an unavoidably sombre one—of the land, the nation, the society, and the individuals that comprise it." [13] *New film* creators numbered themselves among those who favored humanistic, democratic socialism and self-government over Stalinist positivism and bureaucratic statism; who aligned themselves with Marx's earlier notions of *praxis* over ideological dogmatism and conformity; who vigorously and critically confronted collective myths about the National War of Liberation and its aftermath, often endowing these themes with new contemporary relevance and urgency; who explored the sources of humanity's alienation in a society that had theoretically, at least, eliminated its causes; and who created a series of open metaphors about contemporary human and societal conditions which resisted closure and which refused to offer easy and optimistic answers to the questions they posed.

New film tendencies in Yugoslav feature film production followed an uneven course during the sixties and early seventies, and their progress was punctuated by dynamic shifts in the ideological and political climate. For purposes of discussion, the initiation and evolution of *new film* can be divided roughly into three phases: 1) the early sixties, in which "modernist" thematic perspectives and stylistic innovation were first inserted into feature film production and provoked strong and widespread resistance and polemic attack; 2) the middle and late sixties, when new film artists and critics emerged as an increasingly influential vanguard of Yugoslav feature film production; and 3) the end of the sixties and the early seventies, when the counteroffensive against *new film* tendencies was renewed and intensified under the banner of *black film* and resulted by 1973 in the fragmentation and virtual collapse of the movement.

Birth and Early Struggles

The dramatic rise in feature film production which occurred in the early sixties and the relatively free and decentralized structure of Yugoslav film enterprises opened the way for a new generation of filmmakers, who were quick to seize upon the opportunities presented to them. Of the thirty-two feature films produced in 1961, two were singled out as representing the birth of *new film* tendencies in Yugoslav feature film production and as making a sharp break with the past: *Two (Dvoje)*, directed by Aleksandar Petrović, and *A Dance in the Rain (Ples v dežju)*, directed by Boštjan Hladnik. Both films were antioptimistic manifestos which explored failed love relationships, played out in an alienated urban environment. Both were personal, intimate films which experimented in very different ways with new possibilities for film language, in which intricate visual metaphors replaced traditional narrative structure.

Aleksandar Petrović was one of the central and dynamic figures in developing *new film* tendencies. Before making *Dvoje*, Petrović had served his apprenticeship as an assistant director of feature films, as a film critic, and as the director of several award-winning documentary films. Born in Paris in 1929, he attended the film academy in Prague in 1947; he apprenticed in Paris film studios for a short time before returning to Belgrade, where he completed a degree in the history of art from Belgrade University. He began his career in the Yugoslav film industry and as a film critic in 1948. Although Petrović had earlier codirected a feature film with Vicko Raspor, *The Only Way Out* (*Jedini izlaz*, 1958), the film *Dvoje* was his debut as an independent director and writer of feature films. Later in the decade he assumed an increasingly influential role in the development of *new film* as a critic, as a chairman of the Union of Film Workers, as a professor of the Belgrade Academy of Theater, Film, Radio, and Television, and as one of Yugoslavia's foremost feature film scenarists and directors.

Boštjan Hladnik, born in 1929 in Kranj, received his degree from the Academy of Dramatic Arts in Ljubljana, was active in the amateur film movement during the fifties, and directed two professional documentaries, *Life Is No Sin* (*Življenje ni greh*, 1957) and *A Fantastic Ballad* (*Fantastična balada*, 1957). Hladnik spent three years (from 1957 to 1960) in Paris, where he attended lectures at the Sorbonne and worked as an assistant on several films by Chabrol, Duvivier, and Siodmak. He was the first of the talented young directors associated with the amateur film movement of the fifties to move into professional feature film production.

In retrospect, the two debut feature films of Hladnik and Petrović seem rather modest vehicles to sustain the heavy freight of polemic and impassioned critical commentary which their appearance generated. Advocates of *new film* praised them as "the most filmic films yet produced in Yugoslavian cinema" and as representing significant breakthroughs in contemporary thematics and film form.[14] Skeptics regarded them as imitative, pale reflections of French and Italian *nouvelle vague* tendencies which were alien to the distinctive cultural roots and contemporary conditions of socialist Yugoslavia.

The "flavor" of these polemic exchanges is captured in the contrasting reviews of Petrović's film *Dvoje*, which appeared in the Belgrade paper *Književne novine*, under the title "Two Opinions about One Film." Unremittingly negative in his assessment, Dragan Jeremić asserts that the film presents a mechanistic and misanthropic view of love. The true protagonist of the film is not the music student, Jovana, or the architect, Mirko, "but rather 'love' itself . . . her mechanisms, her ascent and fall, the necessity which guides her entrance and exit lines." Jeremić bemoans the film's sketchiness of character and lack of motivation and development. The lovers are presented as marionettes trapped in a "whirlpool which engulfs them," and Petrović is interested not in the "moral meaning or thought" involved in such a relationship but only in its mechanism. "For Petrović, love evidently is a trap into which man involuntarily falls and from which he exits empty, depleted, and satiated." Not only is the theme developed in a mechanical way, but so also is the structure, in which images are presented as "visual phenomena," devoid of analysis "from within." Everything is "shown," not explained, touched, or felt. It is evident to Jeremić that Petrović does not believe in the deeper possibilities of love, and the film is the fruit of his lack of understanding. "Love is presented only as a short and ephemeral illusion—without warmth, duration, or depth." In comparing *Dvoje* to three other films about lovers, *Moderato Cantabile, Lovers,* and *Hiroshima, Mon Amour,* which Jeremić asserts evoke "hymns of love," Petrović's film by contrast is "a requiem to love or a dirge—and a banal one at that." The only saving grace that Jeremić can find in the film is the originality with which Belgrade settings are captured and photographed, so that the "personality" of the city comes through more strongly than the personalities of the characters in the film.

Vuk Vučo takes a different and more positive view of the film. He suggests that the film is not intended to be a conventional or "romantic" love story. The couple in the film did not love in the beginning, in the middle, or at the end of their sterile year—"their end was at the beginning, as in a play by Beckett." Vučo contends that the form of the film is entirely fresh and original, and, as in the new French films, "meaning is transformed into nothingness and nothingness into new creation." By viewing traditional love relationships as if through a concave mirror, the film reflects contemporary "truths" in a way that "opens up new possibilities and directions in our film."[15]

Hladnik's film *A Dance in the Rain* drew equally sharp and conflicting critical assessments. It was condemned by some critics for "aestheticism" or preoccupation with form over content, for the negative and sterile view of modern life and relationships which it presented, and for offering visual complexity without philosophical depth. Others praised the film for its poetic and visually arresting style, for its complex filmic exploration of the ambiguous borders between dream and waking, reality and illusion, and, as in the case of Petrović's film, for opening up new paths of development in Yugoslav feature films.[16]

Undaunted by the controversy that surrounded their first films, Petrović and Hladnik followed them with second films which elicited even more vociferous attacks. Petrović's second film, *Days* (*Dani,* 1963), departed even further from conventional narrative structure in favor of creating a melancholy visual meditation on the empty life of an ordinary young woman, whose inner boredom finds visual equivalents in the cold sterility of her Novi Beograd suburban apartment and soulless urban surroundings. Hladnik's second film, *Sand Castle* (*Peščeni grad,* 1962), is an intensely personal and stylized psychological study of three young people, one of whom had been born in a concentration camp during the war, who find the realities of their life so harsh and alienating that they escape into a world of illusion and games. Neither of these films was accepted for official showing at the annual festival at Pula for Yugoslav feature films, and the *new film* tendencies they represented were sharply attacked by top party officials.

Other films to fall into official disfavor were the multiepisode feature films directed by three amateur film directors associated with the Belgrade kino klub group, Živojin Pavlović, Kokan Rakonjac, and Marko Babac. Their first film, *Raindrops, Waters, Warriors* (*Kapi, vode, ratnici*, 1962), consists of three different episodes, which portray in a veristic, grainy, naturalistic way somber stories from the war years and contemporary life. Their second film, *The City* (*Grad*, 1963), was officially banned by the district court in Sarajevo, and the film negative and all copies were impounded. In summarizing the reasons for banning the film from all public showings, the court stated that the first story "portrays a meaningless view of life, and love is reduced to physical, senseless lust." In the second story, "life is also portrayed as meaningless, and the character of the director, Slavko, a person in a very responsible position, is shown to be a very blasé type, representing capitalist Yugoslavia, who works for the communists but whose heart ailment results from service to the communists." In the third story, the film

> presents a Yugoslav town in such a negative light that it raises the question whether it is worthwhile to live there . . . so negative that the kafanas are full of antisocial types, where life unfolds under the sign of morbid sexuality and hooliganism, through which the hero of the story, a darkly moody invalid, passes lost, gloomy, and isolated to the brink of a pessimistic, sickly precipice, which is all quite obviously the opposite of our social reality and which is put together with a tendency to show negatively the social development of Yugoslavia, thus turning inside out our social reality and spreading ideas which are opposite to our social movement. [17]

Aleksandar Petrović sharply criticized the judgment of the court and stated that because of "a lack of comprehension and understanding, one of Yugoslavia's best films was tossed into the wastebasket." [18]

The well-known Belgrade painter Mića Popović also came under scathing attack with his first feature film, *Man from the Oak Forest* (*Čovek iz hrastove šume*, 1963), which was subjected to several reedits before eventually being released. [19] Živojin Pavlović's film *The Return* (*Povratak*), made in 1963, was also held up for three years before finally being released in 1966.

In a speech at the Seventh Congress of Young People in 1962, and again in his New Year's message of 1963, Tito himself attacked various foreign, antisocialist influences in the cultural and artistic life of Yugoslavia. He warned against a part of the intelligentsia which "places itself above society, which lives outside our socialist reality, and which, falling under various foreign influences, becomes the bearer of prowestern, bourgeois, nonsocialist ideas and understandings; which criticizes and negates all the results of our development." Tito called for a renewed struggle against these "decadent phenomena from the outside which have a negative influence on our people—above all on the young." [20] The text of Tito's remarks was widely circulated among Communist party *aktivs* positioned in cultural commissions, film studios, and other cultural enterprises, and touched off widespread discussion and debate.

In December 1963, Veljko Vlahović, the president of the Ideological Commission of the Central Committee of the Communist party in Serbia, delivered a speech to a meeting of Communist party film workers and *aktivs*, in which he oulined what he considered to be the weaknesses which had developed in film work over the past few years. The most important of these was the increasing tendency toward "ideological and aesthetic straying," which he asserted was tied to "unhealthy relations" within the self-management bodies of the film studios. Evidently, he stated, the "talented cohabit with the untalented," and those "who manage well sit together with spendthrifts and adventurers, who together dispose of the resources of the society." This deplorable state of affairs has led to the squandering of rather scarce social resources on questionable projects, which, in some cases, "borders on the criminal."

In explaining the nature of these ideological and aesthetic "strayings," Vlahović expresses his strong disagreement with film aestheticians, critics, and artists who treat the theme of alienation "in the same way as their colleagues in the West." Many film artists, he insisted, "do not see that socialism began as a system in bitter struggle against alienation—for the rehabilitation of man." Some artists do not see "that in their nihilism they, in fact, sever the constitutional branch upon which our society and the entire system rest, and thus come into latent conflict with the state."

Vlahović strongly objects to what he terms a Bergsonian-derived intuitive and personal approach to creativity, and he especially objects to some film critics who attempt to establish film aesthetics and film creation as an autonomous realm disconnected from literature and aesthetics in general, from philosophy, and from larger social values. Such critics, according to Vlahović, evaluate a work only in terms of its visual form and interreferential symbolic connections, while disregarding its content or thematic substance. Vlahović insists that "there are no values that are exclusively and specifically aesthetic and which stand separate and apart from societal values."

Reflecting the continuously emerging role of the Yugoslav Communist party during this period as a social animator rather than a dictator of cultural policies and norms, Vlahović reminded his audience that the struggle against negative *new film* tendencies should rely "on the strength of persuasion, not on the strength of the Central Committee and the Ideological Commission." He concluded by expressing his own faith in the democratic processes of self-management socialism and the prospect of developing a truly open and creative atmosphere among film artists: one in which individual creators would possess a deeper understanding of the connections between their work and the overall development and values of Yugoslavia's socialist society. In the final analysis, stated Vlahović, "we must all the more rely on the personal responsibility of artists toward their society."[21]

If the primary purpose of Vlahović's speech was to provoke discussion and debate, he did not have long to wait. Far from retreating in the face of such attacks, *new film* advocates increased their efforts to defend, to expand, and to fortify their newly won beachhead in feature film production. In this initial series of polemic skirmishes, it was perhaps Aleksandar Petrović who most extensively addressed the various charges that had been made against *new film* tendencies, in a statement which he delivered at a special conference, "Yugoslav Film and Our Reality," sponsored by the Union of Film Workers of Yugoslavia.[22]

In his address, Petrović provided a lengthy analysis of the films which had come under the most severe attack and argued against the various charges made against them. He argued against the view that because *new film* tendencies in Yugoslavia were part of a worldwide revolution in film stylistics and thematics (in France, Italy, and elsewhere), Yugoslav films were simply mimetic imitations of these trends, "noninventive and inert." He asserted that the roots of Yugoslav *new film* expression can be traced to the documentary work, the amateur films, and the progressive ripening of feature film expression which had occurred in Yugoslavia in the previous decade of the fifties. More significantly, Petrović objected to the various attempts to artificially label any Yugoslav film which touched on the intimate and sometimes tragic dimensions of human existence as nonsocialist or as an infectious import from abroad. Such an ideological line leads, according to Petrović, "to a strange logic that in socialism there are not and cannot be intimate psychological conflicts, individual deaths, and social alienation. . . ."[23]

Perhaps Makavejev best summed up the initial shape and physiognomy of *new film* tendencies as "viewing the world as it is, without literary and ideological intervention."[24] In its initial development, *new film* was practically synonymous with personal films, films that "claimed the right to subjective interpretations of the lives of individuals and society, the right to 'open metaphors,' leaving room for viewers to think and feel for themselves."[25]

New Film Dominance

The maturation of *new film* tendencies was clearly evident at the 1965 annual festival of Yugoslav feature films at Pula. The festival was highlighted by Aleksandar Petrović's third feature film, *Three* (*Tri*), perhaps his most mature and interesting film, which captured first prize and earned international critical acclaim and widespread popular acceptance. Dušan Makavejev, the most original film director of the period, and perhaps the best known internationally, made his feature debut with the film *Man Is Not a Bird* (*Čovek nije tica*). One of the leading creative spirits of the Belgrade kino klub group, Kokan Rakonjac, screened his second independent feature film, *Horn* (*Klakson*). Živojin Pavlović, whose first feature film, *The Return*, was delayed in its release until the following year, stirred renewed controversy with the screening of his second film, *The Enemy* (*Neprijatelj*). The gifted Belgrade director Puriša Đorđević offered the first of his surrealist-inspired tetralogy about the war years and their aftermath with his film *Girl* (*Devojka*). The ripening of *new film* tendencies which these works represented inspired one of the most eloquent advocates of such tendencies, Dušan Stojanović, to declare that "at last we have thematic freedom and lively film." [26]

On the larger political stage, the fall from power in 1966 of Aleksandar Ranković, chief of the State Security Service, secretary of the LCY (League of Communists of Yugoslavia), and a member of Tito's inner circle, was widely interpreted as a further triumph of the "progressive" or "liberal" wing of the Communist party. The forced retirement of Ranković was only one more sign of the progressive liberalization of Yugoslav economic, political, and cultural life which took place in the late sixties.

In this increasingly liberalized atmosphere, *new film* directors and film artists continued to widen thematic horizons and to become more provocative in their confrontation with the revolutionary past and in their critique of contemporary conditions. Since the next two chapters will explore more fully these new thematic and stylistic horizons, it is necessary at this juncture only to identify the principal films and leading figures associated with the *new film* movement and to set this movement in the context of the more numerous traditional and commercially oriented films made during the same period.

The Belgrade Nexus

Yugoslavia's largest center of film production is located in Belgrade, accounts for about half of the feature films produced annually, and was also the most fecund source of *new film* expression. At the cutting edge of *new film* expression and experimentation were the three film directors Dušan Makavejev, Aleksandar Petrović, and Živojin Pavlović.

Živojin Pavlović, a short-story writer, novelist, film critic, and essayist, was from his earliest days as an amateur filmmaker a focus of heated debate and polemics. He provoked and sometimes enraged his critics with an unrelenting assault on received myths and popular shibboleths. His was a scorched-earth policy, a demonic urge to find in film the means to shake complacency, to purge away the dross of collective memory, to confront unpleasant truths, and to explore relentlessly the dark corners of the soul and the broken promises of the new socialist order. He was a pessimistic harbinger of unwanted news and unwelcome visions. His style was naturalistic, often brutally so, but at moments was illuminated by a dark lyricism and poetry. He was, in many ways, an unbending moralist, who aggressively thrust his vision of the world on a recalcitrant audience. Such Old Testament prophets are seldom very welcome in any society—and, as events unfolded, Yugoslavia proved no exception to the rule. His most important films on contemporary themes were *Awakening of the Rats* (*Budjenje pacova*, 1966), a somber and evocative record of human spirits broken on the yoke of the past and living out shattered lives in the contemporary slums of Belgrade, and *When I Am Pale and Dead* (*Kad budem mrtav i beo*, 1967), about the human cost of industrialization. His most controversial film, *The Ambush* (*Zaseda*, 1969), was a bitter recounting of the years immediately after the war, when Stalinism reigned supreme; in it a young, idealistic revolutionary is casually shot on a lonely road by the Yugoslav secret police (OZNA). In the context of the film, it was not only the young boy who was "ambushed" but the revolution itself. Pavlović's film *The Red Wheat* (*Rdeče klasje*) is also set in the immediate postwar period and debunks the failures of collectivization.

If Pavlović was the stern teacher who drove his lessons forward to their relentless conclusion, Makavejev was the ironic, irreverent, sophisticated, and playful gadfly who stung with wit and cunning, lifted the veil of public pomp to expose its empty interior, debunked the rituals of reification and cant, exposed the obscenity of repressive power even when it was dressed in the illusory garb of sanctioned bureaucratic niceties, and celebrated the uniqueness and liberating spirit of the individual. At his best, Makavejev engaged in a self-irony which exposed the irony of irony itself. In his most important films, *An Affair of the Heart, or the Tragedy of the Switchboard Operator* (*Ljubavni slučaj ili tragedija službenice PTT*, 1967) and *WR: Mysteries of the Organism* (*WR: Misterije organizma*, 1970), Makavejev imaginatively explores the actual and metaphorical regions of eroticism as a foil to the obscenities of repressive power.

Aleksandar Petrović probed with increasing complexity and sophistication the regions between human freedom and fulfillment and the sometimes confining and harsh demands of social and historical realities which penetrate the soul and pinion the spirit. He was, among his peers, perhaps the consummate film craftsman. His most important films of the period were *Three* (*Tri*, 1965), set in the years of the war and its aftermath; *I Even Met Happy Gypsies* (*Skupljači perja*, 1967), which unfolds a tragic story of Gypsies portrayed in the contemporary setting of Vojvodina and Belgrade; and *It Rains in My Village* (*Biće skoro propast sveta*, 1969), which eschews picturesqueness and naive romantic visions of village life to portray a ruined world of evil, backwardness, and isolation. His last and most controversial film of the period, *The Master and Margarita* (*Majstor i Margarita*, 1972), based on the well-known Russian novel by Mikhail Bulgakov, is set in Moscow during the beginning of Stalin's reign, and explores the complex relationships of creative freedom and expression in an increasingly repressive atmosphere. An analogy is implicitly drawn between this period and the events which were unfolding in Yugoslavia under the banner of *black film*, and Petrović uses the occasion to savage his contemporary critics.

Other important contributors to *new film* tendencies among the Belgrade directors were Puriša Đorđević, Kokan Rakonjac, and Mića Popović. Popović, a well-known Belgrade painter, followed a unique path of filmic development and contributed visually distinctive, psychologically complex, and highly controversial perspectives on the war years in his films *Man from the Oak Forest* (*Čovek iz hrastove šume*, 1964) and *The Toughs* (*Delije*, 1968). Puriša Đorđević's most important contribution to the period, as previously mentioned, was his surrealist-inspired tetralogy on the War of Liberation and its aftermath: *Girl* (*Devojka*, 1965), *Dream* (*San*, 1966), *Morning* (*Jutro*, 1967), and *Noon* (*Podne*, 1968). Kokan Rakonjac made his first feature film with a negative hero, *Traitor* (*Izdajnik*), in 1964, followed by *Horn* (*Klakson*, 1965), an offbeat portrayal of a small group of guests at a holiday lodge in the mountains who vainly attempt to overcome isolation and alienation. Rakonjac's promising career was cut short by his sudden death in 1969 at age thirty-three. Just before his death, he completed the film *Pent-Up* (*Zazidani*), a searing examination of prison life with strong political overtones.

Relatively minor but not insignificant contributions toward widening the thematic horizons of *new film* were made by the screenwriters Ljubiša Kozomara and Gordan Mihić, who collaborated in writing and directing the internationally acclaimed film *Crows* (*Vrane*, 1969). The Belgrade director Vladan Slijepčević made his debut with *The Real State of Affairs* (*Pravo stanje stvari*, 1964) which provided a quasi-documentary analysis of marital infidelity, followed by *Protégé* (*Štićenik*, 1966), a contemporary portrait of opportunism and bureaucratic corruption. The Serbian Djordje Kadijević also made important contributions, with his films *The Feast* (*Praznik*, 1967), a searing account of the massacre of a Yugoslav village caught in the withering crossfire of rival Chetnik and Partisan forces, and *Expedition* (*Pohod*, 1968), which recounts the desperate efforts of a simple farmer to find refuge in a war-ravaged landscape.

Toward the end of the decade, Belgrade's influence reached out to embrace the Novi Sad group of film creators associated with the newly established Neoplanta film. The most important director of this group was Želimir Žilnik, whose film *Early Works* (*Rani radovi*, 1969), named after Marx's own *Early Works*, was singled out for strong attack and held up as a perfect example of *black film*—a film considered so radically disaffiliated from mainstream assumptions about socialist reality that it was effectively banned from domestic distribution.

The Zagreb Group

The second most important center of *new film* experimentation and creation was Zagreb. Directors who worked out of the studios in Zagreb tended to be less radical politically than their colleagues in Belgrade but were no less inventive in pushing forward the boundaries of film stylistics and expression. The most important directors associated with *new film* were Vatroslav Mimica, Ante Babaja, Krsto Papić, and Zvonimir Berković.

The most restlessly creative and versatile of the Zagreb filmmakers was Vatroslav Mimica, who produced an interesting and varied series of films during this period. His film *Prometheus from Vishevica Island* (*Prometej sa otoka Viševice*, 1964) provides a sympathetic but melancholy portrayal of a middle-aged *stari borac* (old fighter), who had spent his youth in the mountains with rifle in hand and whose contemporary efforts to bring the blessings of electrification and modernization to the island of his birth are met with incomprehension and conservative resistance. The present is infused with memories of the past and brings its share of disillusionment and pain. A stylistically more inventive film is *Monday and Tuesday* (*Ponedeljak ili utorak*, 1966), an abstract meditation on urban ennui, in which a journalist's daydreams punctuate the deadly and monotonous rhythm of his days. Even more abstract is Mimica's film *Kaja, I'll Kill You* (*Kaja, ubit ću te*, 1967), which universalizes the terror and degradation of war and occupation by framing the sudden and brutal killing of an ordinary shopkeeper with visually stylized renderings of parched walls, windswept, narrow, empty streets, and the sound of jackboots on cobbled stone in a nameless Dalmatian town. In his film *The Event* (*Događaj*, 1969), Mimica makes greater concessions to narrative structure and creates a minutely ritualistic and dark tale of greed and violence. In his last film of the period, *Nourishee* (*Hranjenik*, 1971), Mimica experiments with changing shades and gradations of color to transform a concentration camp into a philosophical metaphor where helpless victims try over and over again to achieve a bit of freedom.

Ante Babaja's most important film of the period is *The Birch Tree* (*Breza*, 1967), a visually rich film inspired by a Croatian folk painting, which recounts the tragic death of a beautiful but frail peasant girl, who is metaphorically linked to the slender and vulnerable birch tree of the film's title. The talented scriptwriter Zvonimir Berković made his debut as a director with *Rondo* (1966), which remains his most important film. A literary and cinematic variation on a rondo by Mozart,' the film creates a sophisticated ambience in which a chess game becomes a metaphor for an urbane love triangle. One of Yugoslavia's foremost documentary film makers, Krsto Papić, achieved international acclaim with his third feature film, *Handcuffs* (*Lisice*, 1969), which skillfully recreates the uncertainty, tension, and pervasive ambiguity of the period immediately following Yugoslavia's break with the Cominform in 1948.

Other Visions, Other Voices

Ljubljana continued, as in earlier periods, to be a vital source for film experimentation. The two most important Slovenian film directors associated with *new film* tendencies were Boštjan Hladnik and Matjaž Klopčič. As previously discussed, Hladnik's major contributions to modernist film expression occurred in the early sixties with his two films *Dance in the Rain* and *Sand Castle*. After making these films, Hladnik went to West Germany, where he completed two feature films,[27] and upon his return to Yugoslavia he never recaptured a leading role in *new film* development. In the middle sixties, Hladnik was eclipsed by the versatile and stylistically inventive contributions of Klopčič.

Born in Ljubljana in 1934, Klopčič received a degree in architecture from Ljubljana University and studied film art and literature in Paris. While in Paris, he apprenticed as an assistant art director with Godard and other leading personalities of the French cinema. In the sixties he became one of Yugoslavia's major film critics and a gifted scriptwriter and feature film director. His most important films were *On Wings of Paper* (*Na papirnatih avionih*, 1967) and *Oxygen* (*Oksigen*, 1970).

Among the smaller republican centers for film production (Montenegro, Macedonia, and Bosnia-Hercegovina), only Bosna film in Sarajevo contributed substantially to *new film* tendencies. In the late fifties, the documentary group in Sarajevo had established a well-deserved reputation for stylistic inventiveness and political boldness. Two of its leading documentarists, Bata Čengić and Boro Drašković, emerged at the end of the sixties as leading feature film directors. Čengić provoked widespread critical attention and polemics with his films *Little Soldiers* (*Mali vojnici*, 1967), *The Role of My Family in the World Revolution* (*Uloga moje porodice u svetskoj revoluciji*, 1970), and *Scenes from the Life of Shock Workers* (*Slike iz života udarnika*, 1972). Drašković made an auspicious debut with his first feature film, *Horoscope* (*Horoskop*, 1969), which depicts the emptiness of life in a small town, where pent-up youthful vitality erupts into violence.

No brief survey of *new film* tendencies would be complete without acknowledging the gifted directors of photography who contributed substantially to the creative realization of modernist film expression. Among the most important of these were Tomislav Pinter, Aleksandar Petković, Milorad Jakšić- Fanđo, Rudi Vavpotić, Karpo Aćimović-Godina, Frano Vodopiveć, Mihajlo Popović, and others.

The Traditionalists

While films associated with *new film* tendencies provoked the greatest controversy within Yugoslavia and garnered the greatest attention outside her borders, they coexisted with a much larger number of films produced during the same period which affirmed more orthodox aesthetic values and thematic perspectives. *New films* also coexisted with a growing number of commercially oriented light-entertainment films, which were often so weak in inventiveness and cinematic style that they failed to reach even the low target of audience taste at which they were aimed.

Among the traditional film directors who continued to make well-crafted and often quite popular films during this period were France Štiglic, Veljko Bulajić, Branko Bauer, and Žika Mitrović. The Serbian Žika Mitrović achieved his greatest success during this period with his action-adventure film *March on the Drina* (*Marš na Drinu*, 1964), a dramatic recreation of Serbian military resistance during the First World War. The venerable Slovenian film director France Štiglic continued to make films on war subjects and to experiment with greater film lyricism. His film *The Ballad of the Trumpet and the Cloud* (*Balada o trobenti in oblaku*, 1961), based on a novella by one of Slovenia's major writers, Ciril Kosmač, poetically relates the tale of a peasant who gives up his life on Christmas Eve to rescue a group of Partisans. As previously mentioned, the popular Croatian director Veljko Bulajić turned from his neorealist experiments of the fifties to make well-produced and popular war epics, achieving his most notable successes with *Kozara* (1962) and *Battle on the River Neretva* (*Bitka na Neretvi*, 1969).

Branko Bauer directed two critically and popularly acclaimed films of the period, *Superfluous* (*Prekobrojna*, 1962) and *Face to Face* (*Licem u lice*, 1963). The film *Superfluous* (also released under the English title *It's Michael I Want*) recreates the atmosphere of naive élan among volunteer youth brigades during the postwar period of reconstruction. *Face to Face* treats conflicts within the workers' self-management council and the party organization of a factory, whose general manager resists the new styles of self-management and, in the end, must resign to make way for genuine democratization and face-to-face decision making. A spiritual heir to Pogačić's film *Story of a Factory*, Bauer's film provides a morally uplifting and officially acceptable fable of self-management socialism adapted to the requirements of the sixties.

Among newer directors who followed more traditional subject matter and narrative film form were the Croatian Antun Vrdoljak and the Macedonian Kiril Cenevski. Vrdoljak's most successful film was *When You Hear the Bells* (*Kad cuješ zvona*, 1969), the story of a resistance fighter who gradually forges united resistance among three neighboring and culturally disparate villages: one which answers the toll of a Serbian Orthodox church bell, a second in which the muezzin cries the summons to prayer from a minaret, and a third in which the Catholic church bell is sounded. Kiril Cenevski was the most important talent to emerge from the small production studio Vardar film in Skopje, Macedonia. His film *The Black Seed* (*Crno seme*, 1971) provides a hellish portrait of a prisoner-of-war camp on an island of the Aegean, in which soldiers accused of participating in the 1946 Communist insurgency in Greece suffer torture and hardship under a merciless sun.

Counteroffensive

From about 1969 to 1972, the counteroffensive against *new film* tendencies was renewed and intensified under the banner of *black film*. The most radical films of the period were attacked for their nihilistic and pessimistic view of Yugoslav socialist development and for anarcho-individualistic nonconformism. The campaign was stimulated, in part, by events occurring on the larger political stage: the 1968 student demonstrations in Belgrade, the Warsaw Pact invasion of Czechoslovakia, and especially the Croatian nationalist-separatist crisis of 1971.[28] These events ushered in a period of increasing ideological stringency, aimed at nonestablishment Marxists (especially philosophers associated with the internationally acclaimed journal *Praxis*), members of the non-Marxist "humanistic intelligentsia," radical student leaders, and artists. In the area of film, this campaign led to banning some films and subjecting others to more subtle styles of bureaucratic intervention. Makavejev was expelled from the party and left Yugoslavia to continue film work in France and the United States following the controversy surrounding his film *WR: Mysteries of the Organism*. After a three-month hearing in 1973, Petrović, who was not a party member, was dismissed from his position at the film academy for contributing to a negative atmosphere at the school and for "extreme political negligence."[29] Pavlović was expelled the next year but was later reinstated without faculty rank or teaching duties.

Similar harassments occurred in literature, the press, and theater.[30] In early 1975, eight members of the philosophy department of Belgrade University associated with the journal *Praxis* were dismissed, and the journal was discontinued.[31] These events followed a well-worn script, involving heated and extreme ideological and polemic accusations by party functionaries and members of cultural commissions, the banning of texts either by formal court action or by various arts councils which constitute the organs of social control, and renewed impositions of preventive censorship, in which self-management organs saw the handwriting on the wall and imposed censorship upon themselves—democratically.

No sooner had the curtain dropped on the 1969 Pula festival of Yugoslav feature films than an eight-page supplement to *Borba* appeared, titled "The Black Wave in Our Film." The term *black film* had its origins in the short-lived *black series* of Polish documentary films made in the fifties, the Czech *dark wave* films of the sixties, and the French films of black pessimism of the thirties—especially those of Marcel Carné. The author of *Borba's* special supplement, Vladimir Jovičić, provided an updated version of the term as applied to contemporary Yugoslav film. In the next few years, the lines of attack which he developed were often repeated with varying degrees of emphasis and sophistication. The term *black film* rhetorically replaced *new film* or *open cinema* and dominated the polemics of the time. Even foreign critics picked up on the term and vied with each other in identifying the blackest film of the year—with the palm of blackness usually awarded to Pavlović.

Jovičić begins with the simple premise that literary or artistic freedom should imply some responsibility on the part of the artist to portray the basic realities of the times with "reasonable verisimilitude—though certainly not with slavish imitation or photographic documentation." It is clear to Jovičić that the black wave in Yugoslav film presents a "systematic distortion of the present," in which everything is viewed through a monochromatic lens. Its themes are obscure and "present improper visions and images of violence, moral degeneracy, misery, lasciviousness, and triviality."

Jovičić warns that true artistic freedom does not embrace the right to express negation for its own sake. Freedom practiced in this way "drastically collides with aesthetic, ethical, and social values—values which are the very attributes of true artistic creation." Jovičić acknowledges that "freedom of expression" cannot exclude the risk of failure in the final result; otherwise, without such risk, there could not be genuine creativity. He asserts, nonetheless, that the practitioners of black film cannot be excused under this provision. "Our most recognized film authors are urged on by a whirlpool of tendencies which are not encouraging and are, in the end, unacceptable."

Jovičić also attacks several of Belgrade's most influential film critics,[32] who, he says, support and actively promote black wave tendencies and are apparently blind to "their monochromatic tendencies" and oblivious to the fact that "they overstep the bounds of freedom of creative expression." Such critics "continue to prize and recommend these great shows of misery and horror," apparently cannot see that these works neither are art nor represent life, and cannot hear their "discordant refrain of nihilism and defeatism."

In assessing the social and political roots of black film negativism, Jovičić advances several hypotheses, which were picked up and elaborated upon by other polemicists of the time both within and outside the Yugoslav film community. First, he accuses the films of being fashionable expressions of worldwide political unrest and disillusionment with current political structures. These films merely imitate what is "selling on the world market" rather than anchor their expression in the "unique conditions of socialist development in Yugoslavia—our society and our life."

Second, these films are merely a retroactive and retrograde reaction to the earlier period of socialist realism and naive optimism. But they are equally dogmatic in the other direction. They reflect a "reverse Zhdanovism played in black rather than white—and both are equally false . . . both are a disaster for real art, both equally rhetorical and tendentious, and both provide a false unidimensionality in defining the complexities of life."

Third, Jovičić suggests that, despite the best efforts to solve them, there continued to be social and economic difficulties and differences among the peoples and regions of Yugoslavia, which have provided fertile ground for negative portrayal. Rather than offering some humane vision or way out of these difficulties, the makers of black film have perversely insisted upon choosing their protagonists from the bottom strata—from the outcasts and the alienated, from those "who are condemned from birth and damned for life . . . from the ranks of the antisocial, obscure, freakish, and pathological." Viewing the social order solely from this angle has led to an "invalid cinema of pessimism and defeatism, and an attempt to reject all that is positive."

Finally, Jovičić condemns black films for their lack of communicative power with their audiences. He states that black films contributed to alienating the domestic audience and were partially responsible for the financial crisis of the Yugoslav film industry.[33]

In his conclusion, Jovičić expresses an idea which gained in momentum over the next three years. Black films, he stated, spread ideas of defeatism and suspicion of established values,

> and in doing so, the artist seeks refuge in the liberal idea that artists can express anything, but in relation to the black wave we have ill used the idea of artistic freedom. If some people allow themselves a freedom which cannot be harmonized with any valid concept of social freedom, not even the freedom of artistic creation—to simply negate all that exists in order to affirm themselves—*then it is appropriate that their own ambitions should themselves be negated.*[34]

In the face of mounting criticism both from outside and from inside the film community, the vanguard personalities of the new film movement reaffirmed their tenets of complete freedom of artistic expression and the preeminence of "individual engagement" (*individualna angažovanost*) over different variants of "social engagement" (*društvena angažovanost*). They also reaffirmed that the responsibility of the free, creative individual artist is to serve as a critic of all existing conditions and to continue to oppose dogma and myth in all its forms. The basic position of Živojin Pavlović, Aleksandar Petrović, Dušan Makavejev, and others was very close to the philosophical radicalism of the *Praxis* group, as expressed by Predrag Vranicki:

> We see man as *par excellence* a being of practice, a being who freely and consciously transforms his own life. . . . Man exists and develops by transforming his natural and social reality and . . . in this way he transforms himself also.[35]

The notion of "practice" or *praxis* as it applies to the realm of aesthetics is perhaps given its most radical Marxist-derived formulation by the philosopher Danko Grlić. He first defines what *praxis* is *not*:

> Human practice stands in opposition to all that is passive, merely meditative, noncreative, all that is adaptation to the world and to its particular social conditions. . . . It seeks to attain no *ultimate* and final "results," no life of bliss in this or any other world, in paradise or the promised land.[36]

In defining what creative practice *is*, Grlić argued that it is "opposed to everything established, dogmatic, rigid, static, once-and-for-all determined, fixed,

standard: to everything which has become dug into the past and which has remained hypostatized."[37]

In a round-table discussion at the Pula festival in 1965, Dušan Stojanović expressed ideas very close to those formulated by Grlić. He argued that the critical
moment in the ripening of Yugoslav cinema was a time for the "full individual
engagement of authors." He was opposed to any imposition of group or societal
desires on creative activity, however attractively it may be attired in revised and
updated versions of socialist realist dogma parading under the name of "socially
engaged" films. Any such group-derived norms (however free of the old dogmatism of socialist realism) were obstacles to individual creativity. Stojanović asserted that the true path to "socially engaged" films was to allow film artists to
express themselves in a "free, independent, personal, and, if you like, anarchic
spirit."[38] Stojanović also feared that more benign and flexible aesthetic theories of
"socially engaged" films would serve as a platform for launching the familiar attacks of past years; that they would unleash a "mass of cliches, a flood of sociopolitical vulgarizations . . . and the imposition on the film artist of 'this or that
"social necessity."'" He reminded his colleagues what enormous harm had been
done in the past to art and to the whole of culture under the "fictive 'true be-
liever' slogan of social engagement."[39]

In a slender volume on film aesthetics, *Djavolji film* (*Demonic Film*), published in 1970, Živojin Pavlović also advocated complete freedom of artistic expression, which, in its essence, amounted to a Nietzschean assertion of the creative power of individual human negativity: a radical personal negativity pitted
against received myths and dogma and against what Pavlović termed the "social
mechanism" in all its current forms.[40] Such a position left Pavlović open to the
charges that he was espousing an elitist or aristocratic attitude toward society and
toward everyday human life and that he was promoting negation for its own
sake—i.e., nihilism. Since social and political institutions, by their very nature,
seek to fix, order, preserve, and routinize certain human relationships and to prevent the development of others, the question was raised: In the name of what
vision, or alternative vision, was the total negation which Pavlović espoused
being undertaken? This question was posed by a leading Belgrade film critic,
Milutin Čolić, who had previously been identified as a supporter of *new film*
tendencies, in a sharp attack which he made on black films in the influential
film journal *Filmska kultura*.[41] It was raised in a more extended form by the film
critic and aesthetician Milan Ranković, in his monograph *Društvena kritika u
savremenom jugoslovenskom igranom filmu* (*Social Criticism in Modern Yugoslav
Feature Films*), in which he rejected Pavlović's formulation in favor of a moderate variant of "social engagement" aesthetics.[42]

It became clear that the vanguard personalities of the *new film* movement
were becoming increasingly isolated, not only from "conservative" members of

the film community but also from the more moderate "middle-of-the-roaders," and from former supporters as well. Most of the campaign against black film was waged in the rough-and-tumble of public polemics and in the no-less-intense internal arena of the film community itself. It was not until the early seventies, following the Croatian nationalist-separatist crisis, however, that public pressures became most intense and several films and directors, as previously indicated, were subjected to direct and indirect forms of harassment and bureaucratic interventions.

The result of all these pressures was clearly manifest in the 1973 Pula festival of Yugoslav feature films. The festival was dominated by a long-delayed, expensively produced, three-hour melodramatic color film of the famous Partisan battle at Sutjeska, which starred Richard Burton as Marshal Tito. The only film to retain some spark of *new film* radicalism was Krsto Papić's film A *Village Performance of Hamlet* (*Predstava Hamleta u selu Mrduša Donja*), based on the controversial satirical play by Ivo Brešan.

The ultimate triumph of the black wave counteroffensive was not so much a victory of neo-Stalinist recidivism or of unredeemed Jankovićevites and party centrists who wished to turn the clock backward to the prereform days as it was a part of the general movement in the early seventies to "repair the course" of the sixties and to impede the flow of power concentrations in republican centers: a flow of power which had carried in its wake the revival of old national rivalries and interethnic strife. It was an attempt, as well, to turn the needle of the compass more nearly toward a middle position out of fear, openly expressed at the time, that the social order was gyrating out of control.[43]

While the negative effects on the personal and professional careers of some of Yugoslavia's leading film creators were real enough, the black film counteroffensive, even at its height, fell far short of the Kafkaesque purges of gifted members of the Czech film community which occurred during Czechoslovakia's period of "normalization" from 1969 to 1973.[44] Nor did it reach the scope and paranoid intensity of the Hollywood "blacklisting" which occurred during the McCarthy era.[45] Finally, it seems fair to observe that the black film counteroffensive in Yugoslavia never approached the heights of absurdity or the depths of triviality reached by the various "ban the book" movements which have recently occurred in the United States under the influence of new-right coalitions and the "moral majority."[46]

Despite such qualifications, the bruising battles of the late sixties and early seventies had left the Yugoslav film industry dispirited, beset by severe economic difficulties, and stranded on a sterile shore—rudderless and without a compass. The final chapter will chart the course taken by the Yugoslav film community to adapt to the complex new forms of self-management mechanisms and accountability instituted after the passage of the revised constitution of 1974 and the Law on Associated Labor in 1976, and its gradual progress in the late seventies and early eighties toward a livelier and more interesting cinema. The next two chapters will attempt to provide a deeper understanding of *new film* tendencies as they were worked out in the films themselves.

4

Confrontation
with the
Revolutionary Past

In 1945, Yugoslavia rose anew from the ashes of an exhausting war waged against multiple occupiers and an internal revolution waged by Partisans against contending domestic forces. The National War of Liberation had been fought largely by indigenous forces led by disciplined cadres of Communist leaders. Unlike other countries in Eastern Europe, Yugoslavia did not owe its liberation either to the Red Army or to Western forces.

The Partisan war experience was the founding myth of the new Socialist Yugoslavia. Its heroic deeds, sacred songs, slogans, and icons were transformed into emblems of legitimacy for the postwar leadership. *New film* creators often offended the guardians of sanctioned traditions by reworking the substrata of collective experience into personal filmic visions and by infusing the past with the living present. They painted portraits of false heroes and of fallible Partisan warriors. They moved the viewer through troubling and ambiguous moral landscapes, where "right" and "truth" were not easily discerned. They traced out the dark shadows of the new dawn and unblinkingly and unsparingly exposed the betrayal of dreams and the corruption of high purposes.

Personal Visions

One of the most compelling Partisan films of the period, *Three* (*Tri*, 1965), directed by Aleksandar Petrović and based on stories by Antonije Isaković (who also assisted Petrović in writing the screenplay), presents the war from the personal perspective of the Partisan fighter Miloš, who witnesses three tragic and ethically troubling deaths. The first occurs in April 1941, shortly after the invasion of Yugoslavia by the Germans; the second occurs while Miloš is a Partisan fighter during the war; the third takes place at the end of the war, when collaborators are being rounded up and executed.

The film begins with a series of stills depicting barbed wire, Germans marching, and other scenes of war, punctuated by a drumbeat on the sound track, with titles superimposed. In the opening shot of the first story, two soldiers of the retreating Yugoslav army are bending their ears to a railroad track to see if a train is approaching. Miloš is one of the villagers trying to stay ahead of the advancing

Germans. He walks through and scatters a flock of geese while making his way to the train station. The station is filled with people attempting to make their escape. When the train arrives, it is full of retreating Yugoslav soldiers, and there is no room for further passengers. Some villagers rush to the track, while young boys in army caps sing a song about planting white roses. Soldiers on the train ask a Gypsy to perform with his dancing bear, and they toss coins to him. The crowd is left on the platform as the train pulls out, and the conductor informs them that another train may follow soon. The crowd becomes more tense and anxious. A lone hand-pumped tram, propelled by two men, goes by. The town fool, Zeka, a bearded, crazed man, is taunted by the crowd. The crowd surges toward freight cars on the siding and begins to steal the contents. A war patrol of three soldiers appears to restore order. They ask for papers. A man with a camera claims that his papers were burned during his escape from Belgrade. He is unknown to the waiting crowd of villagers. They are suspicious and fearful that he may be a member of the fifth column, a German spy. The man pleads his innocence and says that his wife is on her way to join him. Miloš intervenes to suggest that the soldiers must wait until the wife arrives to check the story. Others call for the man to be killed. The soldiers shoot him. With his arms outstretched, the man continues to plead his innocence. He is shot again and crumples to the ground with his arms still outstretched. The body is dragged across the tracks, and the crowd falls into hushed silence. The war patrol marches on. The second train finally arrives, and the crowd surges on. A woman appears and tries to get information about her husband, whom she describes as a man with a camera. She receives no answer. A villager watches the scene from the window of her house—a mute witness to a senseless death. The train pulls out of the station. The bearded prophet wanders aimlessly in a circle. The Gypsy walks along the empty tracks with his bear. The drumbeat resumes, and the film fades into the second episode.

Miloš is now a Partisan—alone, being pursued by a German patrol through the woods. A series of quick cuts defines the tempo of the chase. Miloš is nearly smothering in his own breath from exertion and fear. Closeups of the faces of the pursued and the pursuers are intercut with closeups of the muzzles of guns. A shot is fired, and Miloš is spotted—he runs, his breath coming in short takes; faster, dogs, gun, face, feet. He jumps from a small cliff, rolls down the stones, and runs across an open clearing, into a flock of sheep; he hides under the sheep and clings to them like Odysseus making his escape from Cyclops. He escapes the patrol and is running across an open rocky space. With a momentary feeling of relief and safety, Miloš finds a mountain stream. However, he comes upon a German soldier and must kill him in hand-to-hand combat. He takes the German's gun and tries to ward off the patrol, which is now on his trail again. He runs down rocky ravines to the banks of the Neretva River and plunges into the wild and churning water as the Germans fire from the embankment. He makes it

Panic at the train station. First episode of *Three* (*Tri*).

Vagabonds of war. First episode of *Three* (*Tri*).

to the other side, groaning with exhaustion. The Germans find a footbridge and cross it to continue the pursuit.

Miloš finds a cemetery and hides among the tombstones. He is ordered to raise his hands. He turns to discover another Partisan who has been cut off from his unit. They decide to join forces and try to make their way back to the Partisans. The Partisan confesses to Miloš the fear that overtook him while he was alone and hiding. They form a close bond as they make their way through marsh grass and scrub. A German plane spots them and dives to strafe them with machine-gun fire. The pilot smiles and plays a game of cat and mouse—ringing them with bullets but delaying the kill. He circles and fires as they run and dive into the marshy waters. The pilot overplays his hand, and the two Partisans escape into the tall marsh grass. They laugh with relief and triumph. As the men struggle on, they are once again spotted by a German patrol with dogs and are pursued through the marsh. They stumble into a field of wild wheat, with the German patrol herding them into a narrowing circle. They decide to split up. Miloš makes it through the circle. His friend seems about to do the same, when he is spotted and captured. Miloš follows cautiously as his friend is led away. Two German soldiers push his comrade against a straw hut with his back to them. He turns to face them. They turn him back around. The drumbeat begins on the sound track. He faces them. They hit him and turn him back around. He turns to face them, and they throw him into the hut and set fire to it. While the hut burns, the patrol circles and riddles it with gunfire. There is an agonizing scream. The German patrol marches on. Miloš is wild with grief and cries, "My life, my life." There is a panning shot over the marshland, which ends in mist. The drumbeat continues, and the film fades to the final episode.

It is the end of the war, and Miloš is temporarily bivouacked with his brigade in a farm house. Miloš watches a prancing colt, small puppies playing, boys making jack-o'-lanterns. He turns to his typewriter to report the last actions of his brigade. Prisoners are brought into the farm yard. There is a young woman among them who attracts the attention of Miloš, who is looking from the window. She gazes up at him for a long moment. The Partisan who has brought the prisoners—German soldiers, Chetniks, and accused collaborators—announces to Miloš that they will be shot that evening. Miloš wants to know why the necessity for such haste. The Partisan replies that none must escape. Examinations will be conducted, and some may be spared. The woman who owns the farm house asks Miloš how guilt and innocence are to be determined in such cases and takes a special interest in the young and beautiful girl. Miloš gives her permission to take the young girl a melon to eat. The girl looks up at the window. Miloš returns her gaze. The drumbeat resumes on the sound track. Miloš paces, lights a cigarette, looks out the window again. There are closeups of the girl, poised but frightened, eating the melon and glancing up at the window. The

Pursuit. Second episode of *Three* (*Tri*).

Capture. Second episode of *Three* (*Tri*).

farm woman pleads for the girl's life. She is young and can change. Miloš is upset; he paces more insistently. He looks at the prisoners huddled together in the farm yard, waiting. The Partisan in charge of interrogations returns with the typewriter, and Miloš asks him if the girl might not be spared. But her case has been settled. She was in love with a German officer, and there are photographs to prove it. Miloš watches as she is being led away by a soldier with a gun. The girl breaks away and runs, scattering a group of hens. She is easily caught and is taken behind the house. Miloš comes out to the farm yard and slowly follows in the direction the girl was taken. Unseen by the audience, she is executed. A village wedding group passes by with a beautiful young bride and her groom. The film ends with this poignant image of new life for the bride and the end of all such possibilities for the young woman who has been executed.

The film *Three* catapulted Aleksandar Petrović to the first rank of Yugoslav film directors and won wide international acclaim. It captured first prize and the award for best direction at the 1965 Pula festival, won first prize at the International Film Festival at Karlovy Vary in 1966, and was one of the five finalists in the competition for best foreign film at the Academy Awards in 1967. It presented a concrete intimate psychological portrait of an ordinary Partisan warrior caught in the matrix of confused and morally ambiguous events. The protagonist is not so much the author of his actions as he is carried along in the sweep and tide of historical events and concrete human dilemmas. His impulse is to intervene and to prevent the three senseless and cruel deaths in the film. He ends by being a reluctant, helpless, and despairing witness.

The simple events of the film are shot with remarkable economy and richness of visual detail. Metaphor is introduced naturally and unobtrusively. The herding and scattering of the gaggle of geese in the first episode is an effective metaphor for the herdlike behavior and panic of the assembled crowd on the train platform. The lone Gypsy and his bear, left behind to wander along the empty tracks, are exotic and poignant symbols of isolation and of the outcasts and vagabonds of war. The town fool symbolizes the insanity and scourge of war—and evokes, even in his madness, the fearful authority of an Old Testament prophet.[1]

The terrible exactions of guerrilla war fought against forbidding odds are perhaps never better captured than in the middle episode of the film. It echoes the framework established by official historians of the Partisan war, who divide it into seven major offensives in which superior enemy forces attempted to encircle and annihilate Tito's main forces. Each time the ring was broken, and, after suffering terrible losses, the Partisans regrouped, grew in strength, and fought again. In the film, the metaphor of encirclement is evoked in miniature and in concrete human detail as the German patrol closes in on Miloš and his comrade in the tall marsh grasses, and again when the German patrol surrounds and riddles the burning hut with bullets. Harsh and relentless pursuit, complete mastery of the skies, and superior armaments and numbers test the limits of human endurance and take their tragic toll—the cruel death of one Partisan and the agony and despair of the survivor. There are no false heroics, no set little speeches, no attempts to minimize or restrict the full range of human emotions and reactions to such brutal circumstances.

In the final episode of the film, peaceful bucolic images of traditional Yugoslav rural life symbolize the return to normalcy and revitalization. These processes are disturbed, however, by the continuing reprisals of war—symbolized most poignantly by the harsh and perfunctory execution of the young woman.

The Belgrade director Puriša Đorđević also provided original and fresh perspectives on the war years and their aftermath, with his surrealist-inspired tetralogy: *Girl* (*Devojka*, 1965), *Dream* (*San*, 1966), *Morning* (*Jutro*, 1967), and *Noon* (*Podne*, 1968). Of these films, *Morning* received the widest acclaim and provoked the deepest controversy. It is a stylized, poetic evocation of the last day of war and the first day of peace, as expressed in the Serbian town of Čačak. Peace will not be officially declared until the next morning. In a fluid series of visual tableaux and action sequences, Đorđević, who also wrote the film scenario, introduces a colorful cast of characters—victorious Partisans, captured Germans, Chetniks, collaborators, a Russian artillery officer of the Red Army, and local townspeople.

The mood of the film is ironic and lyrical. Partisans shed their inhibitions and relax the harsh puritan discipline that sustained them in the mountains. They seek erotic pleasures and dream of travel and life after the war. The dialogue is often lighthearted and satirical. A Partisan at a local dance asks a young Communist female if she believes in free love and free choice. She happily confirms that she does. He asks a uniformed female if she believes in free love and free choice. She replies, "I don't know, I'm Bulgarian." A Partisan officer seeks his pleasures in the local bordello, which has obviously seen better days. The madam, a Russian émigré, complains that most of her girls have left—some with German soldiers, others with Partisans. She misses the old days before the war and hopes that the new order will recognize that "we are working class, too." A more earnest young Communist (in the beginning of the film) delivers the standard lecture to the townspeople, admonishing them that, now that the war is over, "we must work to change the country and hearts of the people."

Along with these relaxed, ironic, and witty vignettes, there are contrasting motifs in the film which trace out the dark shadows of war and its continuation even into the new dawn of peace. An unredeemed Chetnik boasts of personally killing seventy people—some of them local citizens. Images are intercut of rows of men hanging by their necks on tree branches. Church bells ring, and there are images of blossoms on the trees.

Coffins are being painted with red stars in preparation for a mass funeral.

Liberation. *Morning (Jutro).*

A song speaks of peace but laments that many are dead. "How can these things be told to mother and girlfriend?" And the killing continues. A group of snipers is found and shot. A row of collaborators is lined up on a hill and executed. One man is spared because he freed some Partisans and is allowed to choose another to stand in his place. It is a time for old accounts to be settled. One Partisan cynically comments, "We must complete the killing today because after peace there will be more hearings, judicial proceedings, and investigations than executions." A piano player in a local bistro confesses that he served as a translator for the Germans. He is shot on the spot.

The lyrical yearning for peace and normalcy, contrasted with the harshness and callousness of wartime reprisal, is intricately intertwined in the case of Aleksandra, a young and beautiful Partisan, who, under duress and torture, revealed the names of fellow Partisans. She revealed only the names of dead Partisans, but, unfortunately, the Germans used the information to execute members of the dead Partisans' families. The episode of Aleksandra is lyrically intercut with other motifs and culminates in her execution in the final moments of the film. The execution, ironically, was to have been carried out by her lover—a Partisan lieutenant. She pleads, instead, to be executed at the hands of a German. A captured German officer is dressed in full uniform to accomplish the deed. Aleksandra is led to the bank of the river. She is allowed to escape. She runs through an open field and onto a dusty road. The German pursues her and shoots her. The Partisan lieutenant in charge of the execution then kills the German—his last of the war. The film ends with the cycle of reprisals temporarily, at least, complete.

Morning won top prizes at the 1967 International Film Festival in Venice and at the 1967 Pula festival and was widely discussed and debated among Yugoslav critics. Guardians of Partisan war traditions were highly critical of the lack of discipline shown by some of the Partisans in the film, especially their accession to the demands of the flesh, the whoring behavior of some of the officers, and the unorthodox and hasty manner in which reprisals and executions were carried out. Some critics even descended to pointing out small discrepancies in Partisan dress and military etiquette.[2] Puriša Đorđević, who had quit school at the age of seventeen to fight with the Partisans and had been captured and sent to a concentration camp, trenchantly responded to his critics by observing, "In 1945 there were more brutality and more tenderness than I succeeded in showing."[3]

A fascinating, psychologically complex, and utterly unusual treatment of wartime themes is presented in the film *Man from the Oak Forest* (*Čovek iz hrastove šume*, 1963), directed by the well-known Belgrade painter Mića Popović. The film takes place in a remote village in Serbia at the beginning of the German occupation. The principal protagonist of the film is a lonely mountain shepherd, Maksim, a Chetnik, who undertakes his own program of execution and murder.

Steeped in the bloody historical traditions of the region, Maksim moves with deft grace through the ancient forest, captures wayfarers on the lonely road to the village, and dispatches them in primitive, ritualistic fashion. He takes each captive into the woods, binds the victim's hands, removes a knife from his leg strap, and kills deftly and swiftly. After each killing, he urinates. His alter ego is a young outcast, Maksim the Boy, who plays a wooden flute and conspires with Maksim in carrying out his blood rituals and murders.

Into the remote village from town arrives a pretty young woman on a bicycle, who poses as a smuggler of goods while clandestinely organizing Partisan resistance in the area. Maksim develops a passionate fascination for the young woman and comes to believe (on the basis of a ducat he has found) that she is smuggling gold. The young woman plays on Maksim's primitive passions and invites him to her apartment in town. In the meantime, Maksim the Boy has discovered her identity as a Partisan organizer and reveals this fact to Maksim.

While Chetnik forces in control of the village prepare a foray into town to hunt for Partisans, Maksim makes his own separate journey to the town in order to find gold and wreak vengeance on the young woman. In town, he kills a shopkeeper who he thinks is involved with the girl and the gold. Although armed with a gun, he kills with his knife and urinates afterwards on a sack of flour. He makes his way to the young woman's apartment. She is not there. He shoots down the pictures on the wall and shatters mirrors—one of which breaks into three pieces, reflecting Maksim's shattered countenance in three aspects. He then douses her bed with perfume and stretches himself across it, writhing in sexual motions. As the empty town begins to reverberate with gunfire, Maksim retreats from the house and shoots a young Partisan. He, in turn, is shot by the Partisan young woman, and, though badly wounded, he moves with animallike strength back toward the village—back to the sanctuary of the ancient oak forest. He is shot twice more and left for dead. With primitive determination, however, he struggles on to the dark woods and the ancient graveyard. He dies at the foot of a mighty oak tree, his last waning efforts expended in reaching out to embrace its gnarled roots. A closeup of the ancient bark of the same oak tree is presented abstractly in the opening of the film, with dissonant choral music playing underneath while the titles are superimposed.

An important character in the film is an educated villager, the local sage, who sees and understands the dark tragedy arising from the fierce internecine strife between Partisans and Chetniks which is enveloping the region. He stands apart from the darkness and bloodshed and comments upon it. He is mentor to a young boy whom he calls "son," a village term of affection of an older man (sage, advisor) for a young man. Initially torn in his loyalties, the young man eventually chooses to join the Partisans.

Even in embryo, this film was subjected to strong official attack in the highest

Maksim. *Man from the Oak Forest* (*Čovek iz hrastove šume*).

The village sage (left) and Maksim the Man. *Man from the Oak Forest* (*Čovek iz hrastove šume*).

reaches of the Serbian Communist party and among members of the Ideological Commission. The film was twice banned before being released in a reedited version in 1963.[4] In its initial showing at the Pula film festival, held in the arena of Pula's well-preserved ancient Roman Coliseum, the thousands of spectators greeted the end of the film with stunned and hushed silence. After a brief passage of time, however, the audience erupted in thunderous and prolonged applause.

The film was criticized from its inception to its eventual release for providing ideological variations from accepted dogma about the War of Liberation. Criticism from official party sources was quite intense and focused mainly on the heresy of making a Chetnik the principal protagonist of the film and providing him with a psychologically compelling and interesting characterization. Even worse, the original version of the film suggested that the beautiful young Partisan woman partially returned Maksim's intense erotic fascination for her. That a Partisan could feel anything for such a brute was totally unacceptable. Indications of her sexual attraction for Maksim are muted in the reedited version but not entirely erased. The original version of the film also makes it much clearer that the shooting of Maksim by the Partisan woman was a complex purification rite, in which she purged herself of guilt and rid herself of the strange passion she had felt for him. In the second version, this motivation is obscured, and her shooting of Maksim could be interpreted simply as the act of a "good" Partisan doing her duty in getting rid of a Chetnik murderer.[5]

Such reediting, however, left untouched the cultural and psychological core of the film. The film's deeper meaning lies in its visual ambience and in the close symbolic associations made between Maksim and the dark and bloody traditions and legends of the region. Maksim dwells in the dark oak forest and moves in the environs of the old water mill and the ancient church graveyard. The graveyard is filled with icons of warrior priests and hajduks who had fiercely resisted the Turks during five centuries of domination. It evokes memories of the two great risings against the Turks in the early nineteenth century. The first of these was led by a dealer in pigs, Djordje Petrović, better known as "Black" Djordje or Kara Djordje, who from 1804 to 1813 coordinated a remarkable rebellion, in which peasantry under the leadership of village knezes, hajduk chiefs, and warlike priests routed great Turkish armies, besieged citadels, and finally won partial autonomy. A second spectacular rising, which lasted from 1815 to 1817, was led by another Serb of peasant stock, Miloš Obrenović. The colorful and heroic exploits of warrior priests and hajduks lived in the oral traditions and legends of Serbian villages. Hajduks were brigands and outlaws, bristling with sabers and daggers, who plundered and harassed Turkish emissaries and officials in the mountainous areas of historic Serbia. Modern-day Chetniks were heirs to the hajduk tradition.

The old water mill was also steeped in local history and custom. It was the traditional meeting place for retelling the old legends and reciting ancient epics. It was also a place for clandestine meetings and sharing of secrets. An old saying of the region states, "Ako hoćeš da ti kažem da niko ne čuje, dodji u vodenicu" ("If you want me to tell you something which nobody should hear, come to the water mil!"). The water mill is the favorite meeting place of Maksim the Man and Maksim the Boy as they hatch their plots and form their symbiotic relationship in communion with the spirits of the past. It is also the secret meeting place of the Partisans, whose Marxist sloganeering seems oddly alien to the old ways of the region—and whose meetings are observed by the ever-watchful Maksim the Boy.

The evocation of the region's heroic, bloody, and dark past links Maksim to something deeper than the chauvinistic rhetorical posturing of local Chetniks or Partisan sloganeering. It is to the roots of the old oak tree that sink deep into the bloodied soil of the past that Maksim returns and entwines himself in death.

The distinguished Zagreb director of animation and feature films Vatroslav Mimica lifts the war experience to the level of poetic and philosophical meditation in his experimental and abstract film *Kaja, I'll Kill You* (*Kaja, ubit ću te*, 1967). The film is set in an idealized and poeticized Dalmatian coastal town on the Adriatic during the Italian Fascist occupation. It is a town culturally and geographically light years removed from the remote Serbian village in Popović's film *Man from the Oak Forest*. Isolated from the Balkan hinterland by rugged mountains rising almost perpendicularly above the eastern shores of the Adriatic, the nameless Dalmatian town in Mimica's film enjoys the peaceful and gentle Mediterranean Catholic culture of the region, which is further nurtured by a mild climate and natural lyrical beauty.

The film opens with a title which explains that the town has lived in peaceful and harmonious tranquillity for three centuries. One day evil enters into the very soul of the town and destroys it. A·man of the town comes in twilight to the house of a friend and announces, "Kaja, I'll kill you"—and does.

The film is built upon a complex series of motifs, in which the ruined and desolated town is contrasted with its former graceful, civilized, and harmonious past. The first images of the film are of emptiness, desolation, and ruin. There are images of deserted cobbled streets, rocks crumbling and falling from buildings into the empty town square, the wind whistling among the ruins, and waves crashing against the sea wall. These images are subtly transformed into sunlight glinting across clear blue waters, birds singing, the sound of church bells, and children playing in the shallow sea water. Opening titles are superimposed over these shots of the village as it was—whole and vibrant with life.

A cathedral and a graceful Italianate palace dominate the town square and between them contain the cultural heritage of the centuries—the church with its icons and religious relics, the palace with its library and paintings. The film charmingly depicts a religious pageant in the church, where young children wearing crude, handmade wings act out a religious morality play, with artificial clouds suspended above them forming a light contrast to the mysteries evoked by swelling choral music and ancient relics. The church is an integral part of the town's life—its bell tolls them to daily routines and play.

The town square is teeming with life. Children play in the square and good-naturedly surround the tattered figure of the town fool, who entertains them by imitating animal sounds. A band plays. People cluster and gossip. Early evening brings a fireworks display, and Kaja and four male companions spontaneously join together in singing lyrical folk songs of the region. There are strolls along the stone-walled paths in the hills surrounding the town. Daylight scenes are inter-woven with evening scenes, capturing the seamless harmony and rhythm of life. A man plays sweet strains on a violin, and the camera lazily pans through the cobbled streets, showing a woman cooking, another woman sewing, flowers and birds everywhere, the town clock, serene landscapes.

Into this setting arrive, almost unannounced, the black-uniformed Fascist oc-cupiers and their local collaborators. At first their presence is minimal, and the rhythm of the town goes on as before. As the film progresses, however, Fascist oppression deepens, and its shadow spreads across the town. The growing domi-nation of this alien, dark, and antipodal force is subtly captured in a series of vignettes.

The first significant evocation of the presence of the new Fascist overlords is announced by a morning bugle call (which supersedes and replaces the musical tolling of the church bells). A troop of Fascists in black uniforms is summoned to the town square, where the men stand at parade rest. The town fool attempts to engage them in play and is rudely shunted aside. The rigidity and military gravity of the soldiers provide an absurd and almost comical contrast to the spon-taneous life which still goes on in the square and in the cobbled streets.

A more sadistic expression of domination is captured in a vignette in which a local, urbane aristocrat and town leader goes to the palace where the Fascist ad-ministrator has ensconced himself. He seeks civilized accommodation in the ad-ministration of the town. The Fascist leader cynically expresses interest and offers the aristocrat what purports to be a glass of the light white wine of the region. The wine glass is filled instead with oil, and the aristocrat is forced to drink two glasses of it, to the amusement of the assembled Fascist underlings. The growing oppression is also captured by framing the black-uniformed Fascist overlord of the town standing dominant on one of the balconies of the palace overlooking the town square—surveying his kingdom with a watchful eye.

As the film progresses, Fascists multiply, and the rhythms of the town become increasingly muted. Two film sequences announce the final depredation and ruin of the town. The first sequence takes place at night. The camera pans across church gargoyles. The sky is grey and ominous. Sea water swells and seeps

Threatening the town fool. *Kaja, I'll Kill You* (*Kaja, ubit ću te*).

Fascism in the heart of the town. *Kaja, I'll Kill You* (*Kaja, ubit ću te*).

through cracks in the sea wall. The streets are deserted. Fascist soldiers are walking restless and drunken in the square. The soldiers begin to desecrate the walls of the church with their knives. They destroy icons and saw off the head of a religious statue. They begin singing vulgarly and raucously. They go to the plush interior of the palace and begin to destroy the paintings. One drunken Fascist butts his head through a painting which he has removed from the wall, inviting imitation from his amused companions. Books are thrown over the balconies to the square below and burned. The Fascist overlord drives the "infidels" from his quarters with a whip and then smiles with sadistic satisfaction at the destruction left behind.

The second and climactic sequence involves the killing of Kaja, a gentle man who personifies the culture of the town as it is lived in its dailiness. He is a tall, genial man, who lives in sunlight and among the birds and flowers. He joins in song with his companions in the town square, runs his small shop, and entertains friends in his modest but airy and open home, where they joke, tell stories, partake of the local wine, and dine together on fish and other local delicacies. Among the good companions who surround Kaja is the man who will kill him, Piele. Joining the Fascist forces and donning a black uniform, Piele becomes progressively alienated from his former companions.

On the evening of the killing, Piele is in the music room of the palace. He looks at a photograph of former companions and places a black patch over the image of Kaja—a foreshadowing of the death to come. He salutes his Fascist masters and goes out into the town square. He walks with a limp. The sound of jackboots on cobbled stone is accentuated by one boot that squeaks. The streets are deserted as Piele makes his way to Kaja's home and shop. He walks into the shop and announces, "Kaja, I'll kill you." A shot echoes in the deserted streets. A long slow-motion take follows Kaja as he stumbles back, clings to the shelves behind him, and brings them down as he falls and dies.

The final sequence of the film recapitulates and amplifies the opening shots of desolation and ruin. Waves pound on the crumbling sea wall. Rank weeds grow among the cracks of decaying buildings. The wind whistles through the deserted streets. The town fool runs demented through the abandoned square, staving off imaginary phantoms and uttering guttural sounds of despair and terror as he leaps among the ruins.

Mimica's somber parable, at one level, expresses the essential vulgarity, dark nihilism, and antihumanism of Fascist ideology. Possessing no culture of its own, it pillages and destroys the cultures it occupies. The ultimate depredation occurs when Piele internalizes this dark and alien ideology and commits himself irrevocably to its deforming evil by killing his former friend and companion Kaja. Piele was always an outsider in this band of convivial companions. His assumption of the Fascist uniform has failed to gain him new status, though Kaja humanely and tolerantly invites Piele to join his old companions at table. Piele's inner deformity and self-hatred are objectively symbolized by his crippled leg. Kaja is the living symbol of all that Piele is not. In killing Kaja, Piele not only kills the living "soul" of the village but also destroys the last vestiges of his own humanity.

At a deeper level, Mimica's parable transcends the parochial boundaries of wartime Fascist occupation and comments upon humanity's darkest impulses—the will to power and domination and the destruction of all that is hateful to those who are full of hate.

The Stalinist Legacy

In this film *Zaseda* (*Ambush*, 1969), Žika Pavlović provides a mordant and stinging indictment of Yugoslavia's immediate postwar period, when Stalinism reigned supreme. The film is set in a village in Serbia soon after the war and focuses upon the progressive disillusionment and eventual death of Vrana, a young revolutionary idealist.[6]

In the beginning of the film, Vrana is caught up in the rhetoric of building a new Yugoslavia based on *Bratstvo i jedinstvo* ("Brotherhood and Unity"), singing heroic Partisan songs, and watching an outdoor projection of a film which idolizes Stalin as the genius head of the fraternal Soviet Union, the "leader and teacher of progressive humanity," and which captures a characteristic pose of Stalin benignly presiding over a military parade in Red Square.

The reality which unfolds for Vrana is quite different. As the new order takes shape, Communist party members recruited almost solely from Partisans assume the reins of power, progressively take on special privileges, meet in secret, and peremptorily impose their decisions on others. A successful local lawyer, suspected of bourgeois and antirevolutionary sentiments, undergoes a show trial which results in the confiscation of his house for a hospital and the removal of his civil rights for a period of five years.

Vrana is romantically interested in Milica, the beautiful young daughter of the lawyer, but is warned by his Communist superiors to avoid any entanglement with her. A school class is interrupted so that Communist members can retire in a secret meeting to discuss the possible baneful influence that Milica's father may have had upon her. At a local dance, non-Communists are asked to leave—so that the others can remain and sing Partisan songs.

Representatives of the Yugoslav security service, OZNA, are increasingly ubiquitous. An especially loutish one is elevated to the position of cultural deputy. OZNA (Odeljenje za zaštitu narodna, Department for the Protection of the People) had been organized by Ranković in 1944, with its mission, as defined by Tito, "to strike terror into the bones of those who do not like this kind of

Yugoslavia."[7] In the context of Pavlović's film, members of OZNA are principally occupied in conducting mopping-up operations against diehard Chetnik
bands who continued guerrilla resistance against the Tito regime after the war,
meddling in personal affairs and local government, and having sexual intercourse with peasant women. As depicted in Pavlović's film, sexual intercourse
OZNA style is quick and to the point, without foreplay or tender aftermath—
wham, bang, and not so much as a "thank you, ma'am."

Vrana, who was earlier victimized by a Chetnik raid which resulted in the
death of a companion, eagerly cooperates and joins forces with an OZNA search
party to seek out and destroy the wily local chieftain of the Chetniks, Vojvoda
Marko. After a long and strenuous search and a skirmish in which Vrana's
fondest companion, Zeka, is killed, Marko is tracked to his lair. Unfortunately,
the aging leader has died peacefully in bed. Captain Jotić, leader of the OZNA
search party, who aspires to be mayor of the village, fakes a killing of the legendary and already dead Marko in order to enhance his credentials for heroism.

Thoroughly disillusioned, and despairing over his friend's death, Vrana jour-
neys back to the village. On a lonely road, he is confronted by the local militia
and, in a mixup over identification papers, is summarily executed.

The last images of the film are those of the newly installed mayor of the village, Jotić, standing on a review stand in the village square, framed by flags and
outsized pictures of Lenin, Stalin, and Tito, benignly presiding over a village
parade. Jotić is thus mimetically and symbolically linked to the images of Stalin
presiding over a military parade in Red Square which were introduced in the
opening scenes of the film.

In the context of Pavlović's film, it is obvious that it was not only the young
Vrana who was ambushed but also the revolution itself. The song of liberation
and freedom and the dream of a new Yugoslavia founded on brotherhood and
unity had died in the throat. Pavlović's film was not kindly received. After a brief
run in Belgrade, it was banned for domestic circulation and was screened only at
the 1969 Pula film festival.

A very different filmic treatment of Yugoslavia's complex and ambivalent relationship to its Stalinist past is presented in Krsto Papić's internationally acclaimed
film *Handcuffs* (*Lisice*, 1969). Papić's film is set in 1948, soon after Tito's break
with Stalin and the expulsion of Yugoslavia from the Cominform. It deals with
the tense and traumatized atmosphere of the time when the Yugoslav leadership
was attempting to purge its ranks of Stalinist sympathizers and those potentially
disloyal to a Tito-led government.

The action of the film takes place in the vicinity of a small village at the foot of
Mount Dinara, in the sterile and rocky Karst region. Opening shots of the film
capture a barren, rock-strewn landscape, with a local folk song on the sound
track intoned in the high, nasal style of the locality. The camera pans over the

landscape and comes to rest on a medium shot of the backs of two men sitting on a rock. A man on a bicycle comes into view, making his way toward the two men on the rocky path. He turns over a message to them, and the cyclist, together with the two men, goes to a farm house to arrest the owner, an elderly man. The cyclist then resumes his journey down the path. The two men lead the farmer at gunpoint behind a cluster of rocks, where, unseen by the camera, he is executed.

Farther along the same rocky path there is a small wedding procession heading for the village. The man on the bicycle passes by and waves. At the head of the wedding procession, acting as flag bearer, is a revered village leader, Andrija. The young bride, Višnja, and the groom, Ante, desire only to pass their wedding day in peace, with the usual gaiety, religious ceremony, and celebration which mark such occasions in this hard and flinty land. The party stops at a wayside house on the outskirts of the village for food and drink. The two executioners, dressed in scruffy civilian garb, are seated at one of the two long, crude plank tables outside the house. The wedding party joins them, and an air of uneasiness and suspicion settles over the group.

The two executioners join the wedding party as it makes its way into the village. Villagers greet the bride and groom with festive joy and pay particular homage and tribute to the renowned local leader, Andrija. There is feasting, dancing, and singing. The village men form a circle and dance a local variation of the Kolo, which is done without musical accompaniment—the rhythm of the dance is measured out by the sound of feet pounding against the hard, rocky ground.

The film introduces several vignettes which define the customs of the wedding and the relationship between the bride and groom. Višnja and Ante express a gentle tenderness and respect for one another and reveal a natural grace and refinement, which are contrasted to the flinty and tough coarseness of the other villagers and the hardness of the land. One scene shows Višnja preparing herself for the wedding, assisted by three young peasant women. The three young women mimic the lovemaking which will take place that night. One girl mounts another, loosens the other girl's peasant blouse, and exposes her breast. There is much giggling and lifting of each other's skirts. Višnja adopts a good-natured but poised separateness from these innocent crudities.

Participating in the gaming and festivities of the village, Andrija falls and strikes his head against a rock. With much concern he is taken to Višnja's bridal room to be nursed and bandaged. Some of the villagers remain outside to assure themselves that he is all right.

Višnja, like the other villagers, is somewhat in awe of Andrija, who has made his mark in the outer world and is regarded as the leading citizen and leader of the small village. She nurses Andrija's wound with care and gentleness. Her blouse is loose, and Andrija eyes her with the same interest he had briefly shown in earlier scenes in the film. He goes to the door and closes it. The sound of feet pounding the earth in musicless dance is heard on the soundtrack as the village men resume their celebrations.

Alone with Višnja, Andrija attempts to caress her but is deflected. He then becomes more aggressive and, after an intense struggle, rapes her. Višnja, knowing that she is now "spoiled" in the eyes of the villagers, pleads with Andrija not to tell what has happened. He responds to her sobbing pleas by raping her a second time.

In the meantime, the man on the bicycle has arrived in the village with another message for the two executioners. When Andrija finally emerges from the bridal room, he is greeted with cheers and shows of relief from the villagers. In the midst of the villagers' expressions of relief and joy, the two executioners move deftly to Andrija's side, handcuff him, and place him under arrest. It was Andrija's name on the summons brought by the cyclist. He is accused of being a Stalinist sympathizer. The villagers are thrown into confusion and crowd menacingly around Andrija and the two executioners. One villager gives Andrija a flagon of wine, from which he takes a long and manly draft. As the tension and uncertainty mount, a somber Ante, who has just discovered the ruination of his bride, places a hat on Andrija's head and reveals his brutal act to the villagers. The villagers retreat and let the executioners pass with their prisoner.

Ante returns to Višnja. She is still seated on the floor, weeping softly. Ante's tender impulse to comfort and console her struggles against his pride and the hard custom of the village, which views her as now being soiled and ruined. They sit apart in silence, with no apparent way to resolve their complex feelings of shame and desolation.

The men of the village resume their dance with increasing fury and wildness. Reaching a pitch of intoxication and primitive passion, they break into the bridal room, beat Ante unconscious, and rudely seize Višnja and take her away. They force her along the stony path to the hills, chant their nasal, joyless song, and begin to tear off her clothes. Višnja breaks away and runs. They pursue her and tear away more clothing. She seems about to make good her escape, when one of the villagers shoots her with a rifle, and she falls among the rocks.

In the meantime, Ante has regained consciousness and is in pursuit of the villagers who have abducted Višnja. His panic and desperation increase as he finds torn and discarded articles of her clothing. Before Ante finds the place where she has been shot, he observes at a distance Andrija being escorted on the stony path by the two executioners and the man on the bicycle. As before, the cyclist separates from the other two men and continues down the path. The two executioners lead Andrija behind a cluster of rocks to complete their work. The film then cuts to the body of Višnja, lying half-naked and broken among the rocks. The last shot of the film is of the cyclist riding away in the distance, presumably to fetch another fateful summons.

The brutalization of Višnja. *Handcuffs (Lisice).*

Papić's film vividly captures the tension and stress of the period immediately following Tito's dramatic break with Stalin and the pall which it cast even in a remote and backward village. In the context of the film, the deforming spirit of Stalinism is personified in Andrija, whose authoritarian personality is masked by charisma and shrewd deception. His wanton act of domination and brutalization of Višnja on her wedding day violently and fatally breaks with the traditional customs of the village, in which weddings are a spiritual and joyous break from the harshness of life lived on the edge of bare subsistence. The worst spirit of provincial atavism and primitivism is unleashed by the discovery.

It is not Andrija alone who casts a pall on the village wedding and whose actions eventually shroud it in tragedy and death. The two executioners who act as avenging angels for the threatened established order are portrayed as little more than bounty hunters, whose legitimacy is thinly maintained by mysterious summonses delivered by bicycle from a distant provincial town. After Andrija is arrested, the more unsavory of the two executioners removes a pen from Andrija's pocket and nonchalantly places it in his own inside jacket pocket. Alongside Andrija's pen is a row of others, collected from previous victims of this special kind of justice—not all of whom presumably were guilty of raping virginal brides on their wedding day. The film suggests that the spirit of Stalinism was not entirely absent from those who were doing the purging.[8]

Socialist Reconstruction Revisited

In perhaps his most effective film, *Scenes from the Life of Shock Workers* (*Slike iz života udarnika*, 1972), the Bosnian documentarist and feature film director Bata Čengić, collaborating with the film scenarist Branko Vučićević, recreates the naive enthusiasm and political grotesqueries of Yugoslavia's immediate postwar period of industrialization. The film centers on Adem, a Bosnian coal miner who leads a five-man brigade of shock workers, who compensate for primitive tools and conditions in the mines with extraordinary human effort and labor. Adem and his brigade become the best shock workers in Yugoslavia and even surpass the record of the legendary Russian shock worker Stakhanov. They become celebrities. Their efforts are followed on film and newsreel. The entire Stalinist era is satirized for its naive sloganeering and simplistic ideological atmosphere. After twenty-five years, Adem is retired to the position of guard at a modern factory, alienated from the stream of workers who enter its gates, his past glories forgotten, trapped on the periphery of a social order he labored so enthusiastically and naively to help create. The sharp social irony and satire of the film are advanced by a series of vignettes or "scenes" from Adem's life.

Beneath the lush Bosnian landscape, Adem and his fellow miners toil with primitive tools in an antiquated coal mine, which is dimly lit, rat-infested, and poorly ventilated. One evening, as the miners are assembled to watch a badly performed scene from the opera *Faust*—part of the "bring culture to the workers" movement of the era—the foreman and party chief of the mine mercifully interrupts the performance and announces that coal production must be dramatically increased. The news from Belgrade suggests that without more coal, all trains will stop. This increase in production will require great exertion and extra human effort. A new drill has also been sent from Belgrade to increase production. The party chief is cheered. Adem, who has already demonstrated enormous vitality and enthusiasm for work, is selected to form a brigade of shock workers composed of the five best workers in the mine. They are reminded of the legendary Russian shock worker Stakhanov, whose brigade mined 102 tons of coal in a single shift.

Adem and his brigade tackle their new assignment with exemplary enthusiasm. They dig furiously, shirtless and covered with sweat and coal dust. When the horse cannot pull the car heaped with coal, the shock workers lend their own backs and muscles to the task. They dig ceaselessly, not even pausing to check and put up new supports. Before the shift has ended, the foreman announces that 102 tons of coal have already been mined. A new championship team of shock workers is born.

Adem and his brigade become national celebrities, win a trip to Lake Bled in Slovenia, and later travel to Moscow. Giant photographs are made of Adem, and a bust of him is distributed throughout the land. Publicity accelerates as Adem and his team win competitions throughout the country. Film crews are sent to Bosnia to record staged pieces of propaganda. One sequence in the film shows a brass band walking over the countryside to greet Adem and his brigade. There is a big celebration. A giant wheel graph shows dramatic increases in production. There are huge photos of Stalin, Lenin, and Tito. Adem's team is shown walking, proud and smiling, into the mine. The whir of cameras continues under the title "Victories at Work."

There is a propaganda sequence of Adem and his brigade receiving a red banner as a reward for their victory in competition. In the midst of the large banquet assembled for the occasion, the brigade rises and volunteers to do an extra shift for "Tito and the Country." Another staged piece shows young boys in front of a giant photograph of Adem, vowing to eat well and grow strong so that they, too, can one day be shock workers. Publicity films at competitions show Adem's brigade taking heart tests and height measures while women raise large cardboard hearts to show how big are the hearts of the shock workers.

Interwoven with these satirical vignettes are scenes from Adem's personal and domestic life. These scenes, too, are shot in a posed and stylized manner—much like moving shots from a family photo album. Such stylized treatment suggests the posed existence which Adem's new celebrity status has thrust upon him.

Near the beginning of the film, Adem is shown seated in a chair in the front yard of his small white house, which is situated on a grassy knoll. A new bride, a Moslem, is brought to him by her escorts, accompanied by the sounds of a brass band. She is introduced to Adem's five children, who are lined up neatly to greet their new mother.

Another, more intimate, scene shows the seemingly inexhaustible Adem lying very tired in bed. His five children come into the bedroom, line up, and recite some political doggerel which they have learned at school—little optimistic manifestos about the better future to come—and conclude by reciting that "man is the master of the world." In a moment of shared tenderness, Adem's demure and docile wife suggests that he is working too hard. He is working double shifts, and the children need him. Adem acknowledges the wisdom of her words and also expresses wistful regret that he has never learned to read or write.

Adem attempts a little social reform among his friends at a party when he asks the women to unveil. He begins by unveiling his own wife. Because Adem is now a man of some importance, the other men follow his lead. While Adem

Adem's triumphant return. *Scenes from the Life of Shock Workers* (*Slike iz života udarnika*).

Onward and upward! *Scenes from the Life of Shock Workers* (*Slike iz života udarnika*).

is away at a competition in Slovenia, however, the father of his wife comes to take her back home for disgracing the family by removing her veil. She resists but is forcibly taken away by the father, leaving the children deserted and forlorn.

The redoubtable Adem, however, finds a new wife, a female shock worker, Stefka, whom he brings back to his children. In a charming scene, Stefka and Adem arrive at the small house on the knoll, riding a great white horse presented as one of many gifts for Adem's heroic deeds. The horse slowly circles the five children, and with each circle Stefka lifts another child to the back of the horse—until all five are now joined with their new mother and reunited as a family.

Adem's new wife, more forcefully than the last, chides him for neglecting her, his health, and his family for endless work and competitions. Adem's time has been further consumed by working more closely with the Communist party—a development which offends some of his coworkers. In one scene he joins Communist party members at the mine on a raid to arrest and discipline suspected reactionaries. One of these is a man who had earlier warned Stefka that Adem was coming too close to the Communists and that there might be trouble. This man is confronted by the Communists, and his Moslem pride is deeply offended when his wife is stripped naked in his presence.

Returning from a disillusioning trip to Moscow, where he is treated as nothing more than a propaganda prop, Adem is greeted by a red sign painted on the front door of his home which reads "Death to Adem." Inside the home he finds the body of his murdered wife.

With his children now numbering six, the last an infant born of Stefka, and his remarkable vitality beginning to wane, Adem's life is further complicated by serious injuries sustained in a mining accident. While recovering in the hospital, Adem's children are brought to him and recite further lessons learned in school, which joyously speak of building a better future by "swinging the hammer and sickle." Adem is touched and inspired to return to the mine before his injuries are fully healed. His health collapses under the strain.

In the last sequence of the film, Adem is shown twenty-five years later as a gate attendant at a modern factory—unnoticed, unremarked, and unremembered by the streams of workers that file past. Čengić's film succeeds admirably in combining a poignant and sympathetic portrait of the film's naive protagonist with witty, satirical, and sometimes somber evocations of an era filled with political and propaganda excesses and grotesqueries.

As will be seen in the next chapter, the complex and ambivalent revolutionary legacy of Yugoslavia's war years and their Stalinist aftermath is sometimes critically evoked in films with contemporary settings and themes. It is a legacy which continued to haunt, inform, and partially shape Yugoslav contemporary realities as *new film* creators dealt with them in the sixties and early seventies.

5

Contemporary Reality: Critical Visions

After a quarter of a century of power in the postwar state, Tito and the League of Communists could look with understandable pride and satisfaction at their achievements. By the late sixties and early seventies, Yugoslavia had accomplished a remarkable transition, from a predominantly rural and small-town culture based on an agrarian economy to an increasingly modern, urbanized, and industrial state. Despite backward areas, poverty, unemployment, and inequalities, the general lot of the nations and nationalities constituting Yugoslavia had steadily improved. New towns and suburbs sprang up around the major cities to accommodate the steady influx of people from the countryside, consumer goods proliferated, the university system was greatly expanded, new roads were built, and political and economic freedoms were greater than in any other Communist state.

Along with the progress were the problems and contradictions carried in the wake of rapid material development. Modern Yugoslavia was now blessed with blocks of concrete high-rises, traffic jams, an unfavorable balance of payments, rising inflation, housing shortages, and the inability to absorb increasing numbers of university- and professionally educated young people into the economy. Rural and small-town values were assaulted, and agriculture was stymied or neglected in its development. A proper balance or equilibrium had not always been struck between the needs of town and country, agriculture and industrialization, the underdeveloped South and the more prosperous North, local or individual initiative and central control and, in the international sphere, between East and West.

Such tensions and contradictions offered fertile material for filmic expression. The modernist spirit of *new film* creators claimed for itself the right to reflect critically on *savremene teme* (contemporary themes) and to express sometimes somber images of society's disruptions, dislocations, and social ironies. They viewed the social order from angles of vision refracted through the prisms of their own personal feelings and experience; commented upon the breakdown of human love and communication, urban ennui and alienation, and ethnic isolation and provincial backwardness; and celebrated the uniqueness of the individual and individual creativity over conformity and social repression.

111

Intimate Film

The first two feature films singled out as heralding the birth of *new film* tendencies in Yugoslav feature film production and making a sharp break with the past were *Two* (*Dvoje*, 1961), directed by Aleksandar Petrović, and A *Dance in the Rain* (*Ples v dežju*, 1961), directed by Boštjan Hladnik. Both are personal, intimate films which explore failed love relationships, acted out in an alienated urban environment.

Petrović's film is set in Belgrade and traces a love affair between Jovana, a student at the Academy of Music, and Mirko, a young architect. Breaking from traditional narrative structure, the film creates a fluid sequence of images of Belgrade cityscapes, which act as objective correlatives to the inner dynamics of love's progress. The lovers meet by chance at an outdoor cinema, where Mirko offers Jovana an extra ticket. While the film is in progress it begins to rain, and Mirko offers to walk Jovana home under his umbrella. She goes with him to a corner near her street and then suddenly breaks away, runs, and disappears down the street without telling him her address. Mirko becomes obsessed with meeting her again. He finally does so at a dance; he learns that she is betrothed to another, but he persists in arranging to meet her the next day. She agrees but does not show up at the appointed hour. Mirko follows Jovana and her boyfriend one evening to Kalemegdan Park, where several young lovers are kissing on the benches, and observes her embrace and kiss him. He follows her to her apartment to talk to her. She goes to a small café with Mirko, where she explains that she had not missed their appointment but was late, and he had already departed. He wants to see her again. She expresses uncertainty and leaves. Later Mirko is informed that Jovana called the café to say that she could not meet him. Mirko sends a note to Jovana, which she receives while attending a lecture at the music academy. Finally, Jovana agrees to meet Mirko in front of the academy, and he takes her for a ride on his motorbike to a building which he has helped to design. They go to a concert and hold hands tenderly. After the concert they stroll in Kalemegdan Park and kiss each other passionately. In his apartment, Mirko gently moves Jovana away from the window and slowly unbuttons her blouse. The strains of music from the concert are still playing on the soundtrack as he carries her to bed. They make love tenderly, while their clothes casually adorn the mantel.

The springtime of love between Mirko and Jovana is captured in a series of scenes of the two of them happily together in Belgrade's city parks, main squares, and cafés; still shots of the two of them together are captured in a series of photographs by Mirko's friend Mario, a young photographer.

Passion begins to wane for Mirko as the briskness of fall weather brushes against the light summer airs of his romance with Jovana. The trees in Kalemegdan Park

Chance encounter. *Two (Dvoje)*.

Springtime of love. *Two (Dvoje)*.

are now leafless, and the fountain no longer sends up its spray of water; Mirko's apartment is cold and lifeless. Jovana awakes one morning in the apartment to find Mirko already gone and the fish in his aquarium dead.

In the evening they walk on a bridge across the Danube, with Mirko silent and uncommunicative. He absorbs himself in his work and one evening sees an automobile accident in which two young people have been killed. Mirko experiences a series of flashbacks, in which he tries to revive the images of his own "dead" relationship. The images are shown in negative, symbolizing the flip side of the relationship—its cold and empty negation.

Mirko tries to revive the former light gaiety of the romance by taking Jovana to a fair. There are moments of the old laughter, artificially induced by swirling side by side in merry-go-round swings, where all is blurred around them, and when they playfully take their knocks in the bumper cars. Afterwards there is only Mirko's distant, distracted, and perfunctory conversation.

In the last sequence of the film, the reversal in the relationship is complete. It is now Jovana who must suffer broken appointments and late arrivals, and it is Mirko who cannot decide whether to continue the relationship or break it off. The ending of the relationship occurs in the same settings as it began. Mirko and Jovana slowly walk through Kalemegdan at night. The benches are empty, the trees leafless; the fountain is turned off. Mirko watches a lone couple kissing on a bench. He rehearses in his mind how to break it off. They go to the same small café. Mirko finally tells Jovana what she expects but dreads to hear, "It is finished." He walks away. The face of Jovana is reflected on the surface of the table—sad and disconsolate. The waiter wipes the table with a cloth, and Jovana's image on the table top is blurred and disappears as the film fades to black and ends.

Hladnik's film *Dance in the Rain* deals with a love relationship which has already reached its autumnal phase. Set in Ljubljana, it concerns a painter and teacher, Peter, who has grown weary with his life and his affair with a middle-aged actress, Maruša, who clings to him affectionately and from force of habit. Peter lives in a cramped, grey, and cluttered room and is haunted by dreams of an idealized woman and of his lost youth and sexual vitality. The film is structured so that dream and reality merge seamlessly. The film opens with a night scene, with low-angle shots of water being sprayed on the streets by street cleaners. Maruša makes her way through the wet streets. She comes to Peter in his room, turns off the light, takes off her clothes, and sits at the foot of the bed with her nude torso turned to Peter. They make love.

Peter is haunted by a recurring dream. He walks through the dark street at night toward a lighted window with the silhouette of a nude woman outlined on the drawn night shade. As the film progresses, further details are added to the dream. In the most complete version, the street is lined with men in black carrying white coffins. Peter runs toward the window with the silhouette of the nude

Maruša and Peter—love's autumnal phase. *Dance in the Rain* (*Ples v dežju*).

woman, climbs up to the window, and passes through it, only to find himself once again on the street lined with coffins. He runs faster and climbs toward the vision a second time.

Maruša is also in a state of crisis and is increasingly given over to fantasies of lost youth and her former promise as an actress. She progressively retreats into her fantasy world, loses her position at the theater, and continues to cling to the worn and comfortless relationship with Peter.

The perfunctory barrenness of the relationship is accentuated by scenes in the small café where Peter and Maruša frequently meet. It is a dark café; the customers wear tired expressions, and sad songs fill the air. Camera angles emphasize the separateness and alienation of Peter and Maruša even when they are together.

One scene shows Maruša and Peter going to bed but not making love. Dogs are barking outside. The sound of the dogs barking is heightened and intensified on the soundtrack, emphasizing the forlorn quality of the room, the shabby building in which it is located, and the joyless relationship between Peter and Maruša.

A young admirer of Maruša's invites her to a restaurant. He is sexually at-

Peter's nightmare. *Dance in the Rain (Ples v dežju)*.

Maruša's fantasy in the dress shop. *Dance in the Rain (Ples v dežju)*.

tracted to her and finds her fascinating. Peter arrives at the restaurant and claims Maruša by sitting beside her and taking her arm. The young man leaves. When Maruša and Peter leave the café, a young couple takes their place. The camera remains on the young couple as they assume attitudes of intense interest in each other. Their loving attitude contrasts sharply to the tired, clinging relationship between Peter and Maruša and also symbolizes what their relationship might have been in its springtime beginnings. This motif runs throughout the film.

The progressive disintegration of Maruša is unnoticed by Peter, who is absorbed in his own feelings of failure and ennui. Maruša is shown sitting alone in her nicely appointed and well-furnished apartment. She is shown waking up in Peter's room, in his bed, alone. She has a nightmare, in which she is in a crowded train station being rudely jostled. A man places his hand over her breast and leaves a large black handprint on her dress. She fantasizes being elegantly gowned, swirling out of a dress shop and delighting passersby on the street and in the park. She fantasizes walking on a country road, being given a ride on a cart, and enjoying the slow ride through the beautiful rolling hills.

It is Peter's neighbor and confidant who is first alarmed at Maruša's slide into fantasy and depression, and, sensing impending peril, he and Peter go together to her apartment. She has committed suicide and is sitting dead in a large armchair.

There is a scene of the body being removed from the apartment and carried down the stairs. The rain is pouring down. Peter sits numbly in the chair where Maruša died. He walks outside in the dark street in the pelting rain. As he walks, a young couple enters at the bottom of the film frame and begins to dance. While the young couple continues to dance in the rain, Peter disappears in the darkness.

On Wings of Paper (*Na papirnatih avionih*, 1967), directed by Matjaž Klopčič, is a thematically and visually more complex and sophisticated film dealing with love's fragile and illusory quality. Set in Ljubljana, the film centers on the photographer Marko, who becomes enamored of the image of a beautiful young woman momentarily captured on a film of street scenes which he has helped to shoot for a television program. Marko, who is approaching middle age, and his friends and professional colleagues Ratko and Mirko live a chic but empty life attending endless parties and submerging themselves in the ambience of filmed television and photographic images rather than a world of substance and reality. Marko is beginning to sicken of the sweet life and is captivated by the innocent charm and unspoiled beauty of the young woman in the photograph. He meets her by chance at the modern art gallery. The young woman, Vera, is a promising ballet dancer, who lives with her attractive and cultured mother in a tastefully furnished apartment overlooking the lovely center of Ljubljana. Marko gradually overcomes Vera's youthful reserve and innocent shyness and begins to awaken in her the promise or illusion of a romantic and unique relationship.

Vera's idyllic interlude in the Alps. *On Wings of Paper (Na papirnatih avionih)*.

Their love is consummated in an idyllic setting in the Alps near Ljubljana. As
the film progresses, Marko peers into the emptiness of his life and the illusory
quality of his photographs, which he pronounces mere "wings of paper." He also
comes to realize that the emptiness of his life cannot be bridged by an improbable affair, which, if it ended in marriage, would lead to submergence in medi-
ocrity and an endless round of mistresses such as those enjoyed by his friends
Mirko and Ratko, who, like him, have not really achieved anything in life or art.
Vera is ultimately cushioned against hurt and disillusionment in her idyllic and
brief romance by the protective and worldly advice of her ballet teacher and by
the sophisticated understanding and warmth of her mother.

The film ends as it began, on a note of transience, illusion, ambiguity, and
impermanence. Marko and Vera's love affair was an ephemeral as the snow melt-
ing from pine trees and the frost receding from the cabin window where they
made love. Marko's photographs captured frozen moments, poses, and gestures
but could not replace, extend, or deepen human experience.

Another sophisticated variation on the theme of love's labor lost is provided in
the film *Rondo* (1966), directed by Zvonimir Berković. Set in Zagreb and cinematically patterned after a musical rondo, the film adopts as its principal theme a
series of Sunday afternoon chess games shared between a middle-aged, world-
weary, sophisticated judge, Mladen, who lives an impeccably ordered but lonely

Mladen (left), Neda, and Fedja at Sunday dinner. *Rondo*.

bachelor existence, and the younger, warmer, and more optimistic Fedja, who is a successful painter and sculptor. Fedja's lovely young wife, Neda, who studied music but subordinated her ambitions to those of her husband, amuses herself and the two men while they play chess, and after the game the threesome enjoys dinner and engages in intellectually brittle and stimulating conversation.

The two most important subordinate themes in the film are the growing friendship between Mladen and Fedja (who originally met by chance in a café, discovered their mutual interest in chess, and initiated the series of Sunday afternoon games) and the growing sexual attraction and eventual consummation of an adulterous relationship between Mladen and Neda. The moves in the game of adultery are as subtle as the moves on the chessboard. In a conversation, Neda expresses her love for Mozart's music. The next Sunday, Mladen surprises her with a gift of a recording of Mozart's "Rondo." Neda is touched by the gift and plays the recording while the two men are absorbed in their chess game. Quicker film sequences follow of Sunday get-togethers, in which Neda and Mladen increasingly exchange glances and Neda draws physically closer to Mladen while the three of them are looking at photo albums. The displays of fondness between Neda and her husband continue, but there is a curiously distracted and passionless undertow to their relationship.

Winter arrives, and there is a scene of Mladen assisting Neda as she lights

Mladen and Neda draw closer together. *Rondo.*

Yielding to temptation. *Rondo.*

candles on the Christmas tree. Neda trips on the ladder, and Mladen breaks her fall. The physical touching arouses them both, but its implications are resisted and passed off lightly. After a Sunday game and dinner, Neda escorts Mladen to the gate outside the apartment building. They begin with a social kiss goodbye, which becomes more passionate. Both are shaken by the experience, and at the next session of chess they attempt to avoid each other's glances and touches. Mladen concentrates fully on the game and plays brilliantly. Neda moves closer to her husband, becomes involved in the game, and advises Fedja on his moves. Mladen swiftly and deftly defeats Fedja, despite Neda's assistance. Neda breaks into tears and runs to the bedroom. Fedja goes to comfort her, and she tearfully expresses the fidelity of her love for him. Fedja is now confirmed in his suspicion of the building attraction between Mladen and his wife but has no moves to counter its forward progress.

The attraction between Mladen and Neda finds its consummation at an anniversary celebration, at which friends of Fedja join the threesome in drinking and jazz improvisations. Fedja becomes tipsy and leaves with his friends, clearing the board for Mladen and Neda. They kiss tentatively and then more passionately. They go to bed but find the consummation so devoutly desired rather empty and unsatisfactory. In the end, Mladen is checkmated by Fedja's trust and friendship

and by his own inability to release long-suppressed needs which disturb the ordered life which he has chosen. He is better at chess than adultery. Neda is
checkmated by her inability to compensate for frustrated ambitions and a subordinated wifely role with an illusory affair which proves more fascinating in its
contemplation than in its actuality.

In the final sequence of the film, Mladen is sitting alone on a bench, watching
two pensioners playing chess. It is a Sunday afternoon, and Fedja appears and
joins Mladen. Fedja matter-of-factly calls Mladen a "swine" but an excellent
chess player and invites him to resume their Sunday afternoon games. The last
scene shows Mladen and Fedja settling down to a game of chess in the apartment.
The subordinate theme of adultery has been resolved and is finished. Mozart's
"Rondo" no longer plays on the soundtrack. Neda sits discreetly apart, reading a
book. The chess game holds the three together despite an estranged friendship
and a brief and unsatisfactory adulterous affair. Neda rises from her chair, goes to
the window, and closes the drapes, signaling the end of the rondo and the film.

Very different in visual form and creative vision, the films *Two, Dance in the
Rain, On Wings of Paper,* and *Rondo* all provide ambivalent and antioptimistic
manifestos on the fragility and impermanence of human relationships in a tran-
sient and rapidly changing urban culture. Temporary relationships are formed on
the basis of chance encounters in cafés, film theaters, and the streets. New high-
rises of concrete, steel, and glass jostle with older, more conventional structures;
classical and folk culture jar against new movements, fads, and fashions in art
and lifestyles; frustrated ambitions, self-doubt, rootlessness, and spiritual ennui
and lassitude enter the soul and sap vitality and enthusiasm. A cinema of appear-
ances is created, in which the hazards of chance intervene and the wires of con-
vention and causality are severed and left dangling.

Dušan Makevejev, in his first two feature films, *Man Is Not a Bird* (*Čovek nije
tica,* 1965) and his international success *Love Affair, or the Tragedy of a Switchboard Operator* (*Ljubavni slučaj ili tragedija službenica PTT,* 1967)[1] leaves the
world of students, intellectuals, artists, and professionals to comment ironically
upon love among the proletariat. The film *Man Is Not a Bird* is set in an industrial town in eastern Serbia, where a large copper factory is undergoing modernization. A highly skilled engineer from Slovenia, Jan Rudinski, is brought in to
direct the installation of new machinery and speed up production. He is middle-
aged, serious, stolid, and devoted to his work. He finds a modest sleeping room
with a family, whose daughter, Rajka, is a vivacious and pretty young hairdresser.
Rudinski and Rajka are attracted to each other, and a love affair develops. It is
Rajka who takes the initiative in overcoming Rudinski's conventional reserve and
doubts when they first make love in his room. Rudinski, however, becomes more
deeply involved in his work and sees Rajka less and less. One evening while they
are walking across the bleak expanse of the factory yard, with its piles of grey slag,

Rajka chides him for working too hard and for being married to his work. As Rajka and Rudinski become increasingly separated, she is pursued by a virile and ruggedly handsome young truck driver, Žarko. A strong physical attraction develops between them.

When Rudinski has completed his work, a symphony orchestra is brought from Belgrade to celebrate the event. Before the concert, Rudinski receives a medal and a commendation for his exceptional achievement. The orchestra plays Beethoven for the edification of the assembled workers. In the meantime, Žarko and Rajka are joyously consummating their mutual desires in his truck to the swelling chords of the last movement of the Ninth.

The next morning, Rudinski wants to know where Rajka was during the concert. She openly tells him that she was with a young man. He wants to know how young. Quite young, she tells him. He fiercely grabs her wrist, having finally determined to ask Rajka to return with him to Slovenia and marry him. Rajka is frightened, breaks away, and runs. The last scene of the film shows Rudinski in a long shot, walking slowly across the grey expanse of the factory yard. He has been rewarded for his work but has lost the opportunity to open his life to spontaneity, tenderness, and joy.

Makavejev frames this simple story of romance with satirical social commentary. Throughout the film the natural, exuberant, and machismo lifestyle of the workers is satirically contrasted to planned and rationalized socialist self-management objectives. Near the beginning of the film, the factory manager is on the phone to Belgrade, arranging for the appearance of the symphony orchestra and commenting on how much the workers are moved by classical culture. The film then cuts to a workers' café, where the men are so inspired by the provocative torch singing of a buxom female entertainer that they dash their glasses against the floor and walls and become so raucous that the local police intervene. The workers are also caught up in the mesmerizing entertainment of a hypnotist, snake swallowers, and other circus performers, who symbolize life as an abundance of sensations and attractions.

In a factory tour, the manager tells the visitors that modern machines have freed man from alienating and brutish labor. His speech is carried over the soundtrack while the film depicts grimy and sweating workers breaking coal and feeding the copper-smelting furnaces. A self-management committee discusses the problem of missing copper wire. The film cuts to Gypsy workers wrapping heavy copper wire around their bare waists and torsos, putting their shirts back on, and smuggling the wire out of the factory. While Rudinski is hard at work directing the installation of machines, a worker is suddenly inspired to swing over the machines on a rope, declaring that he is a bird. Rudinski stolidly proclaims that "man is not a bird"—a statement which proves sadly prophetic in his own case.

Makavejev plays satirically on national stereotypes. A worker, Barbulović, a secondary character in the film, is the quintessential macho Serbian provincial. He plays as hard as he works, and sometimes harder. He drinks in great quantities, sings, fights, and tries to keep his rebellious wife in her place and his mistress happy. In one scene Barbulović curses his crying and whining wife because she has the audacity to complain that he has given to his mistress the new red dress he bought for her. Later, in the town market, the wife meets the mistress, who is wearing the red dress; she attacks her and tries to remove it. The wife and mistress are hauled into the local police station, with an unrepentant Barbulović protesting that he bought the dress for his wife and that he has the right to take it away. In another scene, Barbulović's wife complains to a friend that her husband is like the hypnotist. He tells her what to do, and she has no choice but to listen and obey. In the end, however, the wife becomes involved with her own lover, and it is Barbulović who is left wondering where she has gone and with whom.

Makavejev's ironic documentaristic vision is given more complex expression in his internationally successful film *Love Affair, or the Tragedy of a Switchboard Operator*. The film portrays a warm and humorous love affair which ends in bizarre tragedy.

Isabella, a vivacious, sensual, and free-spirited switchboard operator, who has enjoyed several affairs, meets a kind and serious young sanitary inspector, Ahmed. They end up in Isabella's apartment, where she takes the initiative in prompting their first tender and joyous sexual union. They live together and enjoy an uncomplicated period of idyllic sensuality and domesticity, in which trivialities and offbeat moments are infused with humor and warmth—she preparing delicious food, he bringing home a record player and a new shower.

Ahmed is called out of the city by his work, and during his long absence Isabella has an affair with a young postal worker—an infidelity predicted by her fortune-teller friend, Ruža—and becomes pregnant. When Ahmed returns, the relationship begins to sour, and Ahmed eventually learns of Isabella's infidelity. Deeply wounded, Ahmed gets drunk and determines to commit suicide by throwing himself into an antique Roman well. Isabella follows him, and in her struggle to prevent Ahmed from taking his life, she accidentally falls into the well and is drowned. Ahmed is arrested and charged with the murder.

Contrasted to this sensual and tragic love affair are filmic interjections which portray a modern, rationalized, cool, and indifferent world. Makavejev wittily juxtaposes tender and erotic scenes between Isabella and Ahmed with pedantic lectures by an elderly and distinguished sexologist, Professor Kostić (a name derived from the Serbo-Croatian word *kost*, meaning "bone"), concerning phallic adoration in early cultures, analysis of the nature of coitus and its representation in paintings, and a learned disquisition on the hen's egg as the perfect unit for the study of human reproduction. Scenes of the postmortem examination of

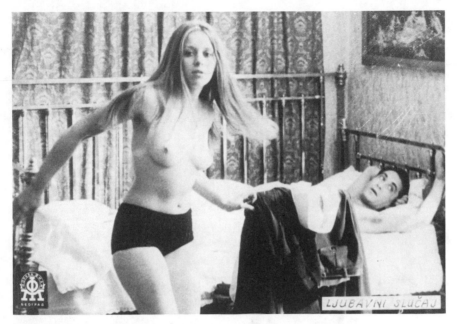

Isabella and Ahmed. *Love Affair (Ljubavni slučaj).*

Isabella's body are accompanied by lectures on detection and identification of corpses. The tragic and bizarre circumstances of Isabella's death are missed alto-gether by rationalized methods of police detection and a learned and beside-the-point criminologist's lecture on the psychology of murder.

Makavejev's film also suggests the polarities and tensions of Yugoslav reality in a period of rapid social change. Isabella is a member of the Hungarian minority in Yugoslavia, attempting to adopt a modern, liberated lifestyle free of Balkan male domination. She has financial independence and her own apartment in the city, and she freely chooses her lovers. Ahmed is a member of the Moslem Slav minority, representing the most traditional and conservative expression of a male-ordered and -dominated social structure. His quiet formality and kindness mask deeper layers of fiery pride and passionate ferocity.

Provincial Ethnicity and Backwardness

Aleksandar Petrović's film *I Even Met Happy Gypsies (Skupljači perja,* 1967), an enormous popular and critical success both domestically and abroad, is set in

Bora (seated left) and Mirka (seated right) are entertained by Lenka and a Gypsy band. *I Even Met Happy Gypsies* (*Skupljači perja*).

the ethnically diverse area of Vojvodina and provides an unromanticized and vibrant portrait of Gypsy life in a region where Gypsies lead a sedentary and economically depressed existence. Ethnographic authenticity is enhanced by filling many of the secondary roles and one of the major roles (that of Tisa) from among local peasants and Gypsies and by using a multilingual soundtrack with Serbo-Croatian, Romany, and Slovak.

The film centers on the business and sexual rivalries of Bora and Mirta, who eke out a marginal existence by buying and selling goosefeathers.[2] Ruggedly handsome and virile, Bora lives in a small, crowded apartment, with an aging, wrinkled, and nearly toothless common-law wife and a gaggle of quarreling children. He travels from village to village, bargaining for goosefeathers and reselling them. His life is punctuated by gambling, drinking, and making love to a sultry Gypsy singer, Lenka, and other women along the way. His macho lifestyle is captured in a series of skillfully composed vignettes. Bora is shown gambling with other Gypsies in an abandoned, decrepit bus. He loses all of this money. He stakes his watch and loses that and finally gambles and loses the shirt off his back. A shirtless Bora goes to his apartment and removes the television set to pawn for cash. His wife follows him out the door, cursing and hitting him, while the children disagreeably express their own displeasure.

In a cheap café, Gypsy men dash their empty glasses on the floor and walls in appreciation of the sultry, deep-throated singing of Lenka, who gives an evocative and soulful rendering of the song "I Even Met Happy Gypsies." A tipsy Bora breaks his drinking glass on the rough plank table, lifts his hands upward, and brings them down hard on the broken shards. With his hands bleeding, he joins Lenka in an undulating dance with his arms outstretched—while she moves seductively toward him and continues to sing. Later they make love.

Bora is relentless and resourceful in bargaining for goosefeathers. He negotiates with the sons of a recently deceased Slovak farmer while they are solemnly marching in the funeral procession. He closes a deal with a priest in an impoverished monastery for goosefeathers extracted from the mattresses of deceased or departed brothers. After driving a hard bargain with a customer, he makes love to the man's wife while the customer is in a drunken stupor.

Bora's chief rival, Mirta, is a muscular, coarsely handsome, and imposing man, who lives in a Gypsy village with small, brightly painted huts nestled together on a muddy plain. Mirta is guardian to the attractive and appealing Tisa, who is the daughter of Mirta's former wife by another marriage. The rivalry between Bora and Mirta centers upon their competition in the goosefeather-gathering trade and over sexual possession of Tisa. Bora is strongly and passionately attracted to Tisa and asks Mirta's permission to marry her in the church, as the priest at the monastery had suggested. Mirta violently rejects the suggestion and tells Bora never to go near Tisa. In order to keep Tisa for himself, Mirta marries her to a twelve-year-old Gypsy boy in the village. After a colorful ceremony, Tisa forcibly ejects the not-ready groom from her bed and spiritedly annuls the marriage. The next morning, Mirta reveals his real intentions toward Tisa by attempting to take her by force. She resists with a knife and makes her escape. Bora finds Tisa, who returns his passionate interest, and they go to the priest and are married.

The next scene shows Bora bringing the young bride back to his common-law wife and the children. He sweetens the pot by also bringing back the television set. While Bora is away on business, however, his common-law wife persuades Tisa that her future would be brighter in Belgrade. The Gypsy singer Lenka had previously given Tisa the same advice, as well as the address of a younger brother who could help her start a career as a singer.

Tisa makes her odyssey to Belgrade but finds it far different from the city which television images had painted it to be. She finds Lenka's brother in Belgrade's Gypsy shantytown, and her "career" consists of singing on the streets and in courtyards for small change. She decides to return home and hitches a ride on a truck. There is an amusing companion in the truck (another hitchhiker), who charms her with puppets and gentleness. She crawls into the back of the cab, and they make love. When the hitchhiker disembarks, the truck driver expresses interest in sharing Tisa's charms. She resists his advances with her knife, and the

Unromanticized views of Gypsy life. *I Even Met Happy Gypsies* (*Skupljači perja*).

truck driver, in a rage, beats Tisa and throws her out of the truck into the mud. He then kicks her unconscious, tosses her in the back of the truck, and dumps her out near her village. A friend of Mirta's finds Tisa and returns her to him.

Bora, in the meantime, has followed Tisa's trail to Belgrade and back and goes to Mirta to reclaim her. The climactic scene of the film is a knife battle between Mirta and Bora in a shed filled with goosefeathers. After a brutal struggle, the two men are locked together under the feathers. There is a heaving up of bodies. Red stains darken the feathers. After a moment of stillness, it is Bora who emerges, his clothes covered with feathers and his knife bloodied. Bora carries the body draped over the back of Mirta's own donkey and slips it into the half-frozen waters of a nearby river.

Tisa is returned to the domestic bliss of Bora's quarrelsome, television-watching household. A police investigation leads to Bora as the prime suspect in the killing of Mirta. The last scene shows the police questioning Tisa, Bora's common-law wife, and Mirta's fellow villagers. There is a wall of silence. The villagers' faces are masks, where no messages can be read. There is a closeup of the face of a wizened and wrinkled woman with a pipe clutched between her teeth; another woman smoking a cigar; the tough face of a boy of only five or six wearing a rakish broad-rimmed black hat, with a cigarette dangling from the corner of his mouth.

The film ends with the shot of a long and deserted road. The title song plays on the soundtrack, with its ironic opening line, "I have been going on a long road where I even met happy Gypsies."

In the context of the film, Bora's virile and passionate spirit beats and rattles against the cages of his confinement. He wants to feel sensibly the pain and joy of freedom. The most potent and subtle metaphor of this longing occurs in an evocative scene in which Bora is riding on the back of a truck with sackfuls of goosefeathers, which he has gathered assiduously through tough bargaining. He rips open a sack with his knife and casts a few feathers into the wind. He is so enchanted by the poetry of white feathers lightly dancing in the wind that he throws handfuls into the air. As excitement mounts, he rips open more bags and fills the air with goosefeathers. Later, when Bora is called into court and fined for littering the highway, the judge asks why he did so. Bora replies simply, "Because they looked like birds." Tisa also offers a touch of beauty in Bora's confined world. Paradoxically, however, Bora is obsessed with trapping this "bird" and imprisoning her in a most unattractive cage. The television set offers illusory images of escape into a larger world. It brings the world into the hovel—but those in the hovel are constrained from entering the world it images forth.

In his film *When I Am Pale and Dead* (*Kad budem mrtav i beo*, 1967), Živojin (Žika) Pavlović, in collaboration with the scenarists Gordan Mihić and Ljubiša Kozomara,[3] paints a dark and sometimes mordantly humorous portrait of under-

"Jimmy" Barka and Lilica. *When I Am Pale and Dead* (*Kad budem mrtav i beo*).

employment, youthful disaffection, and provincial narrowness in the small industrial and agrarian towns near Belgrade.

The film's protagonist, "Jimmy" Barka, is a seasonal field worker who has run
out of employment. Teaming up with his girlfriend, Lilica, also a farm worker,
he tries, without luck, to find a job in the local factories and enterprises. Desperate for money, Barka steals from the workers on a construction site and runs away,
leaving Lilica behind.

Endowed with good looks and provincial charm, Barka begins an eventful
odyssey. He hitches a ride with a small-time female singer, who takes him on as a
lover. She attempts to parlay his practically nonexistent talent into a joint singing
act; she arranges to have a favorable notice placed in a small provincial paper,
and Barka's new career is launched. Unfortunately for Barka, the singer takes advantage of a better opportunity and runs off to Belgrade with a musician who is
beginning to make a mark in the big city.

Barka hops a freight train and hides in the mail car. He is discovered by a
female mail handler. They are attracted to each other and make love among the

mail sacks, and she takes Barka home with her. Her brother finds the newspaper article about Barka's singing prowess, is impressed, and arranges for Barka to give a performance at a small provincial military base. Barka sings a light little soldier's ballad—quite badly—but the enthusiastic reception convinces him that his future, after all, must lie in the field of popular music.

Finding a new girlfriend, a dental assistant, Barka persuades her to go off with him to Belgrade, where he plans to participate in an audition and competition for young singers. The competition is a disaster. Cool young musicians translate rock and roll music inspired by American and British sources into their own distinctive idiom. Barka, in his thin, unmusical voice, sings his simple soldier's ballad to the incongruous backing of a rock band. He is hissed off the stage. Things go from bad to worse for Barka in Belgrade. His dental assistant girlfriend becomes pregnant, and employment prospects are bleak. Beginning to despair, Barka chances to run into his old girlfriend, Lilica, who looks quite pregnant. The pregnancy turns out to be a ruse that Lilica uses to relieve men of their billfolds while they are solicitous of her "delicate" condition.

Barka and the pickpocket, Lilica, are reunited and return to the small town where they began. The same bleak prospects face them as before. Lilica puts on

Death of Barka. *When I Am Pale and Dead (Kad budem mrtav i beo)*.

her pregnancy act and manages to get them a room, with the rent payment delayed. When the proprietor discovers the fake pregnancy, he demands sexual favors from Lilica. She resists, and Barka arrives in time to rescue her and to humiliate the proprietor by making him crawl away on the floor with Barka holding the man's own gun to his head.

The final sequence shows Barka watching a sandlot soccer game. The proprietor arrives, demanding satisfaction for the rent and for his honor. Barka contemptuously dismisses him and leaves the game to relieve himself in a primitive outhouse. While the camera follows the soccer game, several shots ring out. The film cuts to a shot of the privy with the plank door ajar. Barka is seated with one hand between his legs, his body leaning against the wall. Blood trickles down his face from a fatal gunshot wound. The camera holds on this forlorn and shocking image as the film fades to black and ends.

Individual Freedom and Political Repression

The last film which Aleksandar Petrović directed in Yugoslavia dealt with the theme of intellectual and artistic freedom in a period of increasing ideological stringency and administrative-bureaucratic repression. The film, *The Master and Margarita* (*Majstor i Margarita*, 1972), is adapted from the well-known and long-suppressed Russian novel of the same name by Mikhail Bulgakov. It is set in Moscow during the late twenties, when Stalin was consolidating his personal power and centralizing and strengthening Communist party bureaucratic and police control.

The film opens with a series of shots of Moscow and then cuts to a crowded trolley, in which the playwright Nikolai Maksudov, whose brilliance has earned him the title of Master, is making his way to a dress rehearsal of his play *Pontius Pilate*. At the theater, the Master watches the opening scene of the play in the company of the theater manager, Rimsky, and two of his fellow playwrights, Danilovitch and Bobov. In the play, Jesus is presented as an idealistic revolutionary, who declares that "all power is a form of violence" and that a time will come "when there will be no rule by Caesar or any other form of rule." Pilate, who wishes to spare Jesus from the cross, asks if he knows what he is saying and declares sternly that "there never has been, nor yet shall be, a greater and more perfect government in this world than the rule of the Emperor Tiberius!"

Bobov and Danilovitch object to the ideologically unsound character of the play. However, when Rimsky phones the president of the Proletarian Writers' Association, Berlioz, for guidance, his call is inexplicably answered by Professor Woland, a self-proclaimed master of black magic, who is, in reality, Satan. Woland has himself been watching the rehearsals of the play with two rakish and disreputable-looking assistants, Koroviev and Azazello, and he orders that the rehearsal continue.

Berlioz later denies that he had given the order to continue the rehearsals and breaks them off, suggesting that the Master withdraw the play and take a vacation to Yalta. The writers' association denounces the play, and critics, without ever having seen the play, write hostile reviews. Nikolai, however, remains adamant and is supported in his stand by his lovely mistress Margarita, and by Woland and his two ruffian assistants. Strange things begin to happen. Berlioz slips on an oil slick and falls under a trolley, and his head is severed from his body—exactly as Woland had earlier predicted. Later, at the funeral, the head of Berlioz has mysteriously disappeared, requiring that the body be displayed in the funeral cortege with a bouquet of flowers adorning the pillow where his head would have rested. A prominent literary official, Oscar, who also opposes the performance of the play, is mysteriously and instantly transported nude to Yalta, where he stands in a soft rain, covering his genitals with his hands. The critic who wrote the hostile review is attacked by Satan's black cat and is informed by Woland that he will die of cancer in six months. The Master, who has witnessed these strange events, is convinced that Woland is, in fact, Satan, and he attempts to warn the writers' association that the Devil has come to Moscow. He is rewarded by being sent to a lunatic asylum.

Having rather dramatically cut through bureaucratic red tape, Woland arranges for the opening-night performance of the play *Pontius Pilate*, which he precedes with a dazzling display of black magic. In his show, he reveals the venality and corruption of some party officials in attendance and plays upon the audience's greed for material possessions by showering them with money and magically adorning them with new clothing. The theater manager, Rimsky, orders Woland to stop and declares that his tricks are mere illusions. Woland severs Rimsky's head from his body with his cane. The crowd calls for mercy. Woland graciously accedes to the audience's demands; he restores Rimsky's head, and the bewildered theater manager walks off stage. Suddenly the new clothes begin to disappear from the bodies of some of the audience members. Pandemonium breaks loose as members of the audience, their clothes vanishing at an astonishing rate, scramble to the nearest exits and pour outside into the street.

In the meantime, the Master's strait jacket has been mysteriously loosened, and the doors to the asylum have been left ajar, permitting him to come to the theater and make his way through the retreating, nude, and panic-stricken audience. The Master's play opens to an empty house. Woland appears in the author's box with vintage wine sent by Pontius Pilate. Woland confides that he has spoken to Jesus, who likes the Master's play but cannot say how it will end. The play begins with the scene earlier presented in rehearsal, in which Jesus main-

The Master. *The Master and Margarita (Majstor i Margarita).*

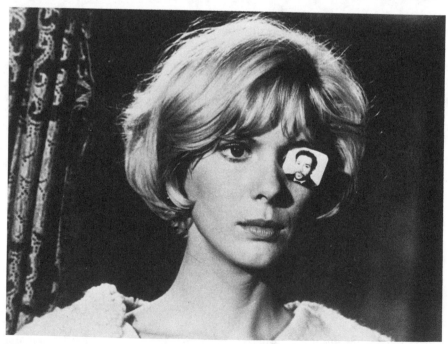

Margarita. *The Master and Margarita (Majstor i Margarita).*

Panic in the theater. *The Master and Margarita* (*Majstor i Margarita*).

tains that all power oppresses, and Pilate warns him against political heresy. Margarita joins the Master in the author's box, and they toast each other with Pilate's wine. The film then cuts to the final scene in the asylum, where the Master is shown dying quietly in bed, with the sheet drawn over his head—leaving open the question how much of what has transpired in the film is real and how much of it is hallucination.

   Petrović's loose filmic adaptation of Bulgakov's novel draws implicit parallels between the early Stalinist period in the Soviet Union and the ideological campaign then going on in Yugoslavia against nonestablishment Marxists, members of the non-Marxist "humanistic intelligentsia," radical student leaders, and artists, which reached its greatest intensity at the time Petrović was making his film. Petrović also uses the occasion to attack contemporary critics associated with the *black film* counteroffensive. In the first scene at the Writers' Union, the Master defends himself against the charges leveled against his play and states that "we must be able to write our own thoughts" and that "I must say what I believe." A slightly tipsy hack writer rhetorically asks why the Master can write what he wants "and I can't." The Master is also accused of using his reputation as a writer to gain special privileges, including a nice two-bedroom apartment. While one writer defends the Master and his right to free expression, the decision of the Writers' Union is against the performance of the play. At a later scene at the Writers' Union, the Master warns that the devil is loose in Moscow and that he has come because "nobody ever writes the truth."

Handsomely produced, with a well-known international cast,[4] Petrović's film won top awards at the 1972 Venice International Film Festival and first prize at the Pula Festival of Yugoslav Feature Films. Subsequent to the festival showing, however, it was banned from domestic distribution. The circumstances surrounding the banning of the film were partially clarified six years later in an interview with Stole Janković, film director and a member of the Central Committee of the Communist party of Serbia. The interview appeared in the influential Yugoslavian weekly *Nin*. Janković informed the interviewer, Boro Krivokapić, that the workers' collective involved with theatrical showings was chiefly responsible for removing the film from circulation on the grounds (which Janković believed to be baseless) that the film was "socially useless":

> Boro Krivokapić: Is this not a form of repression? Stole Janković: It is, in fact, an administrative-bureaucratic measure which replaces public writing and discussion. And that is not good. Each such incident, which precludes full public discussion and polemic, is, indeed, a surrender to repression.[5]

Aleksandar Petrović, who was in Belgrade directing a play, wrote a letter to *Nin* amplifying Janković's remarks and identifying other sociocultural mechanisms involved in the suppression of his film, including the Cultural Commission of Serbia, which had revoked the awards and prizes received at Pula. Petrović then named five persons he deemed most responsible for banning the film from domestic distribution.[6]

In the ensuing four issues of *Nin* there was a heated exchange of letters, which shed little further light on the societal and political processes used to prevent the film from being shown. The persons mentioned by Petrović denied any formal or personal role in the affair but used the occasion to denigrate caustically both Petrović then named five persons whom he deemed most responsible for banning the film from domestic distribution.[6]

> The Editors of NIN deem it unnecessary to continue this polemic over *The Master and Margarita* because it really does not raise any important questions about our domestic cinematography. On the contrary, it simply shows a piling up of personal grievances and disagreements, which are not helpful to anyone.[7]

In the end, the fate of Petrović's film in Yugoslavia was not far different from that of the Master's play.

Dušan Makavejev, in his internationally acclaimed film WR: *Mysteries of the Organism* (WR: *Misterije organizma*, 1970), explores the regions of erotic and sexual liberation as a foil to repressive power. He uses the psychoanalytic theories of Wilhelm Reich as a touchstone for wide-ranging political commentary and satire. Reich developed the theory that, unless a mysterious universal phenomenon called "orgone energy" is discharged naturally through sexual union, neurosis will erupt. He developed an Orgone Accumulator to aid patients in tapping into this energy resource. In the late 1950s, Reich was jailed in the United States for his unorthodox therapeutic techniques; his Orgone Accumulators were confiscated as health hazards, and all of his books were burned (including earlier works that had nothing to do with the Orgone Accumulator).[8]

Makavejev's film is divided into two sections. The first intersperses a documentary account of Wilhelm Reich's life, work, persecution, and death in a Pennsylvania prison with examples of bioenergetic and primal scream therapies of contemporary Reichian practitioners and various scenes and interviews reflecting contemporary America (circa 1969-1970). The second section is a fictional story set in Yugoslavia, which centers on Milena, a liberated young woman, whose attempt to spread the gospel of Reichian sexual freedom to a perfectly formed and handsome but politically conditioned Russian skating star is finally rewarded with decapitation by his ice skates. Milena's roommate, Jagoda, practices Reichian sexual freedom with unusual devotion and pursues the doctrine with unflagging enthusiasm in her sexual couplings with Ljuba "the Cock" and the Yugoslav "natural man" Radmilović.

In the context of the film, the United States and the Soviet Union are monuments to sexuality misdirected into power politics and militarism. The principal symbols of American repression are the right-wing excesses of the McCarthy era, in which pathologies of "Get the Commies" were combined with suppression of intellectual unorthodoxy and the contemporary (at the time the film was made) U.S. militarism in Vietnam.

Stalin is the preeminent symbol of Soviet repression. In the context of the film, he gradually absorbs Lenin and takes on his guise. The contemporary symbol of the repressive Stalinist-Leninist orthodoxy is represented in the politically conditioned Russian ice-skating champion Vladimir Ilyich (after Lenin's first name), whose perfectly formed lips speak nothing but socialist cliches.

Yugoslavia represents a separate path to socialism, espousing a humanistic self-management socialist doctrine but not always living up to its claims. It is Milena's self-appointed task to enliven self-management and self-regulating socialism by preaching the doctrine of liberation through orgasm: "Only by liberating both love and labor can we create a self-regulating worker's society," and she admonishes the workers to "fuck merrily and without fear."[9]

Makavejev assumes an ironic and satirical attitude toward all forms of dog-

Milena exhorting the workers. WR: *Mysteries of the Organism* (WR: *Misterije organizma*).

matism and cant—including an affectionately satirical handling of Milena's
naive and simplistic presentation of Reichian sexual politics. He satirizes both
conventional sexual taboos and mechanical and doctrinaire revolts against them
(from Jackie Curtis's bisexuality to Betty Dodson's paintings of men and women
masturbating). He adopts an ironic view of New Left anti-Vietnam protests by
interspersing scenes of Tuli Kupferberg of the "Revolting Theater" prowling the
New York streets, autoerotically caressing his rifle while the song he wrote for
the Fugs plays on the soundtrack: "Kill, kill, kill for peace."

There are extended scenes of vigorous and joyful sexual intercourse in the film
but, ironically, no orgasms. Scenes of sexual intercourse are separated by dis-
solves and inserts, which provide a structural filmic equivalent to Reich's belief
that we live in an age of incomplete sexuality, in which sex has become subser-
vient to politics, institutionalism, and dogma. This notion is further conveyed in
the repetition of motifs in which arousal is followed by freezing. The most widely
discussed example of this motif is the sequence in which the editor of *Screw*
magazine, Jim Buckley, has his penis manipulated to erection by a female sculp-
tress, Nancy Godfrey, and a plaster cast is made of its erect state. This scene
is followed by a film segment from *The Vow*, Chiaurelli's idealized portrayal of
Stalin, in which Stalin proclaims, "Comrades, we have successfully completed
the first stage of Communism"[10]—a juxtaposition which equates the powerful
but repressive Stalin with a frozen phallus and emphasizes the frozen nature of
the revolution under Stalinist centralized, hierarchical dogmatism.

The complex and ambivalent relationship between Yugoslavia and the Soviet
Union is suggested in the relationship between Milena and the Russian ice skater
Vladimir Ilyich. Milena sees Vladimir perform during a guest tour in Yugoslavia
and falls instantly and romantically in love with him. Despite her views concerning complete sexual freedom, Milena approaches Vladimir cautiously and with
diffidence. In their first encounters, Vladimir speaks in socialist cliches and takes
a condescending view toward Yugoslavia's separate path to socialism: "We Rus-
sians . . . we do respect your efforts to find your own way. You are a proud and
independent people. But we are confident you will learn from your own experience that our way is best!" Milena responds that "time will tell who's closest to
the best," and Jagoda chimes in prophetically, "The closest kin will do you in."[11]

As Vladimir begins to relax in the free ambience of Milena and Jagoda's apartment, he is inspired to observe, "Well, I've been to the East and I've been to the
West, but it was never like this!"[12] On a romantic stroll with Milena along a
snow-covered riverbank, Vladimir declares, "I like being here! I confess there's
much I don't understand. But your people are wonderful."[13] They kiss romantically to the melancholy strings of the Hungarian Gypsy song "Like a Beautiful
Dream." Vladimir at first yields to the sensual moment and then reasserts his
rigid, doctrinaire character: ". . . nowadays if you stroke anybody's head, he'll

Vladimir and Milena—disaffection or rapprochement? WR: *Mysteries of the Organism* (WR: *Misterije organizma*).

bite off your hand! Now you have to hit them on the head, hit them on the head mercilessly . . . though in principle we oppose all violence."[14] Milena attempts to turn Vladimir back to a more sensual mood, but he slaps her face, and she falls down. Vladimir is filled with remorse and asks her to forgive him. Milena begins to hit him hard around the head and shoulders and makes an impassioned plea:

> You love all mankind, yet you're incapable of loving one individual: one single living creature. What is this love that makes you nearly knock my head off? You said I'm lovely as the Revolution. You gazed at me like a picture. . . . But "Revolution" musn't touch! What's a baby to a male? A matter of a second! Everything else is the woman's job!
>
> Meanwhile you put your body at the service of Art! Your magic flood-lit figure serves the needs of the masses!
>
> A bunch of lies is what you're serving . . . the People and the Party! A toy balloon is what it is . . . not a revolution! A petty human lie dressed up as a great historical truth! Are you capable, you rotten louse, of serving the needs of the species by taking the one basic position for an ecstatic flight to the target . . . like an arrow . . . or a vigorously hurled . . . spear?[15]

After this speech, Milena continues to strike Vladimir bitterly and unthinkingly until he stands up in front of her, tears in his eyes, and they kiss passionately. After prolonged and copious lovemaking (not shown in the film), Vladimir severs Milena's head from her body with his ice skates (also not shown), in an effort to reassert his authoritarian rigidity and perhaps, by metaphorical extension, to reclaim his Communist virginity from Yugoslav revisionism.

The last two scenes of the film metaphorically pose the possibility, despite the past, for reconciliation. Milena's severed head, on a white tray in the autopsy room, speaks and bitterly equates Stalinist-Leninist orthodoxy with Fascism but expresses no regret over Yugoslavia's own past:

> Cosmic rays streamed through our coupled bodies. We pulsated to the vibrations of the universe. But he couldn't bear it. He had to go one step further. Vladimir is a man of noble impetuousness, a man of high ambition, of immense energy. . . . He's romantic, ascetic, a genuine Red Fascist! Comrades! Even now I'm not ashamed of my Communist past! [16]

Filled with remorse—his rigid doctrinaire mask dissolved—Vladimir wanders near a Gypsy camp in the snowy landscape. With his arms outstretched, he sings to an unknown God:

> O Lord, my God, my green-eyed one,
> Before the earth stops turning
>   and all our pain is done,
> Before this day is through
> And the fires are still burning
> Grant to each some little thing
> And remember, I'm here too. [17]

Awakened sensuality and love have placed Vladimir in touch with his humanity and the hope of redemption. During the last lines of Vladimir's song, the film cuts to a shot of Milena's smiling head and then to the shot of a photograph of a smiling Reich, the author of this political miracle, and the film ends.

In the Yugoslav section of the film, Makavejev treats with utter irreverence the sacred symbols of the National War of Liberation. In a Kozara snake dance spontaneously organized on the balconies of Milena's tenement building, a Partisan song is sung with new lyrics celebrating love and sexual freedom and ending with "Life without fucking isn't worth a thing." [18] The indefatigable Ljuba is serving his required term in the Yugoslav People's Army and announces to the ever-receptive Jagoda, "I'm Ljuba the Cock. I mount guard by day and girls by night." [19] In one scene, Milena comes to her apartment, where Jagoda and Ljuba are coupling on the couch. Jagoda cheerfully introduces her guest as Comrade Ljuba. "He came for a little rest. He didn't even finish his tea. Ever ready, our military! Ah, the People's Army!" [20] In a particularly vigorous coupling, Jagoda exults, "Onward People's Soldiers,"[21] and in another sequence, Ljuba mounts Jagoda from the rear and triumphantly exclaims, "War of liberation!"[22]

Echoes of the student protests at Belgrade University and elsewhere in 1968 are captured in the character of Radmilović, a tempestuous and angry young radical, who attacks a Mercedes belonging to a high party official, jumps on the hood, and shouts a slogan which had been used in the student demonstrations and festooned on university walls, "Down with the Red Bourgeoisie!"[23] He uses the same slogan in another scene, in which he has blocked traffic and is hosing the cars, shouting, "Screw you all! Down with the Red Bourgeoisie."[24] He scornfully denounces symbols of consumerism, including Steak Esterhazi, Mitsuko perfume, and "Marx Factor."

In his film, Makavejev attempts, in an undogmatic way, to celebrate individual creativity, humor, spontaneity, sexual joy, and irony as mechanisms of counterrepression. He calls his film a confrontation with a dream machine— Makavejev's own attempt to use humor, spontaneity, and irony to challenge received myths, cant, and institutional rigidities, open up new avenues of thought, and possibly provoke social change.

WR: Mysteries of the Organism was shown at a number of international festivals, elicited widespread discussion, and won several prizes, including the Luis Bunuel Prize at the 1971 International Film Festival at Cannes. It ran into a thicket of controversy within Yugoslavia and was effectively halted from domestic distribution by action of the Executive Committee of the Regional Cultural Commission of Vojvodina. The film was subjected to a special screening in Novi Sad, with approximately eight hundred largely hostile viewers in attendance, representing SUBNOR (Veterans of the War of Liberation) and a local community organization in Novi Sad. The screening was followed by heated public discussion, with Dušan Makavejev and representatives from Neoplanta film (which produced the film) in attendance to defend it against polemic attack. Though the film was initially cleared for domestic distribution by the Commission of Cinematography of the Regional Cultural Commission, this decision was later overruled by the cultural commission's Executive Committee, which placed a freeze on the licensing of the film for domestic distribution. In an equally controversial move, the public prosecutor of Serbia restrained the film from being shown at the Pula festival. Widespread protests against these actions were unsuccessful.[25]

Following a structural motif in WR: Mysteries of the Organism, Makavejev's film itself excited widespread arousal but, after a complex struggle, was placed under a freeze, which has lasted to the present time. His film was also one of the last to exemplify the spirit of the new film movement and signaled the end of Yugoslavia's most fertile era of feature film production.

6

Accommodation and Resurgence, 1973-1983

As indicated at the end of chapter 3, the bruising battles and polemic clashes of the late sixties and early seventies had left the Yugoslav film industry dispirited, its finances in disarray, and its domestic audience dwindling in the face of television's rapid advancement and penetration. The period from 1973 to 1977 marked Yugoslavia's lowest ebb of domestic feature film production since the beginning of the sixties, with nineteen films completed in 1973, seventeen in 1974, eighteen in 1975, sixteen in 1976, and eighteen in 1977. In 1978, however, the picture brightened considerably, with a jump to twenty-four domestically produced feature films, followed by twenty-eight in 1979, twenty-three in 1980, twenty-six in 1981, thirty in 1982, and twenty-five in 1983.[1]

The low and flat profile of film production in the mid-seventies was matched by a general lack of thematic boldness and cinematic experimentation. Heroic Partisan films, light comedies, action-adventure films, and historical dramas once again rose to the forefront, and *new film* radicalism receded to the vanishing point. Some spark of it remained in Krsto Papić's film A *Village Performance of Hamlet* (*Predstava Hamleta u selu Mrduša Donja*, 1973), based on a controversial play of the same name by Ivo Brešan. The film is set in the small Croatian village of Mrduša Donja and provides a witty and sharply satirical portrayal of provincial corruption and venality. In 1974, Živojin Pavlović, unable to secure film projects in Serbia and in political trouble at the film academy in Belgrade, went to northeast Slovenia in the Prekomurje to make *The Flight of a Dead Bird* (*Let mrtve ptice*), a passionate and melancholy tale of the collapse of a family of seasonal farm workers under the pressures of modernization and contemporary ethics. A year later, in 1975, Puriša Đorđević stirred up a storm of controversy with his film *Pavle Pavlović*, a witty and irreverent depiction of corruption and illegal acquisition of wealth within the socialist system. Despite the fact that Đorđević's film was made on the heels of an official campaign against these same practices led by Tito himself, it was accused of "ridiculing the system of self-government" and was prohibited from competing in the Yugoslav film festival at Pula.[2]

The Yugoslav film industry was also required to adapt to the complex new forms of self-management structures and financial accountability which followed

143

A Village Performance of Hamlet (Predstava Hamleta u selu Mrduša Donja).

in the wake of the revised Yugoslav constitution in 1974 and the Law of Associated Labor in 1976, which included setting up community self-management
boards with direct decision-making power in approving film projects.[3] Expanded
societal involvement in cultural institutions, however, had the beneficial result
of enlarging the sources of funding for film, along with an increased commitment to provide film expression for the various nationalities of Yugoslavia—this
latter policy leading, for example, to the production in 1979 of the first feature
film made entirely in the Albanian Shiptar language.[4]

Stabilization of socially generated finances and the infusion of new sources of
funding from film and television coproductions set the stage for an upswing in
levels of film production in the late seventies. It also opened the way for a new
generation of filmmakers, who made socially relevant and artistically more interesting films and helped to recapture the attention of domestic filmgoers.

The New Generation

The comeback of Yugoslav film in the late seventies and early eighties has been spearheaded by a group of younger film directors, among the most important of whom are Srđan Karanović (b. 1945), Goran Paskaljević (b. 1947), Goran Marković (b. 1946), Rajko Grlić (b. 1947), Lordan Zafranović (b. 1944), and Miloš Radivojević (b. 1939). All but Miloš Radivojević received their film training at FAMU, the professional film school in Prague, and honed their directing and writing skills by making amateur and short films or films for television. They share a common interest in making films which reflect critically upon *savremene teme* (contemporary themes), but without the radical confrontational impetus of earlier *new film* directors. A close collaborative relationship has developed, in which several of the directors work on each others' films—much in the spirit of the French *nouvelle vague* directors of the early sixties.[5] There is a strong professional commitment to making well-crafted films which will communicate effectively with the audience and make sharp and meaningful comments on the complexities and contradictions of contemporary life in Yugoslavia. As reflected in the films, the attitudes of these young directors toward Yugoslavia's complex struggle and rebirth during the Second World War are less passionate and direct than those of their immediate predecessors and are instead filtered through the gauze of recollection and memory. Seldom do these filmmakers swim against the main currents of received myth and collective belief. They have matured in a Yugoslavia characterized by ever-increasing urbanization and labyrinthine self-management complexities—a system in which *veze* (personal connections) are often the preferred way to get things done; where consumer values and pride in owning a *vikendica* (weekend home) are a national passion; where the problems of high inflation, a growing and serious balance-of-payments deficit, chronic underemployment, and unemployment doggedly resist easy solution; and where social and economic disparities between the more highly developed regions in the North and the poorer regions of the South refuse to disappear.

In dealing with these and other dimensions of contemporary Yugoslav reality, the new generation of film directors adopts an attitude of critical accommodation rather than dialectical confrontation. Much like salmon swimming upstream, they bank and dart rather than plunge headlong against the main current. The results of their creative spawning are best captured by reviewing some of the most significant films made in the last few years, grouped according to overall theme and substance.

The War Years Remembered

While the new generation of directors is primarily interested in making films with contemporary settings and themes, there are two films which stand out as dramatically compelling and evocative filmic recollections of the past: *Occupation in Twenty-six Scenes* (*Okupacija u 26 slika*, 1978), directed by Lordan Zafranović, and *Petrija's Wreath* (*Petrijin venac*, 1980), directed by Srđan Karanović.

Zafranović's film, *Occupation in Twenty-six Scenes*, is set in the beautiful city of Dubrovnik on the southern part of the eastern Adriatic coast during the successive occupations of Germans, Italians, and Ustashis. At first it appears that the graceful and cultured walled city of Dubrovnik will escape the worst outrages of Fascist occupation through clever accommodation. What emerges instead is an ever-deepening portrait of vulgarity and evil. The principal protagonists of the film are three charming companions: a blonde Croatian, Niko; an Italian, Toni; and a Jew, Miho, who all belong to the old prewar bourgeois order of graceful homes, privileges, and culture. They are members of a fencing club, sing light Dalmatian folk songs, and are shown together in the beginning of the film frolicking through the cobbled streets of Dubrovnik at dawn after a costume ball and playfully negotiating with a prostitute to show them her legs and her breasts for a small sum. Before the occupiers arrive, life is carefree, romantically lyrical, gay, and lighthearted.

As the film progresses, Toni falls under the sway of the Italian Fascist occupiers and joins their ranks. Miho and his family begin to suffer increasingly severe persecution. Niko quickly sickens of the smell of Fascism and joins forces with a band of Partisan resisters.

The darkest brutalization of the formerly liberal and cultured lifestyle of Dubrovnik is committed against Miho and his family. Miho is dismissed from the fencing club by the fencing master, Hibička, who is a Fascist sympathizer. In a later scene, Toni leads a band of Fascist soldiers into the shop of Miho's father and mother to close it and confiscate the goods. Each must wear the humiliating star. One soldier fondles the breast of Miho's mother while he is positioning the star. Toni sharply reprimands the soldier, but this act does little to ameliorate the ruin and degradation of this once proud and prosperous family. When the dreaded Ustashis come to town, the final act of brutalization occurs in a scene of unspeakable horror. The Ustashis arrest Miho and his father along with a Serbian Orthodox priest, a Croatian resister, and other minorities. Dressed in nondescript civilian clothes, two Ustashi agents drive the prisoners in a bus up the winding Adriatic highway and stop at a beautiful spot overlooking the old walled city of Dubrovnik, nestled against sun-glint waters. The Ustashi agents have also brought along an elderly blind man, who plays light Dalmatian folk

After the costume ball. *Occupation in Twenty-six Scenes (Okupacija u 26 slika)*.

Before the occupation Niko (left) playfully duels with Toni while Niko's sister Ana looks on—a foreshadowing of the deadlier duel to come. *Occupation in Twenty-six Scenes (Okupacija u 26 slika)*.

songs on his accordion. As the old man plays, the Ustashis matter-of-factly and systematically torture, maim, and kill their prisoners—cutting off the breast of a woman after brutalizing her, cutting out the tongue of the priest, driving a stake through the living skull of one victim, gouging out the eyes of another, smashing the heads of Jews with a sledgehammer, and severing the head of Miho's father. Miho lies on the floor of the blood-spattered bus, miraculously escapes out the back door, and makes his way to the safe sanctuary of Niko's home.[6]

Niko joins with a workers' group of trade unionists and Communists who are attempting to organize Partisan-style resistance. Niko's father, Captain Baldo, who detests the Fascists, agrees to let the group use his home for meetings despite his political dislike for the Communists. Niko's sister, Ana, marries Toni over the strong objections of her father and joins in the vulgar lifestyle of the occupiers. Captain Baldo is eventually arrested by a party led by his new son-in-law, Toni, and is later killed while trying to make his escape. The mothers of Niko and Miho, along with other potential political victims, are smuggled out of Dubrovnik by boat and sent to the sparsely populated island of Mljet for sanctuary.

In the culminating sequence of the film—the last of the twenty-six scenes—Toni has come to confiscate Niko's house for himself and Ana, who has become progressively more unhappy and disoriented over her father's death and the realization that her husband participated in his arrest. Miho comes out of hiding and joins his two old friends. Toni expresses regret that he must arrest Miho but asks that he play a favorite song of the three friends, a Dalmatian folk song, "Dear Companions." While Miho plays lightly on his lute, Niko moves quietly behind Toni and shoots him in the head at close range. Ana comes into the house and shrieks with despair at the discovery of Toni's death at her brother's hand. The film ends with Niko calmly placing his gun on the top of the piano and playing a light classical piece—his way of reasserting the graceful cultural values of Dubrovnik over Fascist decadence and brutality.

In a manner structurally related to Vatroslav Mimica's earlier experimental film *Kaja, I'll Kill You*, Zafranović's film creates an ever-enlarging metaphor of evil. The rigid mechanism of Fascism, with its goose-stepping soldiers, inflated oratory, Mussolini posturing, false pomp, and anticultural vulgarity, is played antipodally against the graceful ease and lyrical beauty of Dubrovnik's Mediterranean culture. The lithesome and fluid movements of the three companions as they dance through the cobbled streets or engage in playful fencing matches in the opening segments of the film are contrasted to the coarse goose-stepping of the Italian soldiers strutting down the Placa (the main thoroughfare of Dubrovnik) toward the Sponza palace, several of whom lose their footing on the slick cobblestones and awkwardly fall out of rank, to the amusement of the Dubrovnik citizens. The musical singing of light Dalmatian airs is contrasted to the decadent merrymaking of the Fascist occupiers. In one scene, a lumpenproletariat Nazi

Arrival of the occupiers. *Occupation in Twenty-six Scenes (Okupacija u 26 slika)*.

Decadence of the occupiers. *Occupation in Twenty-six Scenes (Okupacija u 26 slika)*.

officer dismisses a local ensemble of musicians playing baroque music in order to bang out a schmaltzy little beer-hall ditty on the piano. A strip bar and brothel are set up near the Sponza palace, and a prostitute strikes a nude pose, which is filmically connected to the same pose captured in a classical piece of sculpture. The Fascist and Nazi occupiers begin by vulgarizing the culture and then proceed to vulgarize and brutalize life itself.

The occupiers achieve the deepest level of evil by astutely playing upon and manipulating Yugoslavia's historic national and interethnic rivalries and susceptibilities, prising apart members of the same family, companion from companion, and unleashing the bestiality of the bus scene. The bus, with its nationality and religious mix of victims and perpetrators, is all-Yugoslav in character. The foreign occupiers are in the town below. A light Dalmatian tune fills the air. Sunlight plays upon the windows of the bus. The blue Adriatic lies in the distance. In this romantically beautiful and lyrical setting, the most savage atrocities of the film are enacted.

Apart from the sequence in the bus, Zafranović's film presents a framed, meditative, and sometimes even nostalgic remembrance of the war years; its twenty-six scenes fluidly blend one into the other like a moving mosaic. What emerges most vividly in the film is a reminder to the contemporary audience of the terrible primitivism and brutality which lie beneath the surface of the older forms of national, religious, and ethnic strife. Zafranović's film received widespread critical praise at international film festivals and captured first prize at the Pula festival.[7]

Petrija's Wreath (*Petrijin venac*, 1980), directed by Srđan Karanović and based on a novel by Dragoslav Mihajlović, is another powerful evocation of the years immediately before, during, and after the Second World War as they were lived in a small coal-mining town in Serbia. The film centers on the suffering of an illiterate farm woman, whose personal tragedies are recounted with detailed filmic attention to period setting and the larger events which shaped her individual destiny. The film begins with Petrija's married life before the war with a taciturn and loveless husband, whose hard and embittered mother lives with them. Petrija's life is one of narrow drudgery and work, with little communication or affection. Her husband is tied to his mother, who treats Petrija with cold disdain and mocking cruelty. The most telling scene is the one in which Petrija quits her work in the corn field to go and deliver her first child in a rude shed. She successfully effects the delivery but is so exhausted from her exertions that she falls asleep without cutting the umbilical cord. When her husband and mother-in-law arrive, the infant is dead. The mother-in-law berates Petrija for ignorance and causing the baby's death—having earlier assured Petrija that she would be present to assist in the delivery. In time, Petrija successfully delivers a daughter, Milena, who renews her sense of love and life.

Petrija. *Petrija's Wreath (Petrijin venac)*.

During the war, Petrija's lovely child, Milena, contracts diphtheria. The makeshift hospital in the small town is filled with wounded Partisans, and there is no one to offer the child medical attention. Milena dies in Petrija's arms. Her husband coldly dismisses Petrija from her home, and she leaves with a few personal possessions. She finds a job in a local tavern, the owner of which is an older man who has likewise lost all of his family. He provides her with a place to live and treats her with a respect and kindness she had never before known.

In the harsh aftermath of the war, the tavern keeper is accused of being a capitalist, his tavern is destroyed, and he leaves the town. In the meantime Petrija has met and decided to marry a robust and hard-drinking coal miner, who offers her a sense of joy and sensual fulfillment. Working overtime in the antiquated coal mine, her husband is caught in a mining accident, which crushes his legs. He gradually loses his zest for life, drinks more heavily, and is filled with self-loathing. Petrija remains faithful to him and visits him in the hospital, where he is now confined. During one visit she tells him that she will see him the next Sunday. Before Sunday arrives, she receives a brief message that her husband is dead.

The events of Petrija's life are imaginatively presented through a series of collage arrangements of photographs, which dissolve into the live action of the film. A sense of contemplative distancing is thus achieved throughout the film, which is further reinforced by the voice of Petrija as an old woman acting as narrator.

Petrija's sensual awakening. *Petrija's Wreath (Petrijin venac).*

Her deeply felt recollections from the past are given added psychological weight by scenes of Petrija as an old woman caught in the matrix of dream, hallucination, and reality, in which she mentally evokes her long-dead child, Milena, and talks to her second husband as he was before the terrible mining accident. These hallucinated presences come to visit her regularly and help her to sustain the weight of her suffering, to face the inevitability of her own death, and to compensate for a life limned with sorrow and tragedy. The film reaches into the complex psychological undertow of this one woman's suffering and connects it to national memory of traumatic years which, even after thirty-five years, continued to haunt the imaginations of many yet living. Karanović's film was a strong critical and popular success and captured first prize at the Pula festival.

Youthful Freedom and Social Constraint

Several of the most important and effective films of the new generation of Yugoslav filmmakers center upon contemporary problems of youth seeking independence and the realization of youthful aspirations in the context of serious economic and social constraints. One of the most gifted and versatile of the new Yugoslav directors, Goran Paskaljević, was the first to explore this theme, in his popular and critically successful film *Beach Guard in Winter* (*Čuvar plaže u zimskom periodu*, 1976).

The film dramatizes two interlocking contemporary problems facing the young in Yugoslavia: the problem of finding work (especially work associated with one's education) and the problem of finding housing which will permit the establishment of independent love relationships and marriage. Very often young people find themselves sharing their parents' small apartments well into their late twenties and after marriage.

The protagonist of the film, Karlo, is a gentle but strong-willed young man in his early twenties, who lives with his parents and an unmarried aunt in her fifties. Karlo's father, a train attendant third class, adopts a bluff and smothering attitude toward his son, forever advising him on the course his life should follow, how to stay healthy, and how to be "a real man."

Karlo develops a serious and tender love relationship with a rather shy and attractive young woman, Ljuba, who also lives with her parents and a disabled uncle, who is dependent on her father for support and a place to live. Ljuba's father, an imposing man, also attempts to direct Ljuba's life and to discourage her interest in Karlo.

The love affair that develops between Karlo and Ljuba is thus complicated by interfamilial tensions and by their inability to find satisfactory employment. Karlo meets Ljuba while he is taking temporary employment in a laundry to replace a woman who is on pregnancy leave. The job fills his father with shame— after all, Karlo has completed his vocational training as a leather tanner, and "working in a laundry is woman's work."

As the film progresses, Karlo arrives at a solution which will permit him and Ljuba to marry and have a place to live. He signs on as a guard in winter at a riverside beach resort near Belgrade to replace a guard who has recently died. The manager of the resort, who has taken the former guard's wife as his mistress, offers Karlo rude living quarters in a shed in return for light off-season chores, with the understanding that the salary will still go to the dead guard's wife. This arrangement, as poor as it is, nonetheless offers the chance for Karlo and Ljuba to start an independent married life together. At first, both families are aghast at the arrangement and express strong opposition. When the two families meet to confer on the matter, however, Ljuba's father is so sarcastically and violently opposed to the marriage that Karlo's father reverses his original position and sides with the two young lovers.

Karlo's father arranges for the wedding to take place at his family homestead outside the city, because it "costs too much in Belgrade." On the first night at the farm, Karlo shares a small bed with his father. Early on the morning of the wedding, his father rouses him out of bed to jog in the cool dawn and splash cold water on each other. Karlo is not much taken with the idea, but the father evidently regards it as a potency ritual and an excellent way to prepare for the coming night's ardors. After the wedding, the father has further bright ideas for helping his son and goes to the wedding chamber and knocks on the door. Karlo is able to dismiss his overhelpful father graciously, and the next shot in the film is a very tender one. The two newlyweds are kneeling on the bed in a nude and soft embrace. The camera slowly circles as the two lovers gently descend out of the film frame—their love consummated at last in shared privacy, even from the eye of the camera.

On the train back to Belgrade, Karlo's father once again tries to assert his parental authority. He urges Karlo to go to Sweden as a "guest worker" and earn enough capital to start his marriage on a more secure footing. He reminds Karlo of the *veza* (personal connection) that the father has with Bulajić—a man who has been a great success in Sweden and is coming to Belgrade to recruit guest workers. Karlo resolutely rejects his father's suggestion, and the father angrily withdraws his support of the marriage.

At first Ljuba and Karlo lovingly make the most of their impoverished circumstances, but the precariousness of their future begins to wear away at youthful love. Ljuba suggests that Karlo follow his father's advice and go to Sweden—even if it means prolonged separation. Karlo is wounded at the suggestion, manages to secure some extra income, and proudly returns to their home with bags of groceries and other supplies. Ljuba is gone. The resort manager's mistress informs Karlo that Ljuba's father came to retrieve her, and although Ljuba had resisted, the father's will had finally prevailed.

In great anxiety, Karlo goes to Ljuba's home to win her back. The father resolutely forbids Ljuba to return to such a life, and Ljuba is no longer willing to defy her father's will. Karlo returns to the resort in a mood of despair and defeat. His father comes to him and tries in his clumsy way to persuade him to return home and to "cheer up." In a sudden act of bravado, and in an effort to give to his son the feeling of "being a man," the father strips off his clothes to his undershorts and invites his son to plunge into the icy waters of the river. Karlo scarcely responds to the suggestion. The father jogs out into the chill winter air, beating himself about the torso to stimulate circulation. He goes to the water's edge. In the meantime, Karlo has sufficiently recovered from despondency to race to the window of his shed and to shout to his father not to do such a dangerous thing. The father turns cheerily, shouts "A healthy man can do anything," and plunges into the winter-swollen waters. Karlo races to the edge of the river. His father does not emerge.

The film cuts to the funeral of Karlo's father. The mysterious friend, Bulajić, appears and apologizes for not coming sooner and for missing the wedding and

Karlo's father orchestrates early morning exercises at the farmstead. *Beach Guard in Winter* (*Čuvar plaže u zimskom periodu*).

Karlo and Ljuba on their wedding night. *Beach Guard in Winter* (*Čuvar plaže u zimskom periodu*).

other occasions. He offers Karlo a job as a guest worker in Sweden, and Karlo accepts—his other options have run out.

In the final scene of the film, Karlo says goodbye to his family at the train station. His new protector, Bulajić, however, quickly separates himself from Karlo and goes into the sleeping section of the train, while Karlo crowds in with other new recruits in second class and listens to them chattering bravely about the good life in Sweden and all the pretty girls. The train pulls out and goes through a long tunnel. The last shot of the film is from the rear of the train, which shows the entrance of the tunnel growing smaller and smaller until the screen goes black and the film ends. This poignant and ambiguous ending leaves unresolved the basic economic, personal, and social conditions which face Karlo and thousands like him.

Paskaljević's film is filled with gentle humor and sharp social comment. The naive faith which Karlo's father places in his one important and influential personal connection (*veza*) is forever undermined by Bulajić's relative indifference to the fate of Karlo or the family. The mundane but not unimportant problem of young lovers finding a place to make love in private is underscored in a scene in which Karlo's unmarried aunt joins Ljuba and Karlo at a café. She is supportive of their love and perhaps a little envious that nothing so sweet had ever touched her own life. She adopts an attitude of forced gaiety and joie de vivre, and while Karlo and Ljuba demurely drink Coca-Cola, she gets quite drunk on plum brandy. Karlo and Ljuba help her back to her room, where she passes out on the bed. Seizing their opportunity, Karlo and Ljuba attempt to make love on the same bed, with the principal result that poor auntie is bounced from the bed onto the floor.

A central visual metaphor of the film, and one which recurs in other films by Paskaljević, is that of trains and railway tracks. The opening shots of the film are of the train station where Karlo's father is employed. Railway tracks are shown leading away from the station and seem to beckon toward travel, freedom, escape, and connection with a larger world. The closing shot of the film views these same tracks in reverse angle, symbolizing leaving something behind rather than going toward something new or better—signifying a kind of defeat. The "opportunity" which Bulajić has opened up to Karlo is, after all, no different from that which has been offered to approximately one million underemployed and unemployed Yugoslav "guest workers," who, at any given time, are dispersed over Western Europe, mostly engaged in the hard, dirty jobs that prosperous Europeans are no longer willing to perform—from manning factory assembly lines and building subways to cleaning streets and collecting garbage.[8]

In a fast-paced and skillfully made film, *National Class up to 785 cm* (*Nacionalna klasa do 785 cm*, 1979), directed by Goran Marković, an effective portrait is drawn of a virile and handsome young man, Branko, whose adolescent dependence on his family has stretched to the age of twenty-seven. His parents live a comfortable middle-class lifestyle in the suburbs of Belgrade, with the requisite new model car and *vikendica* (weekend home). Branko's consuming passion is racing in competition with his souped-up Fiat. As the film opens, he is preparing for an all-important race on Saturday, which, if he wins, will propel him into a higher class and a career in speed-car racing. Branko effects a lifestyle to match his ambitions. He is another Martin Floyd, the race driver celebrated in the rock song which plays on the film's soundtrack: "Floyd, Floyd—he is wise, courageous, and drives like mad." Branko's propensity to "drive like mad" is not confined to the race track but also finds its expression on the city streets of Belgrade and the suburbs, creating some of the more amusing visual gags in the film.

Branko is out of work, with no other ambition than racing and no money to put his car into peak condition for the race. The film details his desperate contrivances to borrow money and secure backing from several sleazy race track speculators and a homosexual disco owner, and to defy the self-managed racing club that wants to back a driver with a more dependable car.

A complex social net is rapidly closing in on Branko. His girlfriend, Šilja— also from a well-off and well-connected middle-class family—is pregnant, and the families are forging a pact to force a wedding, which Branko disdains. He also has run out of excuses to postpone his compulsory military service, and the military board is closing in. Fortunately, his father has a *veza* with the military service, Branko's Uncle Kade, who has managed to stay Branko's military service for several years. In the eventful week covered in the film, Branko secures another brief postponement by substituting for his own a urine sample from a friend, Sime, who has a serious kidney ailment. Branko also pretends to be interested in pursuing a career in film by auditioning at the Academy for Theater, Film, Radio, and Television in Belgrade. His knowledge and talents in that field are minimal. In one scene he goes with two fellow aspirants to a film screening of Eisenstein's classic *Battleship Potemkin*. Branko shouts to the projectionist to turn up the sound, apparently unaware that the film is from the silent era.

At the end of Branko's hectic week, which began on a Monday morning, he suffers a series of defeats. He loses the race on Saturday. He is forced to marry Šilja on Sunday. He gets on the train for military camp the next morning.

One of the most effective scenes of the film is of the Saturday race on a mud-splattered track. Driving with balding tires and a patched-up rear-end differential, Branko shows genuine skill, daring, and courage as he pushes his car to the limit. When he is miraculously in sight of crossing the finish line first, however, his car stalls. Another car crashes into the rear and propels Branko over the

Victory in view. *National Class up to 785 cm (Nacionalna klasa do 785 cm).*

Defeat. *National Class up to 785 cm (Nacionalna klasa do 785 cm).*

finish line—a mode of locomotion disqualified by the judges. A poignant shot shows the mud-splattered figure of Branko sitting on the track beside his damaged car, a figure of abject defeat.

A more serious tone is captured in the final sequence of the film. Branko rises from his joyless marriage bed, situated in a cozy little bungalow next to his parents' house, to report to the train station. He passes by the forlorn rows of empty bottles on the tables used the day before for his wedding celebration. There is no one at the train station but his gentle and loyal friend Sime, whose bad kidneys had, in the end, not spared Branko from military service. Branko gives Sime the keys to his most prized possession, the Fiat—a gesture which might ambiguously be interpreted as either resigning himself to defeat and giving up that part of his life, or putting his future into the safekeeping of a true and good friend. Sime gives Branko some oranges to eat on the train. On the train, Branko is alone, solemnly eating an orange. The rock tune "Floyd, Floyd" ironically plays on the soundtrack as the film ends. While this ending is not as stark and pessimistic as those of many *new film* directors, it nonetheless strikes a critical note of lingering ambiguity. It is susceptible to the conservative interpretation offered by Uncle Kade that the military service will make a man out of Branko and teach him to assume real responsibilities. It may be seen also as the defeat of a dream which Branko seemed to have the talent and courage to fulfill, and as an entrapment in falsely imposed and empty social constraints and middle-class values—what the earlier radicals would have called becoming a bona fide member of the Red Bourgeoisie.

Mismanaged Self-Management

Several films of the new generation of Yugoslav directors dramatically explore the dynamic of individual initiative, originality, and ambition playing itself against the intricate surfaces of overlapping and complex self-management institutional and social structures. Two of the most interesting and sophisticated of these films are *Bravo Maestro* (1978), directed by Rajko Grlić, which provides a fascinating portrait of an ambitious young composer who learns how to manipulate the musical establishment to advance his career, and *Breakdown* (*Kvar*, 1979), directed by Miloš Radivojević, which imaginatively illuminates the struggles of a young journalist to maintain his integrity and his sanity against editorial manipulation and a compromised personal life.

Bravo Maestro tells the story of a handsome and charismatic young composer, Vitomir Bezjak, who begins the film as an impoverished and struggling musician living in a cheap and decrepit room and sharing primitive bathroom facilities with several other young musician friends. His first major attempt to gain recog-

Vitomir as a struggling student. *Bravo Maestro.*

nition, with an original composition, "To the Glory of the Sun," fails even to be selected for jury competition.

Vito's fortunes change, however, when he answers a newspaper advertisement and secures a position as a private piano teacher for a family living in a large estate on the provincial outskirts of Zagreb. The mansion was built by a wealthy Jewish merchant in the 1900s and was lived in by Ustashis during the war. Its present owner, Budić, has illegally amassed a sizeable fortune by manipulating foreign currencies. Budić has powerful party connections and wide influence in the musical world. Vito charms his way into the inner circle of the family, and Budić decides to sponsor his musical career. He secures a position for Vito as a choir director, begins a publicity campaign touting him as a fresh and promising young composer, and secures lecture engagements at prestigious conferences of musicians. Budić is later arrested and sent to serve a brief sentence in jail. Vito, however, has learned his lessons well and continues to manipulate the forward progress of his career, always keeping in mind Budić's repetition of an old Dalmatian saying, "If you want to harvest honey, don't batter the beehives."

Pressure begins to mount for Vito to complete a major composition to justify the mystique and puffery which have enlarged his career and reputation. Mired now in the sweet life and political and press manipulations, Vito has lost his creative drive, and his once-radical and -fresh composition "To the Glory of the Sun" is expanded into a hackneyed orchestral and choral composition glorifying national themes. The freshest motif of the piece is plagiarized from an unpublished original composition entrusted to him by his old student friend Stanko. In rehearsal, Stanko, who now occupies a chair for violin in the Zagreb Opera orchestra, immediately recognizes the theft and threatens to expose Vito. Powerful friends of Vito succeed in manipulating the workers' council of musicians into silencing Stanko and clearing the piece for performance.

Vito is by now a ruined personality and drinking heavily. At the end of the premiere performance of "To the Glory of the Sun," he is called onstage to face the enthusiastic applause of the glittering opening-night audience in the ornate auditorium of Zagreb's opera house. At this crowning moment of success, he recognizes the empty shell he has become and stands numb and transfixed before the audience. A lone mocking whistle comes from Stanko, who knows the ruin that has overcome the soul and creative spirit of his once-talented friend, and the film ends.

Grlić's film comments critically and sharply on the ways in which the outward forms of self-management socialism can be subverted and circumvented by astute manipulation and by skillful employment of important connections and personal influence. When Vito's composition is initially rejected for competition, he goes to the chairman of the jury selection committee and bitterly denounces the old-boy network that inhibits entry by talented young musicians. The chair-

Defeat in triumph. *Bravo Maestro.*

man freely acknowledges that Vito is lacking proper connections (*nema veze*), that older and more established composers "must be taken care of," and that his piece, though musically excellent and original, is "not in harmony with social objectives."

While the film takes a critical stance against manipulative cultural politics, it balances this critique against the possibility of pursuing a professional musical career with integrity. Vito's friend Stanko represents the counterpoint to his friend's high-rolling manipulations of the system. Stanko perseveres through poverty and temporary musical employment to achieve a respectable and much-sought-after chair in a professional orchestra. His integrity remains intact, and he "makes it" in the system.

The film *Breakdown*, directed by Miloš Radivojević, captures the moment in a young television journalist's life when he is about to crack under the strain of maintaining a false and alienated social and professional life. As a journalist, Saša is ambitious to use television film as a means of probing beneath surface occurrences and "fluff" interviews to illuminate the deeper problems and contradictions of society. His ambitions are thwarted by the chief editor, who holds his work in the iron grip of censorship softened by the velvet glove of smoothly articulated but empty socialist jargon about "collective responsibility," and who skillfully manipulates self-management meetings to exert his own will.

Saša's personal life is also at the breaking point. His married life is one of convenience, which brings comfort without the rewards of genuine intimacy and sharing. He and his pretty wife live in the bottom half of a gracious, white-columned home in the suburbs of Belgrade, with his father-in-law occupying the top half. Saša's father-in-law is well connected and prosperous and attempts to exercise a benevolent despotism over Saša's life and career.

The emptiness and underlying tension of Saša's marriage are imaginatively captured in the opening sequence of the film. *Breakdown* opens with a quiet shot of a window viewed from inside a darkened bedroom, with the white curtains fluttering against the breeze and framed against the grey half-light of early dawn. Saša's wife stirs and goes softly to the window. She is pensive and restless. The television set is turned on without picture or sound. Restlessly she returns to the large double bed where Saša is sleeping. She tries to interest him in sex. He feigns tiredness and remains passive. She removes her nightgown and attempts to tease him into arousal without success. She leaves the bed and goes to the bathroom. The sound of the clock's ticking is accentuated on the soundtrack. Saša goes to the bathroom and makes a perfunctory sexual advance, which is firmly rejected by his wife. He inspects his penis, and the camera reveals a sore at its tip. He shows his wife this troublesome eruption.

The next shot shows the two of them coming out of the front door of their house. Saša's father-in-law is on the balcony and offers some unsolicited advice to Saša about his future. They drive into the city in silence as the titles of the film are superimposed.

The sore on Saša's penis is diagnosed as herpes, with a possible psychosomatic origin, and a preliminary psychiatric examination is conducted. As the film progresses, it is increasingly obvious that the "corruption" of Saša's intimate sexual life is mirrored, reflected, and conjoined with the "corruption" and compromise which he daily must make as a journalist.

Increasingly teetering on the edge of breakdown, Saša takes a few days away from his job and marriage to find refuge in a mountain retreat. He has a brief affair with an older woman, which restores his sense of potency and "cures" the mentally induced eruption on his penis but does not solve his underlying problem.

In the last sequences of the film, Saša and his wife circle each other in the garden of their home; they painfully face the "lie" that their marriage has become and break it off. Saša also resigns his position as a journalist and severs compromising relations with his coworkers.

The final scene of the film is poignantly and chillingly ambiguous. Saša is shown as a lone passenger in the front of a tramcar, leaning on the hand rail. There is a series of rapid closeups of his back, with the foreground defocused. He slumps on the hand rail, and his head seems to retreat into his body as the film ends.

Saša's brief affair. *Breakdown* (*Kvar*).

The wordless conclusion of the film may signify that the threatened mental collapse or "breakdown" of Saša has finally occurred, on a lonely tram with its destination unknown. It may also signify the possibility that by redeeming his integrity, Saša can now look into himself and find the strength to begin again. *Breakdown* was highly praised by foreign critics and, unlike Radivojević's earlier, more experimental and abstract films,[9] was a domestic success at the box office.

On the Fringes of Society

While *new film* directors often took a bottom-up or outside-in view of the social order by choosing their protagonists from among the alienated, disaffected, violent, pathological dropouts of society, the recent vanguard of Yugoslav directors seldom explores society's fringes. A notable and interesting exception to this tendency is the internationally acclaimed film *The Dog Who Loved Trains* (*Pas koji je voleo vozove*, 1978), directed by Goran Paskaljević. The film centers on three protagonists: a sensitive young man in his late teens or early twenties, called "boy" or "little one," who has just been released from an orphanage with a few personal possessions, including a motorcycle with sidecar; a hard-bitten but attractive escaped female prisoner, Mika; and a former film stuntman, who entertains small-town provincials with a rodeo show and horse tricks.

The film begins with a following shot of the back of a train, which is transporting female prisoners. A male guard is standing on the back of the last car, mopping sweat from his brow. Inside the train car are a group of female prisoners and a female prison guard, who are also suffering from the heat. A hefty prisoner unbuttons her loose prison blouse and crudely and defiantly cups her large breasts to the open air. The female guard takes a dim view of this display, which is soon followed by all the other prisoners seeking similar relief. The male guard comes into the car to help restore order, and in the confusion, Mika and another prisoner jump off the train.

Mika barely makes good her escape by pushing her fellow prisoner in the path of the pursuing guards; she makes her way into a small mining town, swipes

"Boy" joins the rodeo stunt man and Mika. *The Dog Who Loved Trains* (*Pas koji je voleo vozove*).

some clothes from a clothesline, and hitches a ride in the truck of the rodeo stunt man. He offers her a job as his assistant, and their new partnership is sealed by making love.

In the meantime, the "boy" is making his odyssey to various train stations, looking for his lost dog, who loves to hop trains. His father had been a train station attendant before his early death and had taught both his son and his dog the art of hopping trains. The boy was separated from his dog at the orphanage, but he is convinced that his old pet is still traveling the rails. He arrives in a small town, decides to join the rodeo stunt man as an assistant, and meets Mika for the first time.

The film imaginatively captures the small-town atmosphere and hokum of this motley troupe of entertainers and deals sensitively with the growing relationship between the innocent and loving young man and the hardened female criminal Mika. She adopts a rough mothering attitude toward him, shampooing his hair and admonishing him to stay clean. The lonely young man develops a kind of puppy-dog loyalty and devotion to her.

The split-up with the rodeo stunt man occurs when the boy discovers that he plans to abandon Mika at a cheap roadside motel because the police are beginning to close in. He warns Mika of this design, and, while the stunt man is taking a shower in preparation for bedding Mika down for the last time, she takes his money, escapes out the window, and rides off with the boy.

The "little one" takes Mika to a rather shabby sleeping room, where she introduces him to the pleasures of sex. Afterwards she persuades him to take her to Belgrade. In Belgrade she goes to the cheap apartment of her parents to get a wig and some clothes. Her father threatens to turn her in to the police for disgracing the family. Her principal objective is to find her old partner in crime, Žule, who presumably has kept money for her earned in illegal smuggling and drugs. She also wants Žule to forge a passport that will permit her to go to Paris—a lifelong dream. Žule, who is recovering from a gunshot wound, promises to help Mika, but when she returns for the passport, two of his rough-looking assistants savagely beat and rape her.

Mika is in complete despair and is convinced that the "little one" is a burden and a jinx. He has waited loyally for Mika's return and awkwardly tries to offer his sympathetic help and support after her brutal beating and rape. He is now without his motorcycle and sidecar, which were smashed and burned by the stunt man—who adopted this particular mode of vengeance because he did not want to "dirty [his] hands" by punishing Mika.

The boy and Mika hop a train heading back to the small town where he has a sleeping room. On the way back, Mika slips off the train at a rail station and hops another train heading for the border and eventually to Paris. The boy runs after her, collides with an iron post, and bloodies his face just as Mika successfully

Boy "performs" in the rodeo act—a foreshadowing of his later victimization.
The Dog Who Loved Trains (*Pas koji je voleo vozove*).

catches the departing train. Looking back, Mika sees the forlorn figure of her
loyal friend growing smaller as the train accelerates. Her tough facade cracks; she
cries "Little one" and buries her face in her hands. A final irony is introduced
when the long-sought-after "dog who loves trains" nudges its way into the freight
car where Mika is seated. The last shot of the film, as in Paskaljević's earlier
work, *Beach Guard in Winter*, is a reverse-angle shot from the back of the train,
showing a long stretch of empty tracks receding in the distance as the film ends.
In this film, Paskaljević explores the distaff side of the social order, exposes the
sometimes rough and brutal edges of contemporary reality, and does so within
the context of imaginative cinematography and a dramatically interesting narrative structure.

Other Reflections

Enhancing the resurgence of an artistically and socially more relevant era of
Yugoslav filmmaking are several films which do not fall easily into any overall

Between two loves. *Something In-Between* (*Nešto između*).

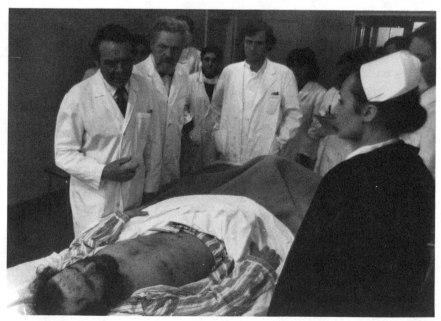

Victim of the smallpox epidemic. *Variola Vera*.

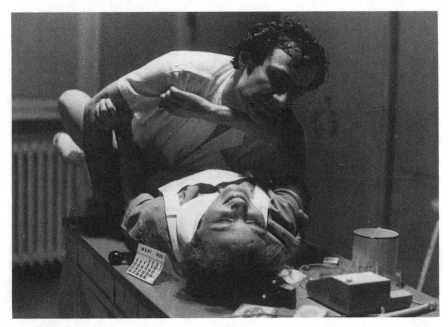

Respite. *Variola Vera*.

thematic or substantive category. Among the most important of these are *Special Education* (*Specijalno vaspitanje*, 1977), directed by Goran Marković, which depicts the efforts of an unorthodox and maverick counselor in a home for juvenile delinquents to break through the wall of silence erected by a sensitive and troubled youth; *Days on Earth Are Flowing By* (*Zemaljski dani teku*, 1979) and *Special Treatment* (*Posebni tretman*, 1980), directed by Goran Paskaljević, which deal respectively with institutional approaches to caring for the aged and the treatment of alcoholics; *Don't Lean Out of the Window* (*Ne naginji se van*, 1977), directed by Bogdan Žižić, which is a sensitive dramatization of the cultural and psychological costs of being a Yugoslav *Gastarbeiter* ("guest worker") in West Germany; and *The Scent of Wild Flowers* (*Miris poljskog cveća*, 1978), directed by Srđan Karanović and winner of the coveted critics' prize (FIPRESCI) at Cannes. This film provides a cinematically complex and ironic portrayal of a middle-aged, world-famous theater actor, who attempts to escape from a life of increasing sterility only to discover that his pursuit of the "scent of wild flowers" is the subject of unending television publicity and of a documentary film. In the end, his "new life" is as fully scripted as the old, and there is no further avenue of escape.

At the time this book is being written, the most significant current film created by a member of the new generation of Yugoslav film directors is *Something In-Between* (*Nešto između*, 1983), directed by Srđan Karanović. It is an engaging and complex portrayal of a young American female journalist in Yugoslavia, who finds herself caught "in-between" her love for two Yugoslav men. At a deeper level, the film explores the ambivalent posture of Yugoslavia, herself trapped "in-between" the political tensions of East and West and the cultural and economic collisions of North and South. Karanović was awarded first prize for best direction at the Pula festival in 1983. The film was highly praised at Cannes, won the top prize at the fourth International Film Festival at Valencia, Spain, and was invited to participate in several major international festivals in 1984. Goran Marković's talent for sharp social satire on contemporary themes is strongly confirmed in his recent film *Variola Vera* (1982), which depicts personal venality and corruption in the medical and public health professions when a virulent outbreak occurs of a rare and fatal strain of smallpox with the medical name "Variola Vera." Marković, who both wrote and directed the film, was awarded first prize for best director and best screenplay at the 1982 Valencia film festival. Miloš Radivojević creates an unusual and skillfully evoked cinematic ambience in his film *Living Like the Rest of Us* (*Živeti kao sav normalan svet*, 1982), in which a talented and idealistic music student from the provinces is progressively disillusioned by the subtle politics and corrupt lifestyles which he finds in the professional conservatory of music in Belgrade.

Among the more than twenty young Yugoslav film directors who made their debut feature films in the eighties, two have achieved widespread critical and popular success. Slobodan Šijan (b. 1946) won the coveted Georges Sadoul award for best debut film by a foreign director in 1981 with his film *Who's That Singing Over There* (*Ko to tamo peva*, 1980), an inventive and humorous portrayal of a group of provincials making their way to Belgrade in a rickety bus, unaware of the tragedy that awaits them on that fatal day, Sunday, 6 April 1941, when Nazi Germany launched its savage bombing attack on Belgrade under the code name "Operation Punishment." All the passengers of the bus are killed in the bombing except for two Gypsy singers, who had previously been verbally abused and beaten by the other passengers and who, at the end of the film, are standing in the rubble and singing of the terrors to come. Another young director, Emir Kusturica (b. 1954), captured the Golden Lion for best first film at the 1981 Venice film festival. His film *Do You Remember Dolly Bell* (*Sjećaš li se Dolly Bell*) is a skillful portrait of a sixteen-year-old boy, Dino Zolje, who lives with his poor family on the outskirts of Sarajevo, and whose painful process of growing into young manhood is poignantly assisted by a tender sexual liaison with a young prostitute, Dolly Bell.

It is too early to assess whether the cinematic promise of Yugoslavia's recently touted *new wave* or *new Yugoslav cinema* will be sustained through the eighties.

Cultural freedom, which steadily expanded in Yugoslavia during the late seventies and seems to have been further enlarged since Tito's death in May 1980, provides a favorable atmosphere for continued cinematic and thematic experimentation. Levels of feature film production have remained high despite very serious economic problems, creating healthy opportunities for new and relatively untried directors and other film artists to express themselves. As in previous periods, however, liberated cinematic tendencies in Yugoslavia (as elsewhere) exist at the thin razor's edge of a much larger politically conformist and commercially oriented cinema.

Conclusion

The path which Yugoslav feature film production has taken from the end of the Second World War to the present has been a complex one, with many fascinating bends and turns. Emerging from the ashes of a devastating war, and with practically no infrastructure or filmic traditions, a unique national cinema has been forged which defies easy description. Its most enduring and distinctive characteristic is the profound social and political commitment which has been made, and repeatedly reconfirmed, to sustain an independent, indigenous film industry capable of expressing the remarkable cultural diversity and languages of Yugoslavia's five nations and more than twenty nationalities and ethnic minorities. In a relatively small country of approximately twenty-two million people, sophisticated structures for film production, distribution, and theatrical showing have evolved in all six republics and the two autonomous regions of Vojvodina and Kosovo. There is scarcely a geographic area, however remote, or an ethnic group, however small, that has not been the subject of filmic portrayal and imagistic confirmation. Complex structures have likewise been introduced to ensure the availability of self-managed social resources and finances to balance and coordinate the overall federal development of film production, distribution, and foreign trade and to forge national unity of purpose from diversity of means and aspirations.

The Yugoslav film industry has also developed within the context of a unique and constantly redefined blend of socialist-determined market incentives and a complex multitiered and sometimes overlapping self-management organizational structure, which seek to prescribe the broad social roles and "collective responsibilities" of film artists. As a result, Yugoslav cinema often suffers from contradictory pressures and ideological limitations imposed, on the one hand, by relying on box office returns to define success (as in the commercial cinema of the West) and, on the other, by the imposition of sociopolitical definitions and restrictions on artistic expression (as in the centralized, bureaucratically managed film systems in Eastern Europe and the Soviet Union). At times, it appears that Yugoslavia has managed to build a system which suffers from the worst as well as the best features of cinema systems in both the East and the West.

What redeems and infuses this complex system with life and vitality, of course, are the creative efforts, ambitions, and personal dynamics of a sophisticated, sometimes quarrelsome and articulate film community of artists, critics, and technical workers, who often chafe against the boundaries of the allowable and produce works of enduring artistic and sociocultural interest. It is a remarkable tribute to a relatively small film industry that there has been scarcely a period since the end of the Second World War when there have not been some films produced which reflect intelligently, critically, and imaginatively upon Yugoslavia's dramatic past and upon the multidimensionality of her evolving present.

NOTES

Introduction

1. Dennison Rusinow, *The Yugoslav Experiment, 1948–1974*, p. vii.
2. Gertrude Joch Robinson, *Tito's Maverick Media*, pp. 13, 229.
3. Mira Liehm and Antonín J. Liehm, *The Most Important Art*.
4. See also Petar Volk, *Svedočenje: Hronika jugoslovenskog filma, 1896–1945* and *Svedočenje: Hronika jugoslovenskog filma, 1945–1970*.
5. Ronald Holloway, "Yugoslavia," pp. 329–35
6. The use of the term *film culture* for the moment begs the question whether there is a *national* Yugoslav film culture or one composed of distinctive culture(s) representing each of the five major nationalities: Serbs, Croats, Slovenians, Montenegrins, and Macedonians. Polemics and debates on this question within the Yugoslav film community are discussed later.
7. Aleksandar Petrović, *Novi film*.
8. Slobodan Novaković, *Vreme otvaranja*.

1. Establishment and Evolution of a National Cinema

1. Mira Liehm and Antonín J. Liehm, *The Most Important Art*, p. 20.
2. Dejan Kosanović; "Razvoj filmske proizvodnje u Jugoslaviji," pp. 10–12.
3. Liehm and Liehm, p. 20.
4. It is estimated that, at the end of the war, approximately two-thirds of the cinema houses in Yugoslavia were damaged and the projection equipment removed or destroyed. M. L., "Nekoliko problema u vezi sa kinofikacijom naše zemlje," *Film*, December 1946, p. 26.
5. Bogdan Denis Denitch, *The Legitimation of a Revolution*, p. 39.
6. Dennison Rusinow, *The Yugoslav Experiment, 1948–1974*, p. 19.
7. Ibid.
8. The most accurate estimate of the number of documentary and film journals (newsreels) produced during the period from 1945 to 1950 is provided by the Institut za film in Belgrade: 542 documentary films, 253 newsreels. "Jugoslovenska kinematografija u brojkama od 1944."
9. Kosanović, p. 17.
10. Ibid., pp 18–19.
11. Ibid., p. 19.
12. Petar Volk, *Svedočenje: Hronika jugoslovenskog filma, 1945–1970*, p. 8. The first Slovenian feature film was directed by France Štiglic, *On Their Own Ground (Na svojoj zemlji)*, and was produced by Triglav film in 1948. Vardar film in Skopje produced the first Macedonian feature film, *Frosina*, in 1952, and Bosna film in Sarajevo produced its first feature film, *Major Bauk*, in 1951. The first Montenegrin feature film was not produced until 1956: *Cursed Money (Zle pare)*, directed by Velimir Stojanović and produced by Lovćen film in Budva.
13. Jakša Petrić, "Opšti osvrt na naše rezultate i slabosti," p. 19.

173

14. Ibid.
15. Ibid.
16. Kosanović, p. 22.
17. By the end of 1946, the new Tito-led government had achieved impressive results in recovery: approximately ninety percent of the prewar rail network was back in operation, industrial production was above 1939 levels, and agricultural levels were returned to the 1933 level. Rusinow, p. 19.
18. Petrić, pp. 22–23.
19. Ibid., pp. 23–24.
20. Ibid., p. 26.
21. Ibid., p. 25.
22. As previously indicated, it was not until 1956 that Montenegrin film facilities were sufficiently developed to enter into the area of feature film production.
23. Kosanović, p. 22.
24. Herbert Eagle, personal correspondence, 25 May 1981.
25. See, for example, Sveta Lukić, *Contemporary Yugoslav Literature*, p. 12, and Liehm and Liehm, pp. 124–25.
26. Aleksandar Vučo, "Naša mlada filmska proizvodnja," p. 4.
27. Ibid.
28. Vučo, p. 3.
29. Ibid., pp. 4–5.
30. Ibid., p. 5.
31. See, for example, "Rezolucija protiv klevetničke kampanje protiv FNRJ," pp. 1–2.
32. Aleksandar Vučo, "Velikoruski šovinizam u sovjetskom filmu," p. 15.
23. Ibid., pp. 16–20.
34. ". . . da se okanimo 'ćoravog posla.'" Vicko Raspor, "Problemi naše filmske umjetnosti i zadaci saveza filmskih radnika Jugoslavije," p. 2.
35. Ibid., p. 3.
36. Ibid.
37. Raspor, p. 6.
38. Ibid., pp. 6–14.
39. Literature dealing with the background and progress of the Partisan war is immense. Some of the more helpful sources are Vladimir Dedijer, *Tito*; Robert Lee Wolff, *The Balkans in Our Time*; Jozo Tomasevich, *War and Revolution in Yugoslavia: The Chetniks*; and Charles Jelavich and Barbara Jelavich, eds., *The Balkans in Transition*. Partisan historians divide the war into seven major offensives. For a brief but clear discussion of these major battles of the war, see Fitzroy Maclean, *Tito*, pp. 60–87.
40. Rusinow, p. 5.
41. Ibid., pp. 2–3.
42. Ibid., p. 5.
43. Ibid., p. 6.
44. Volk, p. 12.
45. Jaskša Petrić, "Još više približiti film narodnim masama," p. 13.
46. *Borba*, 15 May 1947.
47. "*Slavica*—naš prvi umetnički film," pp. 11–19.
48. Teodor Balk, "Problemi našeg filma i film naših problema," pp. 5–7.
49. Jovan Popović, "Iskustva iz šest naših prvih umetničkih filmova i pouke za dalji rad," pp. 3–18.
50. See, for example, contemporary critical reviews by I. Mihovilović, *Kulturni radnik*, nos. 1–2, 1950; H. Grun, *Nova obzorja*, no. 1, 1949; M. Hercog, *Obzornik*, no. 11, 1948; G. Milin, *Borba*, 7 April 1949; and S. Simatović, *Izvor*, no. 5, 1949.
51. Denitch, pp. 31–32.
52. Liehm and Liehm, pp. 76–157.

53. *Život je nas*, directed by Gustav Gavrin, 1948; *Priča o fabrici*, directed by Vladimir Pogačić, 1949; *Jezero*, directed by Radivoje-Lola Djukić, 1950.
54. Maclean, p. 87.

2. Decentralization and Breaking the Mold, 1951–1960.

1. In 1948–1949, Tito's innermost circle of leaders comprised his eight colleagues on the Politburo: Aleksandar Ranković, minister of the interior; Moša Pijade, first vice-president of the Presidium of the National Assembly and chairman of its legal commission; Milovan Djilas, minister of propaganda; Blagoje Nešković, a deputy prime minister and chairman of the State Control Commission; Boris Kidrič, chairman of the State Planning Commission; Franc Leskošek, minister of heavy industry; Ivan Gošnjak, deputy minister of war; and Edvard Kardelj, foreign minister and a deputy prime minister. The most active of these in shaping the new ideological line were Kidrič, Kardelj, and Djilas.
2. Dennison Rusinow, *The Yugoslav Experiment, 1948–1974*, p. 58.
3. Ibid., p. 55.
4. Ibid., p. 58.
5. Gertrude Joch Robinson, *Tito's Maverick Media*, p. 27.
6. Rusinow, p. 59.
7. Bogdan Denis Denitch, *The Legitimation of a Revolution*, p. 154.
8. Slobodan Stanković, *The End of the Tito Era*, pp. 3–5.
9. Dejan Kosanović, "Razvoj filmske proizvodnje u Jugoslaviji," pp. 23–24.
10. Mira Liehm and Antonín J. Liehm, *The Most Important Art*, pp. 247–48.
11. "Jugoslovenska kinematografija u brojkama od 1944."
12. Dejan Kosanović, *Dvadeset godina jugoslovenskog filma, 1945–1965*, p. 84. The tabular summary of film imports to Yugoslavia from the end of 1944 through 1964 reveals that in the first five years after the war, 220 films were imported from the USSR, with only 30 imported from the United States. In the ten-year period from 1951 through 1960, however, imports from the U.S. rose to 579, while only 97 were imported from the USSR.
13. Kosanović, "Razvoj filmske," p. 29.
14. Ibid., p. 30.
15. Sveta Lukić, *Contemporary Yugoslav Literature*, p. 72.
16. Gerson S. Sher, *Praxis*, pp. 23–24.
17. Lukić, pp. 104–105.
18. The Third Plenum of the Central Committee, at which Djilas was arraigned and condemned, was, in unprecedented fashion, broadcast live by radio throughout Yugoslavia.
19. Sher, p. 24.
20. Ranko Munitić, *Jugoslavenski filmski slučaj*, p. 129.
21. Ibid., p. 95.
22. In Yugoslavia, a film which attracts a million or more viewers is considered a substantial box office success. *Father Ćira and Father Spira* attracted 1,621,487 viewers, and Soja Jovanović's second film, *Dr.*, attracted 1,113,856 viewers. See Kosanović, *Dvadeset godina*, p. 80.
23. Lukić, pp. 72–73.
24. For an interesting contemporary analysis of the film, see Dušan Stojanović, *Velika avantura filma*, pp. 53–56.
25. Between making these two influential films, Bulajić directed a comparatively less successful neorealist film adapted from a script by Zavattini and called simply *A War* (*Rat*, 1960).
26. His first epic of the Partisan war, *Kozara* (1962), broke all domestic box office records up to that time, attracting 3,393,632 viewers as well as garnering several interna-

tional awards. His next major film on the Partisan war, *Battle on the River Neretva* (*Bitka na Neretvi*, 1969), was also a huge success. Kosanović, *Dvadeset godina*, p. 80.

27. For a knowledgeable and sensitive description of the leading artists and films associated with Zagreb film, see Ronald Holloway's delightfully written and illustrated book *Z Is for Zagreb*.

28. Liehm and Liehm, p. 412.

29. I am indebted to Dušan Stojanović for recalling some of the leading personalities and films associated with the Belgrade kino klub activities of the fifties. Dušan Stojanović, personal correspondence, 16 May 1982.

30. Liehm and Liehm, p. 413.

3. *New Film* and Republican Ascendancy, 1961–1972

1. Dejan Kosanović, "Razvoj filmske proizvodnje u Jugoslaviji," pp. 31–36.

2. Slobodan Novaković, "Različiti vidici sa iste obale," pp. 1–12; Ranko Munitić, "O vidicima i o obalama," pp. 1–8; Rudolf Sremec, "Film socijalističke Jugoslavije." pp. 1–6.

3. Bogdan Tirnanić, "Nacionalne kinematografije, da ili ne," p. 27 (italics mine).

4. Sveta Lukić, *Contemporary Yugoslav Literature*, p. 181. See also Dennison Rusinow, *The Yugoslav Experiment, 1948–1974*, pp. 224–25.

5. "Jugoslovenska kinematografija u brojkama."

6. Ibid.; 1964—18 films; 1965—19; 1966—18; 1972—20.

7. Kosanović, pp. 34–36.

8. "Jugoslovenska kinematografija u brojkama."

9. Ibid.

10. Gertrude Joch Robinson, *Tito's Maverick Media*, p. 49.

11. Kosanović, p. 33.

12. Dušan Stojanović, *Velika avantura filma*, p. 170.

13. Mira Liehm and Antonín J. Liehm, *The Most Important Art*, p. 429.

14. See, for example, Zoran Petrović, "Naš najfilmskiji film," and Slobodan Novaković, "Dvoje."

15. "Dva mišljenje o jednom filmu," *Književne novine*, 20 October 1961.

16. See, for example, *Vjesnik*, 24 June 1961; *Pobjeda*, 1 July 1961; *Student*, 7 July 1961; *Politika*, 25 November 1961; and *Nin*, 5 November 1961.

17. Okružni sud u Sarajevu, no. K-446/63. Sarajevo, August 13, 1963.

18. Aleksandar Petrović, *Novi film*, p. 175.

19. For an interesting contemporary discussion of the controversy surrounding this film and a review of the film, see Milutin Čolić, *Filmska kultura*, nos. 41–42, 1964, pp. 78–82.

20. Petrović, p. 122.

21. "Stenografske beleške sa sastanka sa filmskim radnicima-komunistima održanog," Komisija za ideološki rad CK SKJ, 14 December 1963.

22. Aleksandar Petrović, "Situacija jugoslovenskog modernog filma," *Delo*, no. 6, 1964; also in his *Novi film*, pp. 152–75.

23. Petrović, *Novi film*, p. 161.

24. Dušan Makavejev, "Kokan Rakonjac ili besciljni pogled kroz prozor," p. 18.

25. Liehm and Liehm, p. 417.

26. "Dvadeset godina jugoslavenskog filma," p. 71.

27. *Erotikon*, 1963, and *Maibritt, das Mädchen von den Inseln*, 1964.

28. For an excellent analysis of these events and the factors contributing to a tightening of the ideological climate, see Rusinow, pp. 232–307.

29. London *Times*, 21 January 1973.

30. For examples, see Lukić, pp. 182–84.

31. For a scholarly and detailed analysis of the issues and events which led to the dismissal of the eight members of the philosophy department of Belgrade University and the banning of *Praxis*, see Gerson Sher, *Praxis*, pp. 194–241.

32. Principally the film critic for *Politika*, Milutin Čolić, and Dragoslav Adamović. Čolić later made a strong attack on black film in the June 1970 issue of *Filmska kultura*; Milutin Čolić, "Crni film ili kriza autorskog filma," pp. 3–25.

33. There was no empirical evidence to support this argument, nor was there any to support equally plausible arguments that the overall drop in viewers for domestic film was caused by other factors. For a thoughtful summary of speculations pro and con on this issue, see Milan Ranković, *Društvena kritika u savremenom jugoslovenskom igranom filmu*, pp. 20–23.

34. Vladimir Jovičić, "Crni talas u našem filmu" (italics mine).

35. Predrag Vranicki, "On the Problem of Practice," p. 42.

36. Danko Grlić, "Practice and Dogma," p. 51.

37. Ibid, p. 52.

38. "Dvadeset godina jugoslavenskog filma," pp. 71–74.

39. Ibid., p. 72.

40. Živojin Pavlović, *Djavolji film*, pp. 232–34.

41. Čolić, pp. 7–10.

42. Ranković, pp. 23–29.

43. Rusinow, pp. 268–71.

44. Liehm and Liehm, pp. 302–305, and especially, Josef Škvorecký, *All the Bright Young Men and Women*.

45. See especially Alvah Bessie, *Inquisition in Eden* (1965), and Victor S. Navasky, *Naming Names* (1980).

46. A list of over four hundred books which have been banned in various local public libraries and school districts, compiled in the summer of 1982 by the American Booksellers' Association, includes among their legions such surprising entries as the *American Heritage Dictionary*, the *Koran*, the *Talmud*, and the *Living Bible*; world classics, including, among others, works by Pierre Beaumarchais (*Barber of Seville* and *Marriage of Figaro*), William Shakespeare (*King Lear, The Merchant of Venice, Tragedy of King Richard II*), Francis Bacon (*The Advancement of Learning*), and Dante Alighieri (*The Divine Comedy*); and a staggering host of school textbooks and works of modern fiction by domestic and foreign writers. See "A List of Books Some People Consider Dangerous," ed. by Mary Ann Tennenhouse and Jan De Deka, American Booksellers' Association, Summer 1982.

4. Confrontation with the Revolutionary Past

1. The name Zeka is possibly a play on the name of the biblical prophet Ezekiel.

2. See, for example, *Borba*, 5 December 1967; *Telegram*, no. 389, p. 13; and *Film novosti*, 1 December 1967.

3. *Gong novosti*, 8 December 1967.

4. See Milutin Čolić, "Čovek iz hrastove šume."

5. Conversation with Mića Popović, 4 April 1980.

6. Vrana is a nickname which means "crow."

7. Quoted in Wayne Vucinich, *Contemporary Yugoslavia*, p. 129. OZNA was later renamed UDBa (Uprava državne bezbednosti, State Security Administration).

8. Some of the excesses committed in purging real or suspected pro-Soviet Communists who opposed Tito's break with Stalin did not come fully to light until after Tito's death. The most recent public controversy in Yugoslavia focused on the Gulag-type concentration camp which Tito's government established in great secrecy on Goli otok (Naked Island), a barren and desolate island in the northern Adriatic. Thousands of al-

leged Stalinist sympathizers passed through the camp and were subjected to, among other things, a system in which prisoners were forced to torture and beat their fellow prisoners. The controversy was set off by the publication in March 1982 of a best-selling novel about Goli otok, *The Instant*, by Antonije Isaković, which is based on extensive interviews with former prisoners.

5. Contemporary Reality: Critical Visions

1. Also known by the English titles *Love Dossier* and *An Affair of the Heart*.

2. The original title of the film, *Skupljači perja*, means "Goosefeather gatherers."

3. Pavlović also collaborated with Mihić and Kozomara in one of his most important films, *Awakening of the Rats* (*Buđenje pacova*, 1967), which also deals with themes of disaffection and alienation, played out in an urban rather than a provincial environment (the slums of Belgrade). Dropouts from society are also portrayed in the internationally acclaimed film *The Crows* (*Vrane*, 1969), which marked the directorial debuts of the two screenwriters Mihić and Kozomara.

4. Ugo Tognazzi played the Master, Alain Cuny the Devil-Professor Woland, and Mimsy Farmer Margarita. Two veteran and well-known Yugoslav screen actors, Bata Živojinović and Pavle Vujisić, played respectively the Devil's assistants Koroviev and Azazello. Other talented Yugoslav actors played the parts of Berlioz, Rimsky, and Bobov.

5. *Nin*, 16 September 1979.

6. *Nin*, 28 October 1979. Those named were Puriša Đorđević, Sofija Mišić, Dragovan Jovanović, Aleksandar Aranđelović, Žika Mitrović, and Dejan Đurković. All but Sofia Mišić responded, along with the writer-translator Milan Čolić and a student, Miroslav Petković. *Nin*, 4, 11, and 18 November 1979 and 9 December 1979.

7. *Nin*, 9 December 1979.

8. These were later reissued in paperback editions.

9. Dušan Makavejev, *WR: Mysteries of the Organism*, p. 31.

10. Ibid., p. 130.

11. Ibid., p. 105.

12. Ibid., p. 127.

13. Ibid., p. 135.

14. Ibid., p. 136.

15. Ibid., pp. 139–40.

16. Ibid., p. 142.

17. Ibid., p. 144.

18. Ibid., p. 88.

19. Ibid., p. 95.

20. Ibid., p. 69.

21. Ibid., p. 76.

22. Ibid., p. 78.

23. Ibid., p. 65. Other slogans which arose out of the student demonstrations in 1968 were: "Into Tomorrow without Those Who Ruined Yesterday," "Let's Dismiss Incompetent Politicians," "Enough of Unemployment," "We Struggle for a Better Man, Not for a Better Dinar," "More Schools, Fewer Automobiles," "Free Information Media," "Down with Corruption," "Down with the Princes of Socialism," and "There Is No Socialism without Freedom, No Freedom without Socialism."

24. Ibid., p. 72.

25. The most complete set of documents detailing the official actions taken with regard to the film and the polemic which surrounded these actions was put together for internal use by Neoplanta film. See *Documentacija za internu upotrebu*, pp. 518–1009.

6. Accommodation and Resurgence

1. "Jugoslovenska kinematografija u brojkama."

2. Mira Liehm and Antonín J. Liehm, *The Most Important Art*, p. 420. Doder has observed that nothing much comes out of these official campaigns against illegally acquired wealth and that the "men who run the campaigns own expensive weekend homes, fancy cars and motorboats, and they would be hard put to explain how they acquired all that on their salaries." Dusko Doder, *The Yugoslavs*, p. 44.

3. Dejan Kosanović, "Razvoj filmske proizvodnje u Jugoslaviji," pp. 40–41.

4. *Kur pranvera vonohet* (*When Spring Is Late*), produced by Kosova film in Priština. It was followed by a second feature film, produced in 1980, *Gjurme te bardha* (*The White Trail*).

5. For example, Rajko Grlić has collaborated on the scripts for several films directed by Srđan Karanović. This role was reversed in the film *Bravo Maestro*, where Karanović collaborated on the script and Grlić directed the film. The talented young cinematographer Živko Zalar has also served as cameraman on several of the most important films directed by his fellow classmates from FAMU.

6. This scene is based on an actual historical incident.

7. In 1981, Zafranović returned to the theme of wartime occupation with his film *Fall of Italy* (*Pad Italije*), which also won first prize at the Pula festival. Released with the English title *Island Chronicle*.

8. There are also a number of Yugoslav professionals—physicians, dentists, architects, engineers, and others—who work and earn very good salaries in Western countries. See Doder, pp. 79–82.

9. Radivojević's first two feature films were highly original and abstract pieces which also dealt with themes of mental breakdown and insanity. The most severely experimental of his early films was *Without* (*Bez*, 1971), a full-length feature film without a word of dialogue.

SELECTED BIBLIOGRAPHY

BOOKS

Adizes, Ichak. *Industrial Democracy: Yugoslav Style.* New York: Free Press, 1971.

Andrew, J. Dudley. *The Major Film Theories.* New York: Oxford University Press, 1976.

Arnheim, Rudolf. *Film as Art.* Berkeley: University of California Press, 1957.

Auty, Phyllis. *Tito.* New York: McGraw-Hill, 1970.

Avakumovich, Ivan. *History of the Communist Party of Yugoslavia.* 2 vols. Aberdeen: Aberdeen University Press, 1964.

Balázs, Béla. *Theory of the Film.* Translated by Edith Bone. New York: Roy, 1953. Reprint. New York: Dover Books, 1970.

Banac, Ivo. *The National Question in Yugoslavia.* Ithaca: Cornell University Press, 1984.

Barton, Alan H.; Denitch, Bogdan; and Kadushin, Charles, eds. *Opinion Making Elites in Yugoslavia.* New York: Praeger Special Series, 1973.

Bass, George, and Marburg, Elizabeth, eds. *The Soviet-Yugoslav Controversy, 1948–1958: A Documentary Record.* New York: Prospect, 1959.

Bazin, André. *What Is Cinema?* 2 vols. Selected and translated by Hugh Gray. Berkeley: University of California Press, 1967; 1971.

Benes, Vaclav L.; Byrnes, Robert F.; and Spulber, Nicolas, eds. *The Second Soviet-Yugoslav Dispute: Full Text of Main Documents.* Bloomington: Indiana University Press, 1959.

Bessie, Alvah. *Inquisition in Eden.* New York: Macmillan Co., 1965.

Boglić, Mira, ed. *Almanac of Croatian Film, 1966–1970.* Translated by Vera Andrašsy and Lina Bernetić. Zagreb: Association of Film Workers of Croatia, 1971.

Brenk, France. *Aperçu de l'histoire du cinema yougoslave.* Ljubljana: Académie de l'art dramatique, 1961.

Broekmeyer, M. J., ed. *Yugoslav Workers' Self-Management.* Dordrecht-Holland: D. Reidel Publishing Company, 1970.

Bulgakov, Mikhail. *The Master and Margarita.* Translated by Michael Glenny. New York: Harper and Row, 1967.

Cameron, Ian et al. *Second Wave.* New York: Praeger, 1970.

Clissold, Stephen. *Djilas: The Progress of a Revolutionary.* New York: Universe Books, 1983.

Cohen, Leonard, and Warwick, Paul. *Political Cohesion in a Fragile Mosaic: The Yugoslav Experience.* Boulder, Colorado: Westview Press, 1983.

Cook, David A. *A History of Narrative Film.* New York: W. W. Norton, 1981.

Darby, H. C.; Seton-Watson, R. W.; Auty, Phyllis; Laffan, R. G. D.; and Clissold, Stephen. *A Short History of Yugoslavia.* Edited by Stephen Clissold. Cambridge: Cambridge University Press, 1968.

Deakin, F. W. D. *The Embattled Mountain.* London: Oxford University Press, 1971.

Dedijer, Vladimir. *The Battle Stalin Lost.* New York: Universal Library, 1972.

———. *Tito.* New York: Simon and Schuster, 1953.

Denitch, Bogdan Denis. *The Legitimation of a Revolution: The Yugoslav Case.* New Haven: Yale University Press, 1976.

Djilas, Milovan. *Conversations with Stalin*. New York: Praeger, 1958.
————. *The New Class*. New York: Praeger, 1957.
Doder, Dusko. *The Yugoslavs*. New York: Random House, 1978.
Dovzhenko, Alexander. *Alexander Dovzhenko: The Poet as Filmmaker*. Translated and edited by Marco Carynnk. Cambridge, Mass.: MIT Press, 1973.
Dragnich, Alex N. *The First Yugoslavia: Search for a Viable Political System*. Stanford: Hoover Institution Press, 1983.
Eisenstein, Sergei. *Film Form*. Translated and edited by Jay Leyda. New York: Harcourt Brace Jovanovich, 1969.
————. *The Film Sense*. Translated and edited by Jay Leyda. New York: Harcourt Brace Jovanovich, 1969.
Fisher, Jack. *Yugoslavia: A Multinational State*. New York: Chandler, 1966.
Giannetti, Louis. *Understanding Movies*. 2d ed. Englewood Cliffs, N.J.: Prentice Hall, 1976.
Graham, Peter. *The New Wave*. Garden City, N.Y.: Doubleday, 1968.
Hibbin, Nina. *Eastern Europe: An Illustrated Guide*. Screen Series. Cranbury, N.J.: A. S. Barnes, 1969.
Holloway, Ronald. *Z Is for Zagreb*. Cranbury, N.J.: A. S. Barnes, 1972.
Huntington, Samuel, and Moore, Clement H., eds. *Authoritarian Politics in Modern Society: The Dynamics of Established One-Party Systems*. New York: Basic Books, 1970.
Ilić, Momčilo, ed. *Filmografija jugoslovenskog filma, 1945–1965*. Belgrade: Institut za film, 1970.
————. *Filmografija jugoslovenskog filma, 1966–1970*. Belgrade: Institut za film, 1974.
————. *Godišnjak 1969: Kinematografija u Srbiji*. Belgrade: Institut za film, 1971. (Momčilo Ilić edited eight more of the annuals, with the last volume covering 1977 and published in 1979.)
Insdorf, Annette. *François Truffaut*. New York: William Morrow, 1979.
Ionescu, Ghita. *The Politics of the European Communist States*. New York: Praeger, 1967.
Jelavich, Charles, and Jelavich, Barbara, eds. *The Balkans in Transition: Essays on the Development of Balkan Life and Politics since the Eighteenth Century*. Berkeley: University of California Press, 1963.
Johnson, Ross. *Transformation of Communist Ideology: The Yugoslav Case, 1945–1953*. Cambridge, Mass.: MIT Press, 1972.
Kosanović, Dejan. *Dvadeset godina jugoslovenskog filma, 1945–1965*. Belgrade: Savez filmskih radnika Jugoslavije i Festival jugoslovenskog filma, 1966.
Kracauer, Siegfried. *Theory of Film: The Redemption of Physical Reality*. New York: Oxford University Press, 1960.
Kuleshov, Lev. *Kuleshov on Film*. Translated and edited by Ronald Levaco. Berkeley: University of California Press, 1975.
Kurzewski, Stanislaw. *Contemporary Polish Cinema*. London: Stephen Wischhusen, 1980.
Leprohon, Pierre. *The Italian Cinema*. New York: Praeger, 1972.
Liehm, Antonín J. *Closely Watched Films: The Czechoslovak Experience*. White Plains, N.Y.: International Arts and Sciences Press, 1974.
Liehm, Mira, and Liehm, Antonín J. *The Most Important Art: East European Film after 1945*. Berkeley: University of California Press, 1977.
Lindgren, Ernest. *The Art of the Film*. New York: Macmillan Co., 1948.
Lord, Albert, and Parry, Milman. *Serbo-Croatian Heroic Ballads*. Cambridge, Mass.: Harvard University Press, 1953.
Lukić, Sveta. *Contemporary Yugoslav Literature: A Socio-Political Approach*. Edited by Gertrude Joch Robinson and translated by Pola Triandis. Urbana: University of Illinois Press, 1972.

Maclean, Fitzroy. *The Heretic: The Life and Times of Josip Broz Tito*. New York: Harper and Bros., 1957.
————. *Tito*. New York: McGraw-Hill, 1980.
Makavejev, Dušan. *WR: Mysteries of the Organism*. New York: Avon Books, 1972.
Mast, Gerald, and Cohen, Marshall, eds. *Film Theory and Criticism*. New York: Oxford University Press, 1974. 2d ed., 1979.
Metz, Christian. *Film Language: A Semiotics of the Cinema*.Translated by Michael Taylor. New York: Oxford University Press, 1974.
Michalek, Boleslaw. *The Cinema of Andrzej Wajda*. Translated by Edward Rothert. Cranbury, N.J.: A. S. Barnes, 1973.
Monaco, James. *How to Read a Film*. New York: Oxford University Press, 1977.
————. *The New Wave: Truffaut, Godard, Chabrol, Rohmer, Rivette*. New York: Oxford University Press, 1976.
Moore, John H. *Growth with Self-Management: Yugoslav Industrialization, 1952–1975*. Stanford: Hoover Institution Press, 1980.
Munitić, Ranko. *Jugoslavenski filmski slučaj*. Split: Marjan film, 1980.
————. *Te slatke filmske laže*. Belgrade: Vuk Karadžić, 1977.
Navasky, Victor S. *Naming Names*. New York: Viking Press, 1980.
Nemeskürty, István. *Word and Image: History of the Hungarian Cinema*. Translated by Zsuzsanna Horn. Budapest: Corvian Press, 1968.
Novaković, Slobodan. *Dvadeset godina jugoslovenskog filma*. Belgrade: Festival jugoslovenskog filma, 1965.
————. *Dve decenije-dve generacije*. Belgrade: FEST 71, 1971.
————. *Vreme otvaranja: Ogledi i zapisi o novom filmu*. Novi Sad: Kulturni centar, 1970.
Obradović, Branislav, ed. *Filmografija jugoslovenskog igranog filma, 1945–1980*. Belgrade: Institut za film, 1981.
Parsons, Howard L., *Humanistic Philosophy in Contemporary Poland and Yugoslavia*. New York: American Institute for Marxist Studies, 1966.
Pavlović, Živojin. *Đavolji film*. Belgrade: Institut za film, 1969.
Petrić, Vladimir. *Razvoj filmskih vrsta*. Belgrade: Umetnička akademija u Beogradu, 1970.
Petrie, Graham. *History Must Answer to Man: The Contemporary Hungarian Cinema*. London: Tantivy Press, 1979.
Petrović, Aleksandar. *Novi film*. Belgrade: Institut za film, 1971.
Pudovkin, V. I. *Film Technique and Film Acting*. London, 1929. Reprint. New York: Grove Press, 1970.
Ranković, Milan. *Društvena kritika u savremenom jugoslovenskom igranom filmu*. Belgrade: Institut za film, 1970.
Robinson, Gertrude Joch. *Tito's Maverick Media: The Politics of Mass Communication in Yugoslavia*. Urbana: University of Illinois Press, 1977.
Roud, Richard. *Jean-Luc Godard*. Bloomington: Indiana University Press, 1969.
Rubenstein, Alvin Z. *Yugoslavia and the Nonaligned World*. Princeton: Princeton University Press, 1970.
Rusinow, Dennison. *The Crisis in Croatia*. New York: American University Field Staff, 1972.
————. *The Yugoslav Experiment, 1948–1974*. Berkeley and Los Angeles: University of California Press, 1977.
Schopflin, George, ed. *Censorship and Political Communication in Eastern Europe: A Collection of Documents*. New York: St. Martin's Press, 1983.
Sher, Gerson S. *Praxis: Marxist Criticism and Dissent in Socialist Yugoslavia*. Bloomington: Indiana University Press, 1977.
Sitney, P. Adams, ed. *The Avant-Garde Film: A Reader of Theory and Criticism*. New York: New York University Press, 1978.

Škvorecký, Josef. *All the Bright Young Men and Women: A Personal History of the Czech Cinema.* Toronto: Peter Martin Associates, 1971.
Stanković, Slobodan. *The End of the Tito Era: Yugoslavia's Dilemmas.* Stanford: Hoover Institution Press, 1981.
Stoil, Michael. *Cinema beyond the Danube: The Camera and Politics.* Metuchen, N.J.: Scarecrow Press, 1974.
Stojanović, Dušan. *Sistematizacija teorija filma u svetu i u nas.* Belgrade-Zagreb: Institut za film-Filmoteka 16, 1974.
————. *Velika avantura filma.* Belgrade, 1969.
Stojanović, Nikola, ed. *25 Godina bosansko-hercegovačke kinematografija, 1947–1972.* Sarajevo: Sineast, 1974.
Stojanović, Svetozar. *Between Ideals and Reality.* Oxford: Oxford University Press, 1973.
Supek, Rudi. *Humanistička inteligencija i politika.* Zagreb: Razlog, 1971.
Tomasevich, Jozo. *War and Revolution in Yugoslavia: The Chetniks.* Stanford: Stanford University Press, 1975.
Volk, Petar. *Moć krize.* Belgrade: Institut za film, 1972.
————. *Svedočenje: Hronika jugoslovenskog filma, 1896–1945.* Belgrade, 1973.
————. *Svedočenje: Hronika jugoslovenskog filma, 1945–1970.* Belgrade: NIP Književne novine, 1975.
Vucinich, Wayne S., ed. *Contemporary Yugoslavia: Twenty Years of Socialist Experiment.* Berkeley: University of California Press, 1969.
Whyte, Alistair. *New Cinema in Eastern Europe.* New York: E. P. Dutton, 1971.
Wolff, Robert Lee. *The Balkans in Our Time.* New York: Norton, 1956.
Wollen, Peter. *Signs and Meaning in the Cinema.* 2d ed. New York: Viking Press, 1972.
Zaninovich, M. George. *The Development of Socialist Yugoslavia.* Baltimore: Johns Hopkins Press, 1968.
Zavattini, Cesare. *Sequences from a Cinematic Life.* Translated by William Weaver. Englewood Cliffs, N.J.: Prentice-Hall, 1970.

ARTICLES, REPORTS, DOCUMENTS

Balk, Teodor. "Problemi našeg filma i film naših problema." *Film,* no. 2 (March 1947), pp. 5–7.
Binder, David. "A Return to Yugoslavia." *New York Times Magazine* (25 December 1983), pp. 20–24.
Bogdanovič, Milan. "Živjeće ovaj narod—kritički osvrt na naš drugi umetnićki film." *Film,* nos. 4–5 (January 1948), pp. 62–69.
Boglić, Mira. "Geografija u kinematografiji." *Filmska kultura,* no. 61 (June 1968), pp. 17–22.
————. "Između politike i šizofrenije." *Filmska kultura,* nos. 68–69 (December 1969), pp. 109–118.
Čolić, Milutin. "Čovek iz hrastove šume." *Filmska kultura,* nos. 41–42 (October 1964), pp. 78–82.
————. "Crni film ili kriza autorskog filma." *Filmska kultura,* no. 71 (June 1970), pp. 3–37.
Dokumentacija za internu upotrebu. Prepared by Svetozar Udovički. Neoplanta film, 1971. (Mimeo report of 1009 pages, which contains all important documents surrounding the controversies over Makavejev's film WR: *Mysteries of the Organism* and Žilnik's film *Early Works.*)
"Dokumenti iz preteklosti slovenskega filma." Belgrade: Jugoslovenska kinoteka, 1969.
"Dokumenti iz prošlosti kinematografije u Srbiji." Belgrade: Jugoslovenska kinoteka, 1969.
"Dokumenti o razvitku kinematografije u Hrvatskoj." Belgrade: Jugoslovenska kinoteka, 1969.

"Dvadeset godina jugoslavenskog filma: Razgovor u Puli." *Filmska kultura*, nos. 46–47
    (July 1965), pp. 61–124. (Report of a round-table discussion involving R. Sremec,
    A. Kostić, S. Stojanović, S. Novaković, M. Miloradović, D. Stojanović, H.
    Lisinski, A. Petrović, Z. Bogdanović, T. Tršar, M. Milošević, V. Bunjac,
    M. Vukos, P. Krelja, B. Tirnanić, A. Peterlić, S. Filomonović, M. Komatina,
    and V. Vučetić.)
"Festival of Yugoslav Feature Films in Pula." *Bulletin* (1965–1983—published in Serbo-
    Croatian, English, French, German, and Russian).
Finci, Eli. "Problemi naše filmske kritike." *Film*, nos. 1–2 (July 1949), pp. 50–58.
Goulding, Daniel J. "Significant Developments in Yugoslav Feature Film Production
    since the Second World War." Paper presented at the Midwest Slavic Conference,
    University of Illinois, Urbana, April 1981.
———. "Yugoslavian New Film and the Counteroffensive, 1961–1972." Paper pre-
    sented at the American Association for the Advancement of Slavic Studies Na-
    tional Convention, Kansas City, Mo., October 1983.
Grlić, Danko. "Practice and Dogma." *Praxis*, International Edition, no. 1 (1965),
    pp. 49–58.
Holloway, Ronald. "Yugoslavia." In *International Film Guide, 1980*, edited by Peter
    Cowie. New York: A. S. Barnes, 1980.
Jeremić, Dragan M., and Vučo, Vuk. "Dva mišljenja o jednom filmu." *Književne
    novine*, 20 October 1961.
Jovičić, Vladimir. "Crni talas u našem filmu." *Borba Reflektor* (3 August 1969), pp. 22–29.
"Jugoslovenska kinematografija u brojkama." Belgrade: Institut za film, n.d. (fold-out
    sheet prepared by Dejan Kosanović).
Kosanović, Dejan. "Razvoj filmske proizvodnje u Jugoslaviji." In *Leksikon jugoslovenskog
    filma*, edited by Dejan Kosanović. Belgrade: BIGZ-Jugoslavija film (in press).
———. "Uvod u proučavanje istorije jugoslovenskog filma." In *Mala biblioteka*, edited
    by Milan Damnjanović. Belgrade: Univerzitet umetnosti u Beogradu, 1976.
Krelja, Petar. "Dvadeset godina jugoslovenske kinoteke." *Filmska kultura*, nos. 68–69
    (December 1969), pp. 142–44.
"A List of Books Some People Consider Dangerous." Edited by Mary Ann Tennenhouse
    and Jan De Deka. American Booksellers' Association. Summer 1982 (mimeo).
Makavejev, Dušan. "Kokan Rakonjac ili besciljni pogled kroz prozor." *Sineast*, no. 10
    (1969–1970), pp. 17–20.
Munitić, Ranko, "Filmska kritika živi leš jugoslavenske kinematografije." *Filmska kultura*,
    no. 70 (March 1970), pp. 25–32.
———. "Jugoslavenski autorski film." *Filmska kultura*, nos. 55–56 (July 1967),
    pp. 87–98.
———. "O vidicima i o obalama." *Filmska kultura*, no. 61 (June 1968), pp. 1–8.
———. "Razvoj filmskog stvaralaštva u Jugoslaviji, 1945–1947." In *Leksikon jugoslov-
    enskog filma*, edited by Dejan Kosanović. Belgrade: BIGZ-Jugoslavija film (in
    press).
"News" (published by Jugoslavija film, Belgrade, 1958–).
Novaković, Slobodan. "Dvoje." *Mladost*, 15 October 1961.
———. "Kuda posle Pule." *Filmska kultura*, nos. 57–58 (November 1967), pp. 1–12.
———. "Različiti vidici sa iste obale." *Filmska kultura*, nos. 59–60 (March 1968),
    pp. 1–12.
"Okružni sud u Sarajevu, no. K-446/63. Sarajevo, August 13, 1963." (Court's judgment
    in the banning of the film *City* [*Grad*].)
Pavlovski, Jovan. "Makedonski film ili smisao za istoriju." *Filmska kultura*, nos. 68–69
    (December 1969), pp. 70–72.
Pekeč, Stanko. "Za diskusiju bez isključivost." *Filmska kultura*, no. 86 (May 1973),
    pp. 1–7.

Perović, Olga. "Crnogorski film danas." *Filmska kultura*, nos. 68–69 (December 1969), pp. 73–76.

Peterlić, Ante. "Tendencije 'političkog filma.'" *Filmska kultura*, nos. 68–69 (December 1969), pp. 101-108.

Petrić, Jakša. "Još više približiti film narodnim masama." *Film*, nos. 8–9 (December 1948), pp. 12–15.

———. "O kadrovima filmskih radnika u našoj proizvodnji." *Film*, no. 1 (December 1946), pp. 19–21.

———. "Opšti osvrt na naše rezultate i slabosti." *Film*, nos. 6–7 (July 1948), pp. 19–26.

Petrović, Zoran. "Naš najfilmskiji film." *Student*, 24 October 1961.

Popović, Jovan. "Iskustva iz šest naših prvih umetničkih filmova i pouke za dalji rad." *Film*, nos. 1–2 (July 1949), pp. 3–49.

"Poslije Pule 1968." *Filmska kultura*, nos. 63–64 (December 1968), pp. 39–90. (Critical articles by Rudolf Sremec, Mira Boglić, Bogdan Kalafatović, Ranko Munitić, and Slobodan Novaković.)

"Pula '77 iz različitih aspekata." *Filmska kultura*, nos. 112–13 (February 1978), pp. 32–79. (Critical articles by Ivan Salečic, Čedo Nedeljković, Ranko Munitić, and Mira Boglić.)

Raspor, Vicko. "Problemi naše filmske umjetnosti i zadaci saveza filmskih radnika Jugoslavije." *Filmska kultura*, no. 1 (1950), pp. 1–14.

"Rezolucija protiv klevetničke kampanje protiv FNRJ." *Film*, nos. 1–2 (July 1949), pp. 1–2.

Roksandić, Vladimir. "O cenzuri-nevezane bilješke s predumišljajem." *Filmska kultura*, no. 83 (July 1972), pp. 51–52.

Shaplen, Robert. "A Reporter at Large: Tito's Legacy—I." *The New Yorker* (5 March 1984), pp. 110–25.

———. "A Reporter at Large: Tito's Legacy—II." *The New Yorker* (12 March 1984), pp. 79–119.

"*Slavica*—naš prvi umetnički film." *Film*, no. 3 (August 1947), pp. 11–19. (Report of a round-table discussion involving Vjekoslav Afrić, Jovan Popović, Milan Bogdanović, Velibor Gligorić, Hugo Klajn, O. Bihalji-Merin, N. Hercigonja, Marijan Stilinović, and Eli Finci.)

Sremec, Rudolf. "Film osvaju boju." *Film*, no. 2 (March 1947), pp. 8–11.

———. "Film socijalističke Jugoslavije." *Filmska kultura*, no. 62 (July 1968), pp. 1–6.

Štaka, Aco. "Škola stvaralačkog iskustva: Putevi savremenog filma u Bosni i Hercegovini." *Filmska kultura*, nos. 68–69 (December 1969), pp. 56–59.

"Stanje i problemi u jugoslavenskoj kinematografiji." *Filmska kultura*, nos. 68–69 (December 1969), pp. 1–26.

"Stenografske beleške sa sastanka sa filmskim radnicima-komunistima." Komisija za ideološki rad CK SKJ. 14 December 1963.

Stojanović, Nikola. "Kao u zrcalu." *Sineast*, no. 5 (Fall 1968), pp. 11–22.

Tadić, Zoran. "*Dvoje, Dani, Tri*—razvoj na linija?" *Filmska kultura*, no. 50 (July 1966), pp. 98–100.

Tirnanić, Bogdan. "Nacionalne kinematografije, da ili ne." *Sineast*, no. 7 (1969), pp. 22–30.

Vranicki, Predrag. "On the Problem of Practice." *Praxis*, International Edition, no. 1 (1965), pp. 41–48.

Vučo, Aleksandar. "Naša mlada filmska proizvodnja." *Film*, no. 1 (December 1946), pp. 1–4.

———. "Velika ostvarenja sovjetske kinematografije." *Film*, nos. 8–9 (December 1948), pp. 8–11.

———. "Velikoruski šovinizam u sovjetskom filmu." *Filmska kultura*, no. 1 (1950), pp. 15–20.

Vukotić, Dušan. "Uzroci (i posljedice)." *Filmska kultura*, no. 86 (May 1973), pp. 8–12.
Vuković, Vladimir. "Bilješka o hrvatskoj kinematografiji." *Filmska kultura*, nos. 68–69 (December 1969), pp. 51–54.
Zečević, Božidar. "Maglovite sfere nacionalnog." *Filmska kultura*, no. 61 (June 1968), pp. 9–16.

FILM PERIODICALS

Ekran
> The major film journal of Slovenia, begun in 1962 under the editorship of Vitko Musek. Publishes ten numbers annually in Ljubljana.

Film
> Forty numbers were published in Belgrade under the initial editorship of Aleksandar Vučo, from April 1950 to November 1952.

Film danas
> Published by Jugoslovenska kinoteka, Belgrade, under the editorship of Vladimir Pogačić. Thirteen numbers were issued between 15 April 1958 and the end of 1959.

Filmska kultura
> A quarterly journal published in Zagreb. The first number was issued in 1957 under the editorship of Stevo Ostojić and Fedor Hanžeković.

Filmske sveske
> A quarterly journal dealing with film theory and aesthetics. Published by the Institut za film in Belgrade, the journal was begun in 1968 under the editorship of Dušan Stojanović.

Sineast
> The major film journal of Bosnia-Hercegovina, begun in 1967 under the editorship of Nikola Stojanović. Published by the kino klub in Sarajevo.

INDEX